DESIGNING MODERN AMERICA

DESIGNING

MODERN AMERICA

Broadway to Main Street   Christopher Innes

YALE UNIVERSITY PRESS   NEW HAVEN AND LONDON

Published with assistance from the foundation established
in memory of Philip Hamilton McMillan of the Class of 1894, Yale College.

Designed by Sonia Shannon.
Set in Monotype Bulmer and Linotype Futura
by Duke & Company, Devon, Pennsylvania.
Printed in the United States of America.

Library of Congress Cataloging-in-Publication Data
Innes, C. D.
Designing modern America : Broadway to main street / Christopher Innes.
p.   cm.
Includes bibliographical references and index.
ISBN 0-300-10804-4 (hardcover : alk. paper)
1. Design—United States—History—20th century. 2. Urban, Joseph, 1872–1933—Criticism
and interpretation. 3. Geddes, Norman Bel, 1893–1958—Criticism and interpretation.
4. Theaters—Stage-setting and scenery—United States—History—20th century. I. Title.
NK1404.I55 2005
792.02′5′092273—dc22
2005008719

A catalogue record for this book is available
from the British Library.

The paper in this book meets the guidelines
for permanence and durability of the Committee on
Production Guidelines for Book Longevity of the
Council on Library Resources.

10 9 8 7 6 5 4 3 2 1

For Eva

Contents

Preface   xi

Acknowledgments   xiii

1 Styling for the Modern Age   1

2 Egos at Work   17

3 Theatrical Fashions   37

4 Stage and Screen   59

5   Society Scenery   83

6   A Century of Progress   101

7   Riding into the Future   119

8   The World of Tomorrow   145

9   Car Culture   155

10   Street Scenes   171

11 Reaching for the Sky   191

12 Suburban Heaven   213

13 Lifestyle Begins in the Kitchen   233

14 Selling Modernity   259

Afterword: Then and Now   289

Notes   295
Index   312

Preface

Once, as a birthday treat when I was a little boy, my grandfather took me to see the classic children's fantasy *Peter Pan*. It was my first time ever in a theater, and I was completely captivated. Wide-eyed, I watched the children flying through the air, the savage redskins prancing in their war dance, the battle against evil Captain Hook and his villainous crew of pirates. When the tiny fairy Tinkerbell was treacherously poisoned and everyone in the audience was asked to help save her, I can still remember crying out, "I believe in fairies!" (we were told that was the only way of reviving her dying spark). Of course, even I could plainly see the wires suspending the children in the air, while those fierce Indian braves were rather plump, with little patches of ordinary pale skin showing between their belts and the rather overly red paint that covered their chests. None of it mattered. The scenery tended to wobble, the lighting was crude—but that simply added to the appeal. The brilliance of the lights, the smell of greasepaint were enthralling; everything on the stage seemed larger than life (played by young adults, the Little Lost Boys were far bigger than me) and more intense. It was magic.

From that moment, I loved theater, and not just make-believe, but the excitement of live performance. Over the years I threw myself into charades and built toy theaters, took up acting, tried my hand at directing plays, designed scenery, and read everything about the stage that I could get my hands on. I always wanted to know how the magic worked, from the ticking alarm clock in the stomach of the crocodile that ate Captain Hook, to the subtle wordless communication of a great mime like Marcel Marceau. So as time passed I took up writing about theater, searching out undiscovered stories about actors or what had happened in performances. That led me to this story, which started off with Broadway stage designers in the 1920s, and turned out to be an unexpected revelation about twentieth-century culture as a whole.

Looking back, I came to realize that childhood experience was also a practical demonstration of how stage performance, with its immediacy and direct contact between actors and spectators, could influence people's lives. (For months after seeing *Peter Pan* I modeled myself on the characters and played in their imaginary world.) On one level, the picture on a stage is always openly fantasy. The life it represents may never be as convincingly real as film, but precisely because theater is so obviously make-believe it can act as a powerful catalyst.

This story about American theater also resonated in another way. Growing up in England after World War II gave me a strong sense of how quickly a culture can change and a new lifestyle emerge. We might have won the battle against Hitler in 1945, but the country remained stuck in the past, held back by bombed-out factories, shattered cities, and the sheer cost of fighting the war. People clung to old, outdated attitudes because there was nothing else, and while I was a child everything around me looked drab and gray. Then quite suddenly in the mid-1950s spots of brightness began to appear everywhere. Going into a store you saw new products, in colorful packaging that leapt off the shelves. Before that, our family—like three-quarters of households in Britain—had made do without a refrigerator. Now everyone had fridges in their kitchens, together with shiny white stoves and washing machines and dryers, which were far easier to use than the old ranges or the tubs with wringers on top. With all this came commercial television, and for the first time in color, bringing this new world right into our living room.

What made the greatest impression on me, being still a boy, was the end of wartime sugar rationing, which had remained in force through 1953. Candy, up to then a longed-for rarity, became freely available and (astonishingly, delightfully) no one stopped us from eating as many pieces as we could buy with our few pennies of pocket money. Cultural assumptions shifted along with personal expectations, and inside a single decade almost everyone was living in a different way. The modern world had arrived—just like that! By 1957 even our droopy-eyed conservative Prime Minister at the time, Harold Macmillan, was declaring, "Most of our people have never had it so good." Tasting the candies, I naturally agreed: the modern lifestyle was great.

Although it wasn't altogether obvious back then—at least not to a youngster like me, barely in his teens—the rapidity with which English society changed around me was because this glossy streamlined culture, so novel to us, arrived already fully formed, from somewhere else. Those new convenience products and the brightly colored packaging they came in, along with the refrigerators and stoves, even commercial television, all came from America or were inspired by practices and styles that had developed in the United States.

This is the story of how that culture came into being. It is also, not coincidentally, a story about theater.

Acknowledgments

Edith Lutyens Bel Geddes most generously and graciously shared with me many insights into her husband's character, which was invaluable to me during my research into his work; and I very much regret that she did not live to see the finished product. I am also deeply grateful to the trustees of the Norman Bel Geddes Estate, both for their kind permission to reproduce so many photographs documenting his work both on the stage and in industrial design, and for allowing me to quote from his unpublished files. In addition, I thank Ms. Laurence Loewy for her enthusiasm on hearing of my project and for her generosity in allowing me to reproduce the photographs featuring Loewy and his work.

I am equally grateful to Columbia University for permission to reproduce photographs of Joseph Urban's work, to the Hagley Museum for providing the photographs of Raymond Loewy, to the Smithsonian for permission to reproduce the photographs of Henry Dreyfuss's work, and to the New York Public Library for the Performing Arts for permission to reproduce two images relating to Maurice Evans's work. In addition I thank Professor Andrew Wood of San Jose State University for providing additional photographs of Art Deco buildings.

I also thank Dr. Tom Staley, Helen Adair, as well as Rick Watson and the photographers at the Harry Ransom Humanities Research Center of the University of Texas at Austin. They were extremely helpful and kind in making it possible for me to examine the massive amount of material in the Bel Geddes Collection, and in advising me on selecting the necessary illustrations. Jean Ashton and her staff at the Butler Library of Columbia University were equally helpful, both in making Joseph Urban's material available, and expediting access, as well as in arranging for so many images to be scanned, as well as generous in their terms for allowing reproduction. The staffs of the Billy Rose Collection at the New York Public Library for the Performing Arts at Lincoln Center and of the Cooper-Hewitt National Design Museum in New York also deserve thanks.

I also thank Mary Butler of the Victoria and Albert Museum for her help, as well as Don Wilmeth of Brown University, Laurence Senelick of Tufts University, and Doug Gibson of McLelland and Stewart for their encouragement and suggestions.

This book was materially aided by generous funding from the Killam Foundation, which provided a fellowship that made it possible to accomplish the extensive research. A grant from the Social Science and Humanities Research Council of Canada supported this project, as did a fellowship from the Ransom Center. These research grants and fellowships made possible extended research at the University of Texas at Austin and at Columbia University. The recognition, encouragement, and the practical aid these research agencies supply is invaluable not only to my own work, but for the whole research culture of Canada.

This project was completed with active involvement from the Performance and Culture Group of the Canada Research Chair at York University; and two former assistants deserve particular mention: Katherine Carlstrom (one of my co-authors on *Twentieth-Century British and American Theatre: A Critical Guide to Archives*, which first uncovered the links between Urban and Bel Geddes), and Allana Lindgren, who helped me gather the archival source material. Another assistant, Chandrima Chakraborty, aided by checking references, proofreading, and indexing.

DESIGNING MODERN AMERICA

1

Styling for the Modern Age

FROM THE BEGINNING, THE "style" of twentieth-century America was deliberately designed, and created by specific individuals. The particular cultural shift we
are following, which emerged through the 1920s and 1930s and has since been widely
copied around the world, marks the start of industrial design in a modern sense.
Perhaps surprisingly, too, this type of design came out of theater. In fact, the magic
of the stage turns out to be crucial to its development, since the people who led the
way in consciously designing a new lifestyle for America made their reputations on
Broadway and carried its theatricality over into everything they did.

The objects and styles—from white kitchens to the Walkman, the modern shopping mall to the prototype of the iPod—created by these individuals, or by their
descendants in the industrial process, surround us still and continue to condition the
way we live. Today we hardly notice their dramatic quality, and they no longer seem
novel—except perhaps when highlighted, as in the current vogue for retro-styled cars.
But looking back at the lives of the people who did the most to bring this about, we see
their legacy nearly everywhere in the world around us. Although many hands were at
work, two extraordinary people stand out in shaping the physical spaces and objects
of American culture, and making it synonymous with "modernity": Joseph Urban and
Norman Bel Geddes. First on the scene, they were instrumental in defining what the
founder of *Time* magazine, Henry Luce, famously labeled "the American Century."

Joseph Urban and Norman Bel Geddes both worked in opera and on Broadway,
directing and designing several shows a year through the 1920s and into the 1930s.
But between these shows, each designed all sorts of other things, from fashion fabrics
and costume jewelry to shopping centers and office buildings. They touched every
aspect of people's existence—in particular the most obvious symbols of modern life:
cars, houses and hotels, kitchens, and household furnishings.

With increasing enthusiasm during the 1920s, even with desperation in the
Depression years, Americans searched for a "real" national identity aligned with the
modern world. Popular catchphrases of the 1930s were "the American dream" (by no
means ironic when first coined in 1931) and "the American way of life" (which had
become so standard by 1939 that George S. Kaufman and Moss Hart used it as the
title for one of their Broadway comedies). It was Urban, followed by Bel Geddes, who
largely defined what that dream, "the American way of life," looked like.[1]

Above all, they were both visionaries. Coming from old-world Europe and looking at America with fresh eyes, Urban was struck by the new conditions he saw around
him. He saw that the modern world, emerging so energetically and chaotically in
this young and bustling nation, needed its own mode of expression. In his view, the
traditional styles, which were still being applied haphazardly across America, would
not do. Nor would the new European design principles, whether Art Nouveau from

Joseph Urban with one of his intricately detailed stage models on which he based the scenes for both his Metropolitan Opera and *Ziegfeld Follies* productions, c. 1922.
Joseph Urban Papers, Rare Book and Manuscript Library, Columbia University.

the turn of the century, or the type of Art Deco that reached its most triumphant expression in the 1925 Paris Exhibition, or the mechanistic geometry of the German Bauhaus.[2] None of these reflected the American experience. Urban set out to create designs that would. The *New Yorker* pointed out that the modern style of "textiles, candy boxes, type fonts, and . . . modern furniture are traceable," quite specifically, "to Joseph Urban." The same article underlined the importance of theater to the development of modern design, remarking that "a number of American artists, many of them stage designers like Urban took up the work, and a piano by Lee Simonson, a bed by Norman Bel Geddes, silks by Robert Edmond Jones were made." The result of their efforts, as Urban's colleague Paul Frankel wrote just three years after that Paris Exhibition, was that "Modernity and America have in fact come to mean, in the mind of the world, one and the same thing."[3]

Bel Geddes, twenty-one years younger, was homegrown and, though too independent in his views to work closely with any other designer, owed much to Urban's vision. He was to some extent a protégé of Urban's, as well as being a competitor. One of his first jobs in the theater was as an assistant to Robert Edmond Jones, helping with the set and costumes for a pageant Urban directed in New York. Then, in the early 1920s when Max Reinhardt was searching for a designer to mount his production of *The Miracle* in New York, it was through Urban that Bel Geddes met Reinhardt. *The Miracle,* his very first major commission, made Bel Geddes a major player on Broadway overnight; and even though Urban (who knew Reinhardt well) was upset to be passed over in favor of the younger man, he willingly helped with the set design when Bel Geddes requested assistance. He also employed Bel Geddes to design part of a club he was building in Palm Beach. And shortly before Urban's sudden death in 1933, Bel Geddes collaborated with him on the Chicago World's Fair. He undoubtedly absorbed a great deal from Urban, and they shared many of the same design principles. Even more uncompromisingly modernistic in his vision, Bel Geddes took up where Urban left off, almost single-handedly creating the entire style of streamlining that became so characteristic of modernistic American design.

Today their names may be almost unknown. But at the time their impact was obvious enough: as a news headline pointed out in 1948, "EVERYWHERE YOU LOOK NOW YOU'LL FIND GEDDES WORK," which "can be seen in every home."[4] And the stylistic concept created by Urban and Bel Geddes influenced other designers in all fields. Through the extraordinary range of the everyday articles, even more so than the public projects they designed, Urban and Bel Geddes shaped the daily environment of the 1930s. They did more than anyone else to create what has been called the golden age of American culture in the 1940s and 1950s, when everything came together in a coherent and identifiable American style.

Norman Bel Geddes as entrepreneurial designer: showing off his styling of the
Nash automobile, c. 1940. Estate of Edith Lutyens Bel Geddes, Norman Bel Geddes Collection,
Courtesy of the Harry Ransom Humanities Research Center.

During the 1920s and on into the 1940s, people in New York, Chicago, or Florida were increasingly likely to go through their lives surrounded by objects Urban or Bel Geddes had created and in décor inspired by them. By the 1950s some people even lived in communities planned by one of them, or in cities where redevelopment was inspired by his ideas. The reach of their influence can be seen in an average day of an American, particularly one living in or around New York, the center of Urban and Bel Geddes' operations, which in part helped to make the city the national leader of fashion for those decades.

He or she—call them Joe and Josephine (to borrow the names another designer, Henry Dreyfuss, gave to the "standard" American couple for his time-and-motion studies)[5]—might well have woken up looking at curtains and wallpaper with Urban's patterns on them, in a bed designed by him, or later in one by Bel Geddes, who also created the styling of the radios that more than half the American population turned on to catch the daily news. This individual would probably then take breakfast from a refrigerator, cook it on a stove or in a toaster, and eat it sitting on a chair at a table in a type of kitchen (the ubiquitous white kitchen), all designed by Bel Geddes. Joe could well have driven to work in a Cadillac styled by Urban, or in a Chrysler, Buick, or Frazer-Nash manufactured to Bel Geddes' design, along a motorway (Bel Geddes' term) constructed according to his plans, to a New York office that either Urban or Bel Geddes could have designed. There, Joe or a secretarial Josephine might well work at an IBM typewriter designed by Bel Geddes, quite possibly sitting at a workstation of his design (or if higher up the office scale, Joe might be behind one of Urban's desks). In their lunch break they might snack on biscuits packaged by Urban and buy a Coke from the dispensing machine Bel Geddes had designed.

Josephine, meanwhile, might be attracted to a Fifth Avenue shop window display by Bel Geddes, then walk into a store decorated by Urban, to buy products of their design. Or she might drop in to an exhibition of their work at the Museum of Modern Art, the Metropolitan Museum, or a Fifth Avenue gallery run by Urban himself. (This phenomenon was not restricted to New York, for their merchandise was sold or exhibited all over the country.)

In the evening, dressed in fashionable clothes inspired by Urban and made of silk with his patterns on it, Josephine might well have gone out with Joe to eat in one of the restaurants Urban had designed. Then, if they were a New York couple, it was on to one of the immensely popular shows staged by Urban or Bel Geddes, or (in the 1920s, at least) one of their films in a theater decorated and perhaps even built by one of them, winding up in a nightclub or dance-hall designed by them as well, to be entertained by one of their cabarets and impressed by their costumes and scenery.

Joe and Josephine's wealthier East Coast cousins would almost certainly have attended a ball with décor by Urban, and might well have lived in or visited a grand house he designed and built, or stayed in one of the hotels Urban or Bel Geddes decorated. When Josephine glanced through a glossy magazine, it was likely that the layout was by Bel Geddes; and Joe may have studied at Urban's New School in New York, or played tennis and swum in a club designed by Urban. Then, if Joe happened to be one of the New York smart set, his favorite meeting place might be the Casino that Urban renovated in Central Park.

Bel Geddes and Urban did not cater just to the upper crust, however. Salesmen from all over the country might gather in a convention hall decorated by Urban, while a worker could be employed at a factory that Bel Geddes had designed, in an industrial park he had laid out, manufacturing objects also designed by him. Housewives across the country who went grocery shopping might well have their produce weighed on shop scales styled by Bel Geddes. Before Disney, children could play at a fantasy theme park created by Urban (the prototype for Sleeping Beauty's castle). Later on, when the combined Ringling Brothers, Barnum & Bailey Circus tried to revive its fortunes by developing a new, contemporary image, the big top, the parade, all the costumes, and some of the acts (as well as the animal cages and even the mechanics of transporting "The Greatest Show on Earth" by rail) had been designed by Bel Geddes.

In short, between them, Urban and Bel Geddes were personally responsible for an overwhelming amount of the physical ambience of America, from which cultural attitudes flowed, at a crucial time in the development of modern society. And among the other designers who followed them, working in exactly the same style, was Henry Dreyfuss, who also came through the Broadway theater. Dreyfuss, who took a design course taught by Bel Geddes and also designed several popular Broadway shows at the end of the 1920s, went on to determine the shape of the Bell telephones in every North American house, the most popular kind of alarm clocks, the interiors of the railway cars most long-distance travelers sat in as well as the streamlined body of the engines that pulled the trains, and the majority of the gas stations where people filled their cars—even the strategy room used by the Joint Chiefs in Washington during World War II. Similarly, Raymond Loewy, who started off in the mid-1920s with fashion illustrations for women's journals (as Bel Geddes himself had done just a few years earlier), continued the modern style created by Urban and Bel Geddes. The competing stoves and refrigerators Loewy designed are indistinguishable from those first created by Bel Geddes; the railway engines he designed directly follow Bel Geddes' principles, as does his trademark Studebaker Avanti, which drew crowds in the streets when it appeared in the 1960s, and the interiors of the space shuttle and Skylab, which were also Loewy's work. Some of these designers are still fairly well known, particularly Loewy, who lived thirty years longer than Bel Geddes and remained active into the 1980s. And as a result of this longevity Loewy has been credited with much that Bel Geddes introduced.

Designers are relentless self-promoters—it's the nature of the profession—and in the battle of egos those who live longest win out. But even when Urban and Bel Geddes' influence was most extensive, almost all the objects or places they designed were known solely by their manufacturers or owners: Standard Gas stoves and GE refrigerators, Chrysler cars, the Coca-Cola vending machine; the Bedell Store on 34th Street, New York, and Franklin Simon on Fifth Avenue; Mallin and Simmons furniture; the Park Avenue Restaurant and the New York Plaza Hotel; the Ziegfeld Theatre, the New School for Social Research, and the Cosmopolitan movie house. Urban and Bel Geddes helped to introduce brand recognition, being responsible for familiar logos like Goodyear Tires and Coca-Cola. But since this was before the era of Calvin Klein and personalized brand names, they were not able to attach a logo of their own to industrial designs or consumer products.

In addition, their versatility—which made possible such a wide influence that they could shape an entire lifestyle—meant that neither designer established a leading reputation in any single field outside the theater. For example, even though at the time other architects admired Urban's buildings, he is not mentioned in histories of modern architecture. Such books tend to deal with those whose careers were dedicated solely to architecture and who made a more obvious mark in this field because (in contrast to Urban) they designed little else. Similarly, Bel Geddes completely changed the way American cars looked, yet because he worked on cars only part-time, the credit goes to automotive executives who headed the styling divisions in Detroit.

If their contribution has mainly been forgotten, in a sense this may be a measure of their success. Paradoxically, precisely because the style and objects Urban and Bel Geddes created have become so ubiquitous, no association with their names remains.

The twentieth century did turn out to be the American century, a truly remarkable cultural shift. In 1900, when people around the world grew more affluent and wanted models for a new way of living, they had looked to Britain or France. This was equally true of Americans, and the "White City" constructed for the 1893 Columbian Exposition in Chicago copied the Beaux Arts design popular in Paris. By contrast, for the last half of the twentieth century, the American lifestyle has been imitated everywhere across the globe and is identified with being "modern."

Over the first decade of the twentieth century Art Nouveau was the style of the age—again derived from France although some of its leaders were American, in particular Louis Comfort Tiffany and Louis Sullivan. The characteristic Art Nouveau signature motif is an elongated "whiplash" curve, like the tendril of some exotic plant. Its dynamic line, which represents organic growth, was carried through into stylized forms taken directly from nature: Tiffany's stained-glass lamps portraying dragonflies and flower-engraved vases, grapevine or seaweed necklaces, enameled trays with the shape of lily pads—or the leaf-like openings around doorways or windows, as in Sullivan's main entry for the Schlesinger and Mayer department store (now Carson Pirie Scott).

In many ways Art Nouveau was the first concerted attempt to express a specifically modern perception of life, and Joseph Urban's designs echo its sensuous, sinuously flowing lines, while the same dynamism and the shapes derived from nature (though far more simplified and abstract) carried over into Bel Geddes' streamlining, which became characteristic of American modernism. At the same time, even though it decorated biscuit tins, billboard posters, public buildings, and entries to the Paris metro as well as lamp shades, restaurant menus, and beer mats, Art Nouveau remained an almost exclusively aesthetic movement. It never freed itself from the ateliers of the art world where it was born. Then too, there is a hothouse quality everywhere in Art Nouveau that Urban largely left behind when he came to America and is completely absent from the work of Bel Geddes.

As its name declares, Art Nouveau looked on itself as a radically new movement, opening a new age. But in fact it became identified with *fin de siècle,* the end of an era. Elitist, exotic, and subtly erotic, it suggests decadence associated with the final stage of a civilization—and indeed the whole movement was brought to an abrupt end by World War I. In 1914 Art Nouveau was at its height. By the time Germany was defeated, the world had changed. Art Nouveau died in the brutal realities of trench warfare and the Russian Revolution. After 1918 it had disappeared completely, as much a casualty of the conflict as the old monarchies of Europe.

Art Nouveau was in a way reinvented in the more angular and exotic style of Art Deco showcased at the International Exhibition of 1925 in Paris. The full title of this event, which defined Art Deco as a style, was the Exposition Internationale des Arts Décoratifs et Industriels Modernes (originally planned for 1915—but the war intervened). It achieved coherence by exclusion, even if this was to some extent inadvertent. Notably Germany did not participate, as the invitation came too late for the Bauhaus and other German design schools to prepare. Nor did the United States, since the Department of Commerce, headed by Herbert Hoover, notoriously turned down the invitation, unilaterally disqualifying all "American manufacturers and craftsmen" as having "almost nothing to exhibit in the modern spirit" to which the exhibition was dedicated.[6]

However wide of the mark this extraordinary denigration (and Hoover's decision was excoriated by Urban and others), it could be said that the American design of the time had little in common with the style showcased by the 1925 Exposition. The Paris style of Art Deco expressed a consciousness very different from the American experience. Even the European victors in World War I had been bankrupted by more than four years of conflict which cost the lives of a generation of young men, and the threat of Communist revolution—which had achieved short-lived workers' states in Germany, as well as power in Russia—continued to stalk the wealthy throughout Europe. Haunted by the guilt and relief of surviving, the new instability of traditional structures, the suddenly apparent fragility of institutions, together with the giddy release of peace, the gilded European youth of the 1920s went on a spree of frenetic gaiety. The blank but highly polished surfaces in paintings by the poster girl for the movement, Tamara de Lempicka, the bright but frequently jarring colors, and the jagged geometries and blatant display of riches in European Art Deco expressed this "flapper" generation dancing over a void. Even more than Art Nouveau, Art Deco was created for the wealthy. It was conspicuously lavish in its use of precious materials, and too expensive for most of the population to buy.

By contrast, America had emerged from the war with comparatively little damage and with the consciousness of having been the decisive factor in victory. Although the 1920s were boom years in the States, far more so than for the European nations, with New York outdoing Paris in conspicuous consumption, America showed none of the desperation that one senses in the postwar pursuit of pleasure on the other side of the Atlantic.[7] American institutions survived unchallenged: while the almost nude Josephine Baker, wildly dancing in her scanty banana-skirt, became a symbol of the period in Paris, the more traditional moral (and often racist) attitudes were still prevalent in the United States, where her act was widely condemned. American society was also intrinsically more democratic. In opposition to the Art Deco designers producing luxury goods and high art products, Urban and Bel Geddes, followed by most of the other American designers, created mass-market furniture, household appliances, and mid-range cars (even though Urban started by designing for the rich and famous). Bel Geddes' Skyscraper cocktail shaker and goblets with the Manhattan tray were chrome plate, in conscious distinction to the solid silver preferred by Art Deco. And contrary to the elitism of European styles, Bel Geddes' modernist design occasionally contained a strongly humorous element that clearly signals its popular appeal. It is therefore not surprising that the style of modernism that America developed was quite distinct.

As in the earlier Art Nouveau, and despite the exclusion of the United States from the landmark Paris Exposition, some American work, such as the Chrysler Building, was defining for European Art Deco. In its Parisian "Moderne" form, too, the move-

Bel Geddes' household designs, c. 1935. The iconic Skyscraper shaker and cups on Manhattan tray (*left*). The "Coquette" lamp (*right*). Bel Geddes' caption for the lamp reads: "Irresistibly chic and saucy, this little lamp is as practical in use as it is diverting in design. The 'eyes' are really clips to hold the 'hat' shade to the frosted glass globe." Estate of Edith Lutyens Bel Geddes, Norman Bel Geddes Collection, Courtesy of the Harry Ransom Humanities Research Center.

ment had some influence on America, as in the photography of Edward Steichen and Man Ray, some of the architectural detail on the RCA Building in Rockefeller Center in New York, or the more extravagant Los Angeles movie theaters of the era. The Wiltern on Wilshire and the Pantages on Hollywood Boulevard, both constructed in 1929–31, combine billowing clouds on the front curtains with angular geometric sunbursts on the ceilings and stylized murals, all in vibrant colors.[8] Yet apart from those deliberately over-the-top Hollywood movie palaces, the American equivalent avoids the primitivistic exoticism and edgy opulence of European Deco. Where European Art Deco favored the apparently primitive features of central African carvings and masks, Hollywood looked to the highly Westernized decadence of an imagined Egypt. And as the dates of these two iconic theaters indicate, the main influence of Art Deco on the United States was limited to a two- or three-year period. In a very real sense, the transplanted European Art Deco style was exotic. While American design of the period has some comparable characteristics, it displays an entirely different design ethic.[9] Joseph Urban with Norman Bel Geddes played a major role in forming this new and uniquely American variant on the visual definition of modernity.[10]

In his characteristic use of bright colors, Urban might well be taken for a typical

Urban's murals in the roof-garden nightclub of the St. Regis Hotel, New York, 1927.
Joseph Urban Papers, Rare Book and Manuscript Library, Columbia University.

Art Deco designer. Yet, sharply contrasting with the jarring combinations and jagged shapes typical of Art Deco, even in Urban's most opulent décor the color scheme is unified. In the roof-garden dining room of the St. Regis Hotel, the white cherry blossoms, scattered in an elaborate tracery over the curving roof and walls, are picked up in the cascading inverted white pagodas of the lamps, in the white tablecloths, and in the flowing, elongated white tails of cockerels perched in the branches, while the red wings of parrots and brown tree trunks are echoed in the orange veils of the window curtains, and all is bound together through the blue of the background and the backrests and chair seats.[11] While the effect here is deliberately light and fantastical, mirroring the purpose of the space and intended to create an atmosphere of stylish levity, Urban's shapes tend to simplicity, as with the uninterrupted sweep of the curving roof and walls. The décor also takes on the quality of a stage setting in conveying an impression of richness with the simplest materials (plaster and paint). In all these ways his principles are essentially different from those of the Art Deco world—and particularly in his melding of form and function, which was to become the basis of all of Norman Bel Geddes' industrial designs.

However painterly those parrots and blossoms, the modern culture Urban and Bel Geddes developed was not artistic in the same way as Art Nouveau or even Art Deco, coming as it did out of the popular entertainment world of theater, rather than from the rarefied atmosphere of ateliers and art galleries. Theatrical design, being very much an applied art, allowed Urban and Bel Geddes to bridge the gap between industrial draftsmanship and the "fine arts" of painters and sculptors who populated the Art Nouveau and Art Deco circles. But American modernity was no less connected with the fallout from global wars than these European movements. World War I was the first time the United States had taken part in a major conflict outside its borders. Entering late, more than three years after the battle had first been joined in France, Americans bore relatively little cost and sacrifice, while victory brought equality with the exhausted European powers, even a feeling of national superiority over the old cultures that up to then had been admired and copied by the New World.

This boost created a public openness to new possibilities, and Urban—who had left Vienna at the end of 1911 and established himself on Broadway by 1915—was well placed to start filling the demands of an emerging consumer society. Bel Geddes, who designed his first Broadway show in 1920, joined him—as did others later, like Henry Dreyfuss, who made his mark on Broadway at the end of the 1920s. British designer Oliver Bernard also began his career on Broadway, and worked with Bel Geddes, before returning to design ceramics, furniture, and the famous illuminated glass foyer of the Strand Palace Hotel in London.[12] And between them, Urban and Bel Geddes established all the elements of the modern American lifestyle, which was in place by the end of World War II.

When the United States emerged as a global superpower in 1945, its new self-confidence led to the enthusiastic adoption of "the American way." During the Cold War this was broadcast through the U.S. Information Agency, which flooded Europe and even China with American culture: concerts by Isaac Stern and Louis Armstrong, plays by Eugene O'Neill and Arthur Miller, as well as Hollywood films, still more directly promoting images of American life. Although American designs have become far more varied and diffuse over the intervening half century, arguably the principles pioneered by Urban and Bel Geddes still underlie a great deal of our contemporary visual context. As yet, no single figure or group of designers since them has established a distinctively new and popularly accepted vision. Raymond Loewy made a major impact in the 1950s and 1960s both in America and, through his offices in London and Paris, in spreading American design directly to Europe, but he was a follower of Bel Geddes, as Loewy's earlier work in the 1930s and 1940s clearly shows. He picked up where Bel Geddes left off, promoting and developing the same vision.

Possibly the main European competitor to Urban and Bel Geddes was not the Art Deco movement, to which historians have sometimes assigned them, but the Bauhaus, founded in 1919, which flourished in Germany from the mid-1920s until Hitler came to power in 1933. The Bauhaus specifically claimed to be in tune with the scientific industrial age, and when some prominent members of the group later found their way as exiles to the United States, like the architect Mies van der Rohe and Walter Gropius, the founder of the Bauhaus school, they contributed to the American brand of modernism. The Bauhaus style, created and defined by architects, was purist in its modernism, however. It simplified forms into rectilinear rigidity and static geometrical shapes. In contrast, both Urban and Bel Geddes, though they too moved toward functional simplicity, produced dramatic curves and dynamic forms abstracted from nature. So Gropius's series of cars for a German manufacturer in the late 1920s were cuboid, very different in form and feel from the streamlined (even if not truly aerodynamic) cars Bel Geddes designed for Chrysler around the same time.

What made the difference is the way the work of Urban and Bel Geddes was rooted in their stage designs. Although the Bauhaus had a theater attached to its school in Dessau, they used the stage to experiment with spatial concepts from their architecture. For instance, in Oscar Schlemmer's *Triadic Ballet,* actors were encased in rigid geometrical costumes, turning the human figure into globes, cylinders, and squares; or they had long sticks attached to their limbs, which extended the angles of motion. The Bauhaus theater never fed back into buildings and décor. In contrast, Urban, followed by Bel Geddes, moved from costumes and scenery to designing the objects people used, the clothes they wore, the buildings that surrounded them, and the image of the society they inhabited—transferring theatricality to the broader culture.[13]

That this transfer from theater to industrial and architectural design was possible is partly due to the way America prided itself on being the new world, liberated from the hierarchical traditions of European empires.[14] This made it more acceptable for people to cross over from one specialization to another. American industrialists looking for designers to create mansions that would display their status, or (more important) to style their commercial products to attract a new breed of customers (now defined as consumers), liked what they saw on Broadway and sought out stage designers for the job. The "new world" ethos also meant there was a general openness to modern styles—and Joseph Urban and Norman Bel Geddes were on hand, with the talents to fulfill these expectations. Even though they came from different backgrounds, both had the sort of driving, outsize personality needed to exploit these opportunities. Their colorful characters and ability to create public images for themselves ensured that they would play a large role in shaping the modern lifestyle.

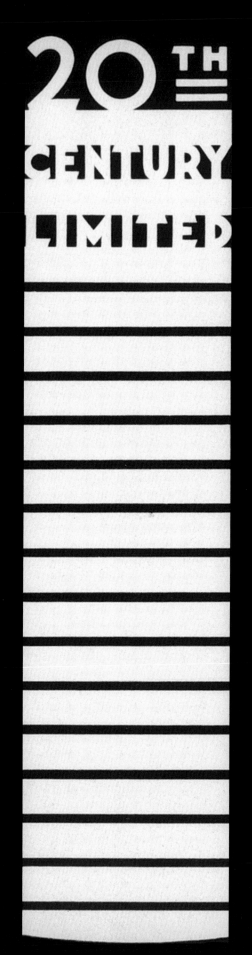

2

Egos at Work

BEING IN THE RIGHT PLACE at the right time—New York, the center of American culture in the 1920s, when a newly self-confident society was demanding expression—is partly what made Joseph Urban and Norman Bel Geddes so influential. With consumer marketing and modern advertising just getting off the ground, they helped create the demand for a new approach to industrial design, and the popularity of their products showed the commercial advantages of artists working with engineers. Still more important, they shared the perception that America was developing into a completely new kind of society: one calling for a distinct and modern style of living.[1]

In addition, the experience Urban brought with him to the New World meant that he was open to the wider possibilities of design. Although initially known in the States solely as a stage designer, back in turn-of-the-century Austria he had already done illustrations for children's fairy tales and designs for postage stamps, undertaken various architectural projects (including a miniature garden-palace for one of the wealthiest aristocrats of the Austro-Hungarian empire), as well as mounting an elaborate day-long pageant celebrating the Imperial Jubilee of 1908. His work for this pageant is in fact an excellent demonstration of the mix of social and artistic skills that made it possible for Urban to have such influence as a designer later in America. He not only designed the reviewing stand for the aging emperor and his court (two matching semicircular colonnades, complete with flower-bedecked banners, bearing columns and an elaborately fantastical canopy topped with a forty-foot-high replica of the crown of the Holy Roman Empire) but also organized the whole day-long procession and scripted historical scenes to be performed by officers and troops in each regiment, even persuading all the ladies of the court to wear white and red dresses (the Austrian colors).[2] Applying the same skills in America, Urban acted as an example for the much younger Bel Geddes, who in turn became a model for other American industrial designers.

Their personal backgrounds could hardly have been more different. Growing up in fin-de-siècle Vienna, the city of Freud as well as Richard Strauss, Urban was exposed to one of the most vibrant cultural centers in Europe. He made his mark on the lively Viennese art scene while still a student and moved in bourgeois, even aristocratic, circles. Bel Geddes was born twenty years later in small-town Ohio and raised in Pittsburgh, where—at least according to the version Bel Geddes assiduously promoted—his family lost all their money in bad investments by his father.[3] In this self-fashioned myth, he grew up penniless, his education was erratic, and as a young teenager he was forced to earn his keep working in his grandfather's grocery store and as a bellboy on an Erie lake boat instead of going to school. Urban arrived in New York as an established presence with a reputation already for groundbreaking and dazzling stage design. When Bel Geddes got there, the only work he could find at first was doing pen portraits of Broadway stars for the Sunday *New York Times*.

At the same time they shared certain qualities. Both had a rebellious streak, fueling the idealism that led them to undertake such an ambitious task as the redesign of society. The young Bel Geddes claimed to have been expelled from two schools for drawing scurrilously satirical cartoons of the teachers. He was finally accepted to study art, but he left the Cleveland Institute of Art after just two terms to follow up his fascination with American Indians by living for a summer on the Blackfoot Reservation (which led him to try his hand at writing an opera based on Native myth, *Thunderbird*). He then—as he gleefully claimed in his autobiography[4]—disturbed the staff of the Chicago Art Institute by insisting on doing his anatomy drawing in the dissecting room of the Cook County morgue, instead of the art studio. He also cut art classes to act as an extra on the stage of the Chicago Opera, which he found completely intoxicating, and supported himself by the most menial of artistic work: doing lettering for fashion plates in the Sears, Roebuck catalogue. Unable to cover his expenses, he left the Chicago Art Institute after a single year, to take a minimum-wage job in Detroit with the Peninsular Engraving Company, where he drew blatantly materialistic advertising posters for *Collier's* magazine and covers for theater programs of shows he never saw. Not surprisingly, perhaps, Bel Geddes developed strong left-wing sympathies and a naïve admiration for the Russian revolution. Such political sympathies were quite fashionable in the early 1920s, although Bel Geddes also took a strongly pacifist stance in deliberate opposition to the patriotic jingoism that swept America after it entered World War I, and was a card-carrying member of the Anti-Establishment League.[5]

For his part, Urban defied his solidly bourgeois family. Making no appearances in any of the law classes his father had signed him up for, he secretly took courses in architecture and aesthetics at the Vienna Polytechnic, then at the Imperial Academy. On discovering from a chance meeting with the dean of the law school that his son had never been seen within its doors, his outraged father cut off all support. Urban was able to complete his studies only by persuading his architecture professor to employ him on a project in Egypt. So, barely nineteen years old, he found himself overseeing the construction of a "European" wing that the Khedive had commissioned for the Abdin palace at Cairo—his first break, which (as he frequently repeated, claiming an exotic background of romance) gave him his feel for strong lighting effects and intense color, with the rich "Urban blue" for which he became famous echoing the "indescribable blue of the Egyptian sky" and the "strange deep blue of the Mediterranean" in his memory.[6] Where Bel Geddes became politically radical, Urban was an

Joseph Urban's prize-winning pavilion at the St. Louis World's Fair, 1904.
Joseph Urban Papers, Rare Book and Manuscript Library, Columbia University.

artistic revolutionary. After initially joining the Vienna Secessionists, he broke away to become one of the founders of the rival, and in art terms more radical, Hagenbund (loosely translated, Nature Fellowship).[7] Urban's group of artists combined the rhythmic fluidity of Jugendstil (the German version of Art Nouveau) with the pragmatism of William Morris and the contemporaneous English Arts and Crafts movement, which aimed to reform society by creating an aesthetic and harmonious environment from the bottom up.

At the Hagenbund exhibition hall in Vienna—an old market building, renovated by Urban, who gave it fanciful towers on either side of a curving Art Nouveau entrance—art (in the "high" form of paintings and sculpture) intersected with the home environment. Furniture, carpets, and vases designed by Hagenbund members were a major part of their shows, and Urban even designed special wallpapers as a backdrop to complement the exhibits in each show. Their exhibitions were so famous they were shown abroad, forming part of the Austrian Pavilion at the Paris World's Fair in 1900, and again at the 1904 Louisiana Purchase Exposition in St. Louis.

Urban came to St. Louis to organize the Hagenbund installation. More strikingly

Heavy (fake) beams and elaborate decoration in the main dining room of the Rathauskeller, Vienna, as designed by Urban, 1899. Joseph Urban Papers, Rare Book and Manuscript Library, Columbia University.

simple than his set-up for any of the Viennese exhibitions, lit entirely through trans-lucent panels covering the ceilings and with plain geometric patterns on the floors, it won Urban a prize for the best-arranged exhibit at the exposition. It also brought him several offers of work in America. Despite his being attracted by the kind of life he saw here, at that point in his life Vienna was still very much the center of Urban's aspirations, and shortly after the exposition he returned to Europe.

The radical simplicity of this display was an attempt to create a modern style specifically suited to the "new world" of America. It went far beyond anything Urban did in Austria, either before or after, and the difference can be measured by two of his turn-of-the-century projects. These were the most important architectural works Urban undertook in Vienna: a bridge to join two buildings, the art gallery, and the concert hall, where a joint exhibition was being held to mark the Emperor Franz Joseph's fiftieth anniversary on the throne; and décor for the Rathauskeller, a series of restaurants in the cellars beneath the newly completed city hall—still a popular dining place today. Both were pastiches of medieval pomp, heavily Gothic, and bearing strong Germanic traditionalism, despite some light Art Nouveau trimmings.

Had he remained in Austria, it is likely that Urban would have continued to work in much the same elaborate and historically dependent style. One or two interiors in a more simplified Art Nouveau manner, which he designed for ordinary people's Viennese houses and apartments, anticipate the future. But in Urban's other commercial designs, right up to his departure for the States in 1911, medievalism and ornate stylization predominate. The Vienna City Hall restaurant was very much a stage setting for the customers, deliberately harking back to a largely imaginary heroic past, and so artificial that in photographs of the time the décor and the top hats of turn-of-the-century diners look anachronistic and wildly incongruous. Urban is, as he did with the Jubilee pageant, applying theater to social appearances, but here expressing the values of a past that was even then vanishing. He might have already begun to envisage a more modern lifestyle. But clearly the Austrian context made it very difficult to define what this "modernity" should look like. Still responding to popular taste, Urban was not serving as an active agent to shape it; that would come only after he reached America.

With all they accomplished, it seems difficult to believe that Urban or Bel Geddes had time for anything outside their work. Truly, the range of their activities in any given year would be daunting for the most energetic and ambitious, with each of them effectively pursuing several full-time careers simultaneously. Yet at the same time both were colorful, consciously high-profile, personalities, with busy private lives that verged on the scandalous.

The media being far less intrusive than it is today, in general they managed to keep the press away from their numerous extramarital affairs and divorces: Urban had two wives; Bel Geddes four, his last (who alone seems to have been able to keep him at heel) being an Olympic fencer and the daughter of the British imperialist architect Sir Edwin Lutyens. Yet they advertised every other aspect of their activities. Quite ready even to pull blatant publicity stunts—like Bel Geddes, who arranged a police cavalcade with sirens and flashing lights to escort him in an open car, with a pair of monkeys he was giving to the new Bronx Zoo, all the way from the docks to their new home—they considered their personal image very much part of their work. Indeed, they promoted their lives as if theatrical performances.

Urban had learned the value of this early. More than most people, he had an extrovert's talent for friendship. Even when newly married back in Vienna, he entertained lavishly; and several of his guests (including the minister of culture at the time,

Baron von Wiener), impressed by the décor which Urban had designed in the new style of his artistic group, commissioned him to do their own homes. Photographs of Urban's Vienna apartment were also used to illustrate a special issue of the *Studio*, one of the leading British art journals, on "The Art Revival in Austria" in 1906.[8] Self-advertising under the cover of reportage was a method of spreading his work that Urban used again, even more extensively, after his arrival in America.

A large man in every sense—highly independent as well as impulsive; generous, extravagant, and flamboyant; corpulent, cosmopolitan, and extremely convivial, with broad interests and intense enthusiasms—Urban himself served as excellent public relations for his projects. Known by the fondly incongruous pet name of Buschi (or "little kid"), he made an instant impression on all who met him. He loved wine and singing—at one time he had even seriously thought of training to become an opera singer—and he loved numerous women, including a whole series of the stars who performed in his shows. In fact, he was an incurable romantic; and almost everyone found him good company, from Austro-Hungarian aristocrats and the new rich of America to his fellow artists, the architects with whom he competed, and the actors who worked for him, even if his early success and the imperial favor he had won caused considerable jealousy in Viennese circles.[9]

Certainly after dealing with the emperor of Austria on a personal basis in managing Imperial Jubilee celebrations, Joseph Urban found it easy to mix socially with the people for whom he worked in America, like the newspaper magnate William Randolph Hearst or the cereal heiress Marjorie Merriweather Post. Much to his first wife's dismay, Urban also mixed with his wealthy customers in terms of opulent equality, even though his income, however high—he was certainly the best paid film director of the time by far, in addition to his earnings for his other theatrical and entrepreneurial activities—could never come close to matching their riches. So while overseeing his architectural work in Palm Beach he hired a large yacht (complete with captain, crew, and butler) to live on, anchored permanently off shore, where he threw wild parties for his clients that lasted until dawn. He was just as adept in cultivating the leading professionals of his day, for instance founding a "Four-Hour Lunch Club" where well-known architects, including Raymond Hood and Frank Lloyd Wright, met every Friday at Mori's Restaurant in Manhattan.[10] (Urban himself was responsible for the cocktail they always warmed up with—his own new and unique recipe that he christened, with typical insouciance, "Nipple Spray.")

All this helped him win clients and contracts, and made him very much a public figure. His dynamic energy and larger-than-life personality, combined with his aesthetic flair, were the source of the influence he achieved in America, which continued even after his early death in 1933. It seduced the rich and powerful, as well as the

Joseph Urban at home in Yonkers with Mary Urban and dogs, c. 1925. Joseph Urban Papers, Rare Book and Manuscript Library, Columbia University.

beautiful and feminine. It also impressed the professionals—some of whom, jealous of his success, surreptitiously blocked his plans for landmark projects—as well as the journalists who wrote about him and reported on his projects.

Norman Bel Geddes was as much a perfectionist as Urban. He too had enthusiasms for everything, and was no less generous in sharing his ideas. Excitable, intellectually voracious, and extremely animated, he tended to swamp everyone he met with high-pressure conversation. But even though he had just as much appetite for women, good food, and wine, Bel Geddes had little in the way of small talk, and in contrast to Urban seems to have had few close friends.

Far more politically motivated, Bel Geddes was a committed pacifist. He was also (despite his interest in highways and cars) a passionate if somewhat eccentric animal rights advocate and environmentalist, which was expressed, however misconceived it might appear by today's environmental standards, in his city planning as well as in the large glass-topped case of ants he kept in his office. He even used the ants as miniscule "actors" for a movie of *Helen of Troy,* while experimenting with high-magnification 16-mm photography (the cutting-edge camera technology of the time). Along with this kind of obsession with detail carrying over into everything he did, Bel Geddes also clearly felt impelled to improve whatever he touched. For instance, instead of simply relaxing in his sailboat around Long Island, he invented the first nylon sails.

Unlike the convivial and faintly aristocratic Urban, who never lost his sweeping foreign gestures or German accent, Bel Geddes was typically American in his combination of idealism and entrepreneurial drive. One might say he spent his life overcompensating for his stature (5-foot-7). A Napoleon of self-promotion, he consciously constructed his own persona—even making his own name part of the image-making process, with the prefix "Bel" being adopted from the middle name of his first wife, Helen Belle Schneider. Presented as a romantic gesture of united love (in a marriage that was to be brief and ended in a messy divorce), the double-barreled name was also intended to signal artistic importance. In addition, from the start, when he got his first theatrical job designing scenery for one of Jessie Bonstelle's Detroit productions in 1915, he founded his own self-published and self-promotional magazine.

Called *INWHICH*—a deliberately capitalized title, explained with typical bravura in the first, August 1915 issue, as "Being a Book IN WHICH is Said Just What I Think"—this short-lived magazine contained etchings and stage designs by Bel Geddes, plus short stories, miniature fables, poems, and brief articles on politics or the arts, all written by Bel Geddes or his first wife. Many of these were designed to drum up business or establish connections with well-known artists (to whom Bel Geddes, naturally, sent complimentary copies). For instance, a piece on film showcased D. W. Griffith, whom Bel Geddes was to work for shortly afterward. One entitled "The Artist in the Theatre" praised Max Reinhardt (the director of the Deutsches Theater in Berlin, known for the vast spectacles that he staged throughout Europe), and with only the barest minimum of experience, Bel Geddes later persuaded Reinhardt to give him the job of designing and mounting the 1924 New York production of *The Miracle,* which made Bel Geddes' reputation. Some of his *INWHICH* essays also contained early signs of the principles that he was later to work into an aesthetic of modernism. As he put it in a 1915 issue, "Simplicity is basic—it is unity," and "concentration on essentials is great living."[11]

There was nothing small about his vision, as his mammoth plans for staging his version of the *Divine Comedy* indicate. This project, which preoccupied Bel Geddes for practically all his working life from 1921 to 1951, involved building a huge theater seating 7,000 spectators as the sole place suitable for performing such a culturally significant dramatic piece. Its stage was planned to be 165 feet deep by 135 feet wide and composed entirely of serried arrays of steps, rising around a central pit to four cliff-like peaks almost 100 feet high. To fill this space Bel Geddes called for more than 500 actors and singers. He designed fantastic costumes and masks and worked out every single movement for all the figures on a scale model of the set, from the exact

Norman Bel Geddes with a costume sketch for his *Divine Comedy,* c. 1921.
Estate of Edith Lutyens Bel Geddes, Norman Bel Geddes Collection,
Courtesy of the Harry Ransom Humanities Research Center.

placement of the members of the chorus on each and every beat to the precise gestures and postures of his two protagonists, Dante and Virgil. He composed a complete score for continuous abstract music, as well as drawing up full architectural plans, elevations, and structural blueprints.

All this he brought together in elaborate directing scripts for the "Inferno" and "Paradise" sections, where—like some multimedia orchestral score—the spoken or sung words (in his own translation and adaptation of Dante) formed one line on each page, with all the separate lines below being filled by detailed instructions on the lighting, the musical notes, the exact positions of the principals and chorus movements, even arm or hand gestures, and special effects. He also made detailed cost estimates: in his mind, a modest $266,000 would do, with an additional $40,000 to rehearse

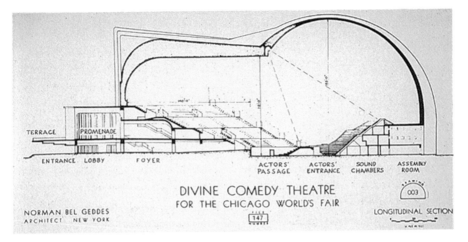

Architectural drawing of the theater for Bel Geddes' *Divine Comedy* (side view).
Estate of Edith Lutyens Bel Geddes, Norman Bel Geddes Collection,
Courtesy of the Harry Ransom Humanities Research Center.

the cast and musicians. At something approaching $4.5 million in today's money, this would have been a significant investment for a building that was designed for a single play—even if Bel Geddes (never one to downplay his genius) anticipated it running indefinitely.

Yet there was nothing inherently impossible about even such apparently grandiose plans.[12] Urban had made a striking success of something very much the equivalent. This was a pageant celebrating the 1916 tercentenary of Shakespeare's death: an event that publicly marked the introduction of the "new stagecraft" to America in the combination of Urban and Robert Edmond Jones (as well as a very junior Bel Geddes) and included Isadora Duncan—so intimately associated with Gordon Craig's "Art Theatre"—as the principal dancer. A sweeping procession of theater history from its ancient Greek origins, titled *Caliban of the Yellow Sands,* this had involved more than four times the number of actors and dancers envisaged by Bel Geddes for his *Divine Comedy* with a cast of 2,000 plus large groups of children, a choir of 450 singers, a complete symphony orchestra, and numerous other onstage musicians. To perform this mammoth spectacle Urban completely remodeled the Lewisohn Stadium of the City College on Amsterdam Avenue in New York into a horseshoe-shaped auditorium holding 25,000 spectators (almost four times as large as the projected audience for the Divine Comedy Theatre). A large circular arena—the "Yellow Sands," mottled with shadowy contours of the continents of the world—fronted a multilevel stage flanked by high lighting towers, which were disguised as brooding statues, the whole being

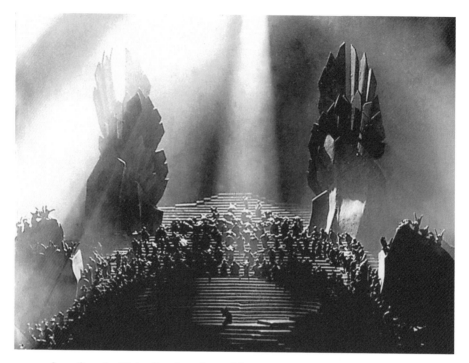

Scene from the *Divine Comedy* on the model stage: the soldiers of Dis and the City of Dreadful Night. Estate of Edith Lutyens Bel Geddes, Norman Bel Geddes Collection, Courtesy of the Harry Ransom Humanities Research Center.

dominated by a tall rocklike pile shaped to represent the snarling mask and open jaws of some monstrous panther (the cave of Setebos, the god on whom Caliban calls in *The Tempest*).

This celebration of theater and its civilizing power—allegorically embodied (as the script by the well-known pageant master Percy MacKaye proclaimed) by Caliban, who represented "aspiring humanity" and became transformed from his bestial shape through the love of beauty instilled by watching scenes from Shakespeare's plays—was highly popular. Performed in New York to packed audiences every night for a week, it was remounted in Boston for two weeks the following year in Harvard Stadium, where it was seen by a further 250,000 people. And it also had a definable social impact, leading to the founding of the Community League of Greater Boston "to encourage and foster the community ideals exemplified in 'Caliban.'"[13]

Among many other examples from the era, a production two years earlier made the scale even of Urban's spectacle look modest in comparison. MacKaye, who wrote the script for *Caliban,* had staged *The Pageant of St. Louis* in May 1914 to celebrate the tenth anniversary of the St. Louis World's Fair (which had marked Urban's

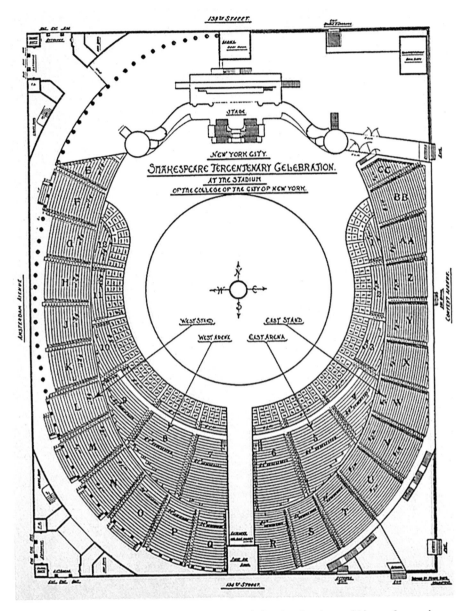

Urban, *Caliban on the Yellow Sands*, 1916, ground plan showing the amphitheater form and playing areas in the Lewisohn Stadium, from the program. Joseph Urban Papers, Rare Book and Manuscript Library, Columbia University.

first contact with America). Performed by a cast numbering more than 7,500 and a 600-voice choir, to an audience estimated at 150,000 people for each of the four performances, it too had mythic resonances, representing the history of triumphalist American colonization as the dream of a Mayan deity, and culminating in the flight of an airplane overhead scattering fireworks—to a great cry of "Eagle's wings! . . . America! Your league rides on his wings and rises towards the stars!"[14] The pageant inspired Charles Lindbergh to name the airplane in which he became the first to fly across the Atlantic *The Spirit of St. Louis*.[15]

Even Hollywood got into the act of staging mass spectacle, with the 1916 performance of *Julius Caesar* (again to celebrate Shakespeare's tercentenary) in Bolton Canyon, future site of the Hollywood Bowl. A self-described "MONSTROUS SPECTACLE" starring Tyrone Power and Douglas Fairbanks, with 5,000 "gladiators, dancers, centurions, soldiers—all Romans," this rivaled later movie spectacles like *Ben Hur*.[16]

The vogue for these community pageants had flourished through the war years with patriotic recruiting masques, and the nationwide pageant movement—the grassroots precursor of the Federal Theater Project organized by the Works Progress Administration in the 1930s—remained a popular social force through the early 1920s. Against this context, Bel Geddes' *Divine Comedy* was by no means so impractical (a label used, particularly by competing designers, to dismiss the achievement and minimize the influence of his industrial work). It remained a visionary idea and was never staged. Yet as such, Bel Geddes' *Divine Comedy* became possibly the most widely known unperformed theater piece ever. The designs were reviewed, exhibited, published, and republished all through the 1920s,[17] and the Divine Comedy Theatre intended to house Bel Geddes' production was one of the buildings announced for the 1933 Chicago World's Fair. It remained unconstructed only because the whole artistic program was cancelled due to the Depression. But Bel Geddes never seems to have become discouraged. He was still publishing proposals for the project in the 1940s—yet it brought more immediate returns. An exhibition of *Divine Comedy* designs and renderings in Amsterdam in 1922 persuaded Reinhardt to approach Bel Geddes about mounting the New York edition of *The Miracle*, which proved so central in advancing his career.[18] More: the scale of this Dantean vision carried through into Bel Geddes' campaign to redesign the way Americans lived their lives.

Throughout his career, Bel Geddes planted stories about himself in the daily newspapers: whether admiring or controversial, any sort of publicity would do. He kept meticulous "case histories" on every aspect of each production or project that emphasized their significance or novelty, for feeding the right angle to journalists (and quite possibly with an eye to posterity, too). He published his ideas in books—*Horizons* (1932) and *Magic Motorways* (1940)—that not only promoted his vision and conditioned the way his work should be received, but also served as highly effective advertising to attract clients for his nontheatrical business. He mounted publicity campaigns for his own work, or persuaded others to do so on his behalf, as well as continually publishing statements on future plans that also served as advertisement. All this self-generated publicity, quite as much as his actual stage work, was what won Bel Geddes his design jobs outside Broadway.

Urban, and more so Bel Geddes, might be said to have been the first industrial designers, a profession that had not existed before the 1920s. Up to then—with perhaps the signal exception of William Morris, who had set the style for late Victorian living in England[19]—the different aspects of what is now considered an industrial designer's work had been largely kept separate, with architects sometimes also designing furniture to go with their buildings (as Charles Rennie Mackintosh had done in the 1890s, defining the Glasgow revival), or painters and sculptors designing conventionally artistic objects from ceramics to jewelry, while engineers backed up by industrial draftsmen designed everything mechanical. However, with the emergence of a consumer culture, fueled by the spread of wealth in the 1920s, particularly in America, and promoted by increasingly effective advertising, there was a need for differentiating products (such as cars and kitchen appliances) and making them more attractive. This meant involving artists with industrial production, and as the *New Yorker* specifically asserted, "Until a few years ago the designers employed by manufacturers merely corrected the ugly lines created by machinery or stuck on meaningless decoration. The first break came . . . under the aegis of Joseph Urban."[20]

This was possible precisely because, as a stage designer, Urban was already to some extent practicing as an architect and a mechanic—not to mention interior designer and couturier, as well as a scene painter. He was also an entrepreneurial businessman, running a factory (that primarily manufactured scenery) and employing a workforce that rose from 60 in his Boston days to around 150 people once he was fully engaged with the New York stage, as well as a Fifth Avenue gallery and an architectural design office. He was therefore well equipped to take on the new demands, indeed, to move from field to field, bringing his art to bear on every kind of product. Bel Geddes expanded on Urban's range in engineering and mass marketing, and a whole group of designers followed Urban and Bel Geddes.

The followers who established the highest profiles were Raymond Loewy and Henry Dreyfuss. There was also Walter Dorwin Teague, born in 1883—the same year as Bel Geddes—who opened an office for industrial design around the same time. All these, together with Bel Geddes, contributed major buildings and exhibits for the 1939 New York World's Fair—the most concentrated expression of American modernism anywhere. Bel Geddes was hailed in 1934 by *Fortune* magazine as "the father of streamlining."[21] And all three adopted his streamlined principles—with Loewy even carrying streamlining to absurd excess in a teardrop-shaped pencil sharpener (its spaceship lines being ridiculous, as Dreyfuss pointed out, for something screwed down to a desk).[22] Significantly, Dreyfuss too started off designing scenery for Broadway hits and was demonstrably under Bel Geddes' influence. Not only had he attended a course in design taught by Bel Geddes himself, but also was an employee of the Walter Thompson Agency during the period from 1929, when Bel Geddes redesigned their corporate offices (providing a whole context of streamlined machine-age modernism) to 1937, when Walter Thompson worked with Bel Geddes on a landmark advertising campaign for Shell Oil, which Dreyfuss clearly echoed in the display he designed for the 1939 New York World's Fair. By contrast, Teague came to industrial design through advertising, while Loewy, who had trained as an engineer in his native France, started off as a fashion illustrator for *Harper's Bazaar* and *Vogue* when he first reached America in the 1920s. Yet, as well as being applied artists whose work overlapped with both Urban and Bel Geddes (who had also designed costumes, including some of the fashions that Loewy illustrated, and theater posters and programs in direct competition to Teague), by the time Teague and Loewy established their design offices, the theatricality introduced by Urban was already very much the fashion.

Each of these other designers competed hotly with Bel Geddes in designing some of the standard accoutrements of modern America: the Kodak camera and standardized and utilitarian Texaco gas stations (Teague), the Hoover vacuum cleaner and Singer sewing machine as well as the Bell telephone (Dreyfuss). Notably, Bel Geddes had earlier designed exactly the same range of objects—but for General Electric (vacuum cleaners, radios) and Standard Oil (gas stations). Similarly, while both Loewy and Dreyfuss designed magnificently streamlined railroad engines, or the streamlined interiors of the carriages for trains with names like the *Twentieth Century* (something Bel Geddes never did), their concepts were lifted directly from his book *Horizons.* And whereas Teague turned to the more eccentric side of modernism, for instance, designing modernist grand pianos for Steinway, while Dreyfuss came to specialize almost exclusively in the lucrative but mundanely mechanical design of agricultural machinery and particularly John Deere tractors, after World War II Bel Geddes was working on broad-scale city planning and studio designs for what was already becoming the major disseminator of lifestyle imagery: television. Only Loewy, due to his far longer career, outpaced Bel Geddes, and the competition between them was fierce, as is all too clearly demonstrated by a skit Loewy himself performed at his firm's 1944 office Christmas party. Sung to the tune of the Richard Rodgers hit "Pore

Judd Is Dead," this singles out Bel Geddes (as the ostensible singer) in a parody of all the competing designers, who are notionally rejoicing at Loewy's going on holiday to Arizona. It went like this:

> I'm Norman Bel
> Yes, Geddes am I,
> A fellow much respected by the press—by the press.
> My Futurama's gone, and the other things I've drawn
> Are pretty—but they can't be built, I guess—built I guess!

The song ends with a chorus, representing Bel Geddes in harmony with Dreyfuss and Teague singing a happy farewell to Loewy:

> We're glad to see you go; it was getting tough, you know
> To find designing jobs you DIDN'T do—didn't do![23]

It is hardly surprising, then, to find Loewy continuing to deny that Bel Geddes had any influence on his work. The comparison made in a 1949 *Life* article, clearly inspired by Loewy and hailing him as "The Great Packager," includes a line that was to become standard for design historians and commentators. While acknowledging that "Loewy's work does not have the imaginative sweep of Bel Geddes' visions" (a word selected to show Bel Geddes' impracticality), it asserts that Loewy "has had a greater influence on current designs and modern living . . . simply because his pen is in so many different inkpots."[24]

Many others figure in the story, both as competitors and contributors to the modern American lifestyle. No two individuals, even as gifted as Urban and Bel Geddes, could have had so complete an impact alone. Although they never formally headed a "school," they needed the multiplication effect provided by their followers, professional acquaintances, and even rivals. Among them are visionaries and eccentrics—architects, from Frank Lloyd Wright to populists like Morris Lapidus—and women of fashion like the notoriously shocking modiste Lady Duff Gordon and Gordon Conway, both of whom helped to set the style of the 1920s.

All these either worked with Urban or were directly influenced by Bel Geddes. It was these two who figured out the design principles and developed the ideas that the others applied, with Dreyfuss, for example, substituting the term "cleanlining" for "streamlining."[25] Together these followers helped to push the lifestyle envisioned by Urban and Bel Geddes into every corner of American society—and even when they themselves had no stage experience, they carried on the theatricality Urban and Bel

Henry Dreyfuss, logo for the *Twentieth Century* train. Printed by
permission of the Cooper-Hewitt, National Design Museum, Smithsonian Institution.

Geddes had introduced. For example, the most famous train pulled by Loewy's S-1
engine for the Pennsylvania Railroad was named the *Broadway Limited,* while the
brilliantly titled New York Central Railroad train designed by Dreyfuss became the
subject of a Broadway musical: *On the Twentieth Century.*

　　Nowhere else but in the United States did people whose primary job was theater
play a significant role in architecture and industrial design. Part of the reason that
Broadway stage designers achieved such dominance can be traced to an inherent

theatricality in much of American life. This is still present today in the intersection of entertainment and public life: a former movie actor as president in the 1980s and one as governor of California (the job Ronald Reagan had held) in the first decade of the present century; a character actor in *Star Trek* being invited to join NASA's board of directors; an airport named after an actor and a highway after a comedian. However, this blurring was particularly evident over the early decades of the twentieth century. In the 1920s, when first Urban and then Bel Geddes started their careers as industrial designers and architects, the American society was primed for influence from the theater.

3

Theatrical Fashions

THE PERSON WHO FIRST MOVED out from Broadway to design everyday things for Main Street was Joseph Urban. He started off small, with his costume designs being taken as patterns for evening gowns by just one or two well-connected ladies in Boston. But by the time America emerged from World War I with a fresh sense of national confidence, he was in a position to influence fashions of dress and décor. Fashion may seem something trivial, yet it colors our experience of everything around us, and Urban played a significant role in defining the vibrant, elegant twenties.

His example was the catalyst, encouraging other scene designers to move outside theater and opening the eyes of industrialists to the potential advantages of using aesthetics from the stage for commercial products. When Urban was recruited to head the Boston Opera in 1911, no one could have predicted this—and indeed his appointment very nearly did not happen.

It all came about because a small-time but highly energetic impresario named Henry Russell, finding his little touring company from the West Coast stranded in New England, managed to persuade Boston society that their civic pride required an opera house.[1] Up to then his only claim to fame had been as a voice coach for famous singers of the time, most notably the Australian soprano Nellie Melba. But during its first season, which opened with considerable fanfare in November 1909, the fledgling Boston company staged an amazing total of nineteen different operas. Among these were major spectacles like Verdi's *Aïda* and Wagner's *Lohengrin*; and, to say the least, such an ambitious program must have strained even Russell's chutzpah. So the following summer, when he was in Paris visiting the Belgian playwright Maurice Maeterlinck, hoping to get *Pelléas and Mélisande* (his latest piece) for Boston, and happened to meet Urban, who was there for discussions about staging the same opera in Vienna, Russell offered him the job of artistic director on the spot.

It is quite astonishing, in light of his influence on America, that Urban's arrival was due so much to sheer chance. A further coincidence was that just then Urban was at odds with colleagues in Austria, deeply hurt by a malicious rumor about the immense cost of the imperial jubilee procession, which focused on (of all things) a diamond ring that the emperor had given him as a token of appreciation. But Urban embraced his new home with enthusiasm, and had soon moved beyond opera into new fields.

At the same time, he continued to work in opera all his life, and his first impact was to revolutionize the American theater world. He staged no fewer than twenty-eight productions during his two and a half years in Boston, where everything except the music was his responsibility: scenery, costume, props, lighting and direction, even posters and programs. These performances won him an instant reputation, and he went on to work for the Metropolitan Opera in New York, even after he had branched out into other fields of design, creating another fifty-five productions between 1917 and 1931 (several of which were still in use at the Met up to at least 1959).

Controlling every aspect of the staging, Urban was able to impose complete imaginative and visual unity. This was his guiding principle, and he extended it beyond opera to culture. For Urban, achieving this kind of unity meant discarding all practices and conventions from the past. To be effective, everything—in designing a lifestyle, as on the stage—had to reflect the dominant ideas of the period.

His Boston productions were certainly eye-openers. "Nothing like them has ever been seen in any opera on the American stage," the *Evening Transcript* commented in 1912.[2] Repeated groupings of characters created dominating visual rhythms, reinforced by striking and vivid color schemes. Urban was also the first to use an inner frame (which later came to be known as "portals"), cutting down the dimensions of the proscenium to create a sense of intimacy. This frame could be fitted with doors in each side which opened to show other scenes behind—a set-up that Urban was to build into his plans for the new Metropolitan Opera House in 1928. Or they were decorated like the broad borders of his fairy-tale illustrations, as with one of his first Boston productions, *Hansel and Gretel*. He was also one of the first to recognize that, as he put it in a 1913 article on modern stagecraft, "Under the new lighting conditions, the colors in stage scenery are no longer constant. They change like the colors of nature itself."[3] And in order to realize this potential Urban developed a pointillist technique (similar to Georges Seurat's paintings but on a far larger scale—the cyclorama of the Boston Opera House being 64 feet high by 170 feet wide).

Laying the enormous canvas cloths for the scenes flat on the floor of his workshop, a huge shed in Swampscott on the outskirts of Boston, assistants drew outlines with charcoal on the ends of long sticks, then spattered paint with huge semi-dry brushes, directed by Urban standing on a platform high above. For a sky backdrop the blobs might be three or four shades of blue, with sparser spatters of red, green, and silver. In ordinary white light the result was neutral gray—but under amber it appeared golden sunlight; with red light it turned the rosy pink of sunset; and when a strong blue light was thrown onto it the effect was the intense and transparent, atmospheric, deep blue that became Urban's trademark. As reviewers noted again and again, the result was magical.[4]

This sort of scenery revolutionized the position of the designer in American theater. Apart from such little experimental theaters as the Washington Square Players, the general practice at the time, surprising as it may now seem, was to order complete

Joseph Urban, sketch for the proposed Metropolitan Opera House, showing the inner frame and "portals." Joseph Urban Papers, Rare Book and Manuscript Library, Columbia University.

sets of scenery ready-made from commercial workshops: Dodge and Castle, Lee Lash Studios, and others. Opera companies, with greater aesthetic pretensions, went to European firms and had their sets shipped across the Atlantic. All these commercial settings tended to be standardized and highly conventional. By contrast, Urban's sets and costumes were original, keyed to the vision of that particular production. And the new elements and principles that Urban introduced were adopted by American theater almost overnight. His inner frames became commonplace around the stage proscenium. His methods of lighting were widely copied, as was the way of painting scenes at his Swampscott studio (which became known as "the greatest factory of illusion in our country").[5]

Still more influentially, American theaters rapidly began hiring a specific designer for each show. All experimental little theaters, such as the Washington Square Players, where Lee Simonson started his career in 1915, already did; but Urban's practice predated both that and Robert Edmond Jones's breakthrough with the design for *The Man Who Married a Dumb Wife,* also in 1915, which is generally credited with initiating a new era of scene design in the United States. By then Urban's Swampscott scenery shop had been in operation for more than three years, offering a highly effective example, if by no means so nonnaturalistic as the "new stagecraft" championed by these much younger designers. Urban had effectively started a new theatrical profession in the United States, one that would have significant implications for American society as a whole.

The qualities that Urban's settings epitomized not only made his stage work unique. The intensity of color, harmonious patterning, rhythmic lines, and visual unity, simple means creating unusually rich effects, and above all the use of light, together with an unconventional approach, combined to embody an idealized image of life, which Urban then translated into fields of design outside the theater. As Urban put it in his 1929 book, *Theatres,* the function of the stage is "to establish a relation between man's life and his environment."[6]

And in Urban's view this environment had to be specifically American, because the United States was the only country capable of forming a new culture for the modern age. A 1919 entry in his wife's diary records his view that "America, to him the New and Truly Great," had yet to find its own style, and that "there must be an absolute break with the past" if America was to express itself.[7] Ten years later, in the conclusion of *Theatres,* Urban made the point even more explicitly: "America is free from the influence of the dead which in Europe crushes the vitality of the living with the weight of history and tradition. The weight of the old form is an obstacle which hinders every living movement. American life belongs to the living and the future!"

If by 1929 America had been liberated from the historical and imported styles that were standard at the turn of the century, it was partly Urban's work. He was instrumental in creating a specifically contemporary American image—and his theater won Urban his first opportunities for other types of design in America.

One of the Boston socialites of the time, a relative of the well-known art patron Isabella Stewart Gardner, admired Urban's costumes for *La Bohème* so much that she acquired the sketches and had dresses made from them for herself. And the lavish spectacle of another opera, *Monna Vanna,* in the spring of 1913, led the Broadway impresario George Tyler to hire Urban for *The Garden of Paradise,* a play adapted from Hans Christian Andersen's "The Little Mermaid." The script of this was so awful that not even Urban's spectacular scenery could save the production. But his visions of an undersea world won enthusiastic praise and attracted the attention of Florenz Ziegfeld who, on seeing the twelve striking settings and more than seventy fantastic costumes he had designed, immediately hired Urban for the *Follies.* And through Ziegfeld's annual revue, the show that was already the most popular (in all senses) on Broadway, Urban rapidly gained far wider influence.

The *Ziegfeld Follies* had first hit the New York scene in 1907. Disparagingly, but all too accurately described as a mix of tall girls and low comedy, it was modeled on the Parisian Folies Bergère, and each annual show had always been a scandalous success. But its raunchy, down-market reputation kept more refined people away. On being taken by Ziegfeld to see the 1914 edition of the *Follies,* the last of the older, cruder shows, Urban remarked: "Advertising posters! The best of their kind in America today, perhaps. But how much more can be done!"[8] Offered the chance, he turned the revue into a high-quality lifestyle advertisement.

When he first joined up with Ziegfeld, the *Follies* were being presented at the old-fashioned Century Theatre, hardly décor to suit the modern sophisticated shows Urban envisaged. So instead he had the interior repainted in turquoise and yellow, with portraits of the beauties of the chorus as murals in the lobby and corridors, to set a mood of fashionable frivolity in addition to pushing the glorification of "the American Girl" (the Ziegfeld trademark). And he transformed the revue itself by unifying the short scenes, dances, and comic skits to give each show a dominant image that reviews referred to repeatedly as "sumptuous," "exotic," "vivid," "dazzling."[9] Strikingly imaginative and highly colorful, these scenes of Urban's were also on the cutting edge of fashion—displaying his variant of Art Deco modernism in extremely stylish contexts, as in the entirely black-and-white sequence of "Here Comes Tootsie" in *Around the Map,* his 1915 show for the New Amsterdam Theatre, or later at the Met

The black-and-white cabaret theater in *Around the Map* (act III, scene 4), complete with
Urban's characteristic chairs (later manufactured by the Mallin Furniture Company), 1915.
Joseph Urban Papers, Rare Book and Manuscript Library, Columbia University.

in operas such as *Johnny Spielt Aus* (1929).[10] The impact of this fashion was frequently
reinforced by combining it with patriotic emblems—as in the finale of *Johnny Spielt
Aus,* where a whole array of the Stars and Stripes formed the scenery, stylized into
an Art Deco pattern surrounding the Statue of Liberty, or by overlapping the stage
setting with the audience's own space—for example, setting a scene of *Around the
Map* in a cabaret theater—in a way that became typical of how Urban promoted his
new styles. The dramatic material and dialogue of such revues might be minimal, but
its very frivolity was an advantage in giving a lightness and gaiety to Urban's designs,
while offering little to distract from this subliminal advertising, which was reinforced
by the beauty of the actresses and dancers.

At the same time as Urban became involved in the *Follies,* Ziegfeld also recruited
Lady Duff Gordon, an English aristocrat turned couturier, newly arrived in New
York with a bevy of elegant models. At her London salon, Lucille's of Hanover
Square, in 1897 she had mounted the very first fashion show—training salesgirls in

deportment and having them parade her gowns while tea was served to the consumers. She shocked Victorian society by opening a Rose Room, where what she called her "glorious girls" modeled scanty and transparent lingerie (to select consumers, male voyeurs, as well as women customers). In 1915, having crossed to New York, she staged a public fashion parade of "dream dresses" in aid of the British war effort at her 57th Street salon. Ziegfeld was so taken by her daring use of chiffon—as well as by one of her models—that he used her creations (and the model) in that year's revue.[11]

From then on, with Urban and Gordon collaborating on costumes that were strikingly lit by Urban and displayed in his gracefully stylish settings, the *Follies* became a byword for chic. Widely patronized by the New York smart set, the revue spawned a whole number of imitators in the 1920s—the Shuberts' *Passing Show,* George White's *Scandals,* Earl Carroll's *Vanities,* Irving Berlin's *Music Box Revues,* and the *Greenwich Village Follies.*

Hailed by headlines like "Urban's Triumph" (1916) or "Memorable Dream of Splendor" (1919), each of the annual *Follies* was described in detail by reviews. Photographs of the scenes and costumes, even of Urban's sketches, as well as of the stars were regularly published in the daily press, frequently taking up a full-page spread in journals, and reviewers implicitly recognized the advertising potential of the shows in referring to the scenes as "a series of vivid poster pictures."[12] Newspapers began printing the names of the high society line-up attending the openings—for instance, listing the presence of more than fifty notables (mainly women) at the 1919 *Follies:* Belmonts, Vanderbilts, Huttons, Condé Nasts, and Guggenheims, foreign nobility such as the Duchess de Chaulnes, as well as a major-general of the American army, and even the New York police commissioner.

The *Follies* had joined mainstream American fashion with a bang. Up to then women's images had been almost solely the province of magazines, where fashion-plate sketches had launched the famous Gibson Girl—otherwise known as the "Outdoors Girl" or, in more sophisticated guise, the "Beautiful Charmer." New female roles were consciously showcased by *Vogue* and *Vanity Fair.* Together with competing journals like *Harper's Bazaar*—where Raymond Loewy was to start his career—these promoted the image of modern woman through advertising beauty products and leisure services, as they still do today. But during the glittering 1920s, with Urban staging the *Follies,* the focus for new fashions switched to the theater.

By around 1919 the links between New York magazines and the popular stage were already close, and, of the many crossovers between the designers of fashion plates and

GREETINGS

Gordon Conway
1920 — 1921

Gordon Conway's Christmas card, 1920, featuring an image of herself. Courtesy of the
Harry Ransom Humanities Research Center.

revues, one of the earliest and most notable was Gordon Conway. A socialite with considerable artistic talent who had joined the staff of *Vanity Fair* in 1915, Conway herself presented the chic look of the fashionable New Woman (like her friend Dorothy Parker, who was also on the Condé Nast team). Throughout her career, sketches or photos of her, in dresses of her own design, were featured in the magazines she worked for. She created a special female character—redheaded, like her—which gained the status of one of America's dream girls in 1919 through a nationwide advertising campaign. And she even served as a highly recognizable model for the modern heroine of a novel about the fashion world of the 1920s, *Smart Setback,* by Wood Kahler.[13]

Not only the clothes shown in her fashion-plates, but the poses of the figures she drew, their facial look, and even body type suggested the new status of women (now that they had the vote) and the type of life they should aspire to. And more than any other magazine artist's, Gordon Conway's style of drawing epitomized the feminine ideal at the opening of the modern period. Before the age of air-brushing, drawings were far better at capturing an ideal body shape (anorexically elegant) or dress (sleekly fitting and uncreased) than photographs, where wrinkles and reality always intruded. Drawn images were thus the engine of fashion; and the clean lines of Conway's sketches, slim forms and flowing shapes, stylized simplicity and directness, flat planes of color and sharp edges, all express the essence of liberated independence, self-assured sophistication, and modern glamour. In particular, the women of her drawings are in motion. They leap and dance, lithe, unconstrained, demonstrating pace and grace in a way that is immediately recognizable as the image of the twenties.

So it's hardly surprising that Conway hooked up with Dorothy Dickson, one of the most popular American dancers of the time, providing all her costumes. Conway also worked on revues for almost all the major New York producers, and collaborated with Joseph Urban on one of the first of the late-night cabarets that made up Ziegfeld's *Midnight Frolics.* Perhaps her most characteristic Broadway show was a 1920 satire on the straitlaced image of the New Woman, tellingly titled *The Charm School* (a fantasy, with music by Jerome Kern, where a young car salesman inherits a girls' school and hires his bachelor friends to teach these would-be feminists "charm"). Conway designed the whole concept, from posters and programs through scenery and costumes. Her billboards for musicals like Jerome Kern's *Rock-a-Bye Baby* drew such large crowds that they stopped traffic in the New York streets. Yet while she contributed so much to setting the style at the beginning of the 1920s, she left the American scene in 1921—marrying a dashing Frenchman who took her to live in Europe.[14] Through the mid-1920s and early 1930s Conway became one of the fashion-setters in Paris and London, designing women's clothing for major stores like Harrods and Debenhams, as well as continuing to costume the London shows of Dorothy Dickson—and from 1928 on she designed numerous British films, becoming head of the Gaumont-British/Gainsborough costume department. So Conway became a highly effective publicist for the new American style of fashion through Europe, leaving Urban, and the glamorizing effect of his theater, as the leading influence on the developing images of the New York lifestyle.

The way Urban's work spread to the wider society can be graphically seen in the rooftop cabaret he designed in 1918 above the New Amsterdam Theatre, the new home of the *Ziegfeld Follies*. There, after the main revue ended, spectators could dance and drink champagne (at least until Prohibition closed down all the bars) or dine while watching *Midnight Frolic*—the first ever dinner-theater—which *Hotel Review* noted as "a New Novelty for Blasé New Yorkers."[15] It became the fashion to go from one Ziegfeld show to the other. Patrons, very possibly wearing dresses inspired by the *Follies,* saw the same stars and costumes in intimate surroundings, and when they danced they were in the same space as the cabaret stars, moving against the same scenery. In the same way, several editions of the *Follies* included rooftop cabarets, whether idealized or bohemian, in their scenes. Lifestyle merged with theatrical display on every level.

Urban continued to design the annual edition of the *Ziegfeld Follies* every year through 1926, and again in 1931, as well as providing scenery and costumes for a series of spectacular musicals mounted by Klaw & Erlanger, one of the commercial firms that dominated New York theater, starting with *Around the Map* in 1915. This production, and his 1916 edition of the *Follies* under the title of "The Century Girl" at the newly reopened Century Theatre, set the tone for the next decade. Both were little more than vehicles for fashionable décor and clothing. *Around the Map* was reviewed simply as "a gorgeous fashion show which moves in steady procession across three and a half hours,"[16] while "The Century Girl" had no story at all, just staircases that appeared to stretch into the heavens, down which came "A Dream of Fair Women" starring Helen of Troy and Cleopatra, culminating in "The Century Girl" herself—America outshining the past.

"The Century Girl" *Follies* was hailed as "The Beauty Show of the Century," while subsequent editions of the *Follies* set their subliminal advertising firmly in an idealized present by parading fashions against a heavily romanticized New York skyline. The 1917 *Follies* even featured a penthouse view of what is clearly a prototype for the Chrysler Building more than a decade before it was planned. Although there is no evidence that the architect William Van Alen saw this, the similarity of the iconic

Urban's rooftop cabaret at the New Amsterdam Theatre with the set for Ziegfeld's *Midnight Frolic,* c. 1920 (*above*); rooftop cabaret used as a set for a cabaret performance in the 1915 *Ziegfeld Follies* (*opposite*). Joseph Urban Papers, Rare Book and Manuscript Library, Columbia University.

shape he gave to the Chrysler Building is a sign of the way Urban's general influence permeated the design world.

By 1917 newspapers were remarking that "Ziegfeld has out-Urbaned Lady Duff-Gordon" with the "unequalled display of colorful costumes" in that year's *Follies* (which also featured a nude Venus inside a huge iridescent bubble as part of a "Garden of Girls"). Commenting on the new look that Urban had brought to the *Follies,* in 1919 the leading magazine of interior design, *Arts and Decoration,* took particular note of the way his work was defining public taste, pointing out that "the audience which had come for frivolous entertainment was quite unconsciously absorbing the beauties of color and light, line and mass."[17] It is significant that rather than the arts pages of the daily press, this comes from a trade journal, like so many of the comments

on Urban's work, indicating the widespread impact of his theater on manufacturing and commerce. The *Follies* spread Urban's style of dress as well as décor throughout East Coast society. And from the *Follies* it was a short step to fashion shows. Even before joining forces with Ziegfeld, in 1915 Urban had become involved in a "Fashion Extravaganza" at Carnegie Hall (sponsored by *Vogue* to promote American designers now that Parisian imports were blocked by the war), the event that introduced the "shockingly revealing" short skirt that came to characterize the twenties.[18] In 1920 a piece in the *Cincinnati Commercial Tribune,* citing Urban as its sole example, was headlined "Spring Styles Copied From 'High Art' Sources."[19]

His influence grew rapidly. As the *Buffalo News* reported (with evident pride), the new fashions of 1924 and 1925 were for the first time American, not imported from Paris, with "great masses of women appearing in myriads of colors," the most widespread being "Urban blue." Indeed Urban was directly responsible for some of the fabrics in these dresses, having designed the popular "Franco Prints" (manufactured by Frank Silk Mills) that were made into women's dresses, as well as being used in handbags and shoes. In fact Urban's influence on fashion was so extensive that he became uniquely identified with the "American" style. So a year later the more sober-minded *Minneapolis Journal* commented, in a sour, backhanded compliment:

"Those of us who have resented the fact that fashion has been full of color as a Joseph Urban stage set may look with satisfaction upon the new modes just arrived from Paris" for the 1926 season, which by contrast promoted a "vogue of black, navy and gray."[20]

Other stage designers also contributed to the fashion scene, if somewhat later and in more minor ways. In the early 1930s Henry Dreyfuss's first commercial jobs, while he was still designing scenery for Broadway shows, were creating a range of belt buckles, men's neckties, and women's garters, as well as perfume bottles. Similarly, Norman Bel Geddes designed costume jewelry for Trifari, Krussman, and Fishel, as well as packaging for Yardley cosmetics.

At the same time, Urban's settings for the *Follies,* and later for the *Midnight Frolics,* provided the décor and social contexts for such clothes and accessories. Although many of the scenes for these revues were exotic or extravaganzas, there were also American cabaret scenes, which prefigured the kind of styling he was to apply to various hotels, and contemporary boudoir and living room scenes.

Urban's first *Follies* had been hailed by the *New York Sun* as "dazzling as a jewelry store window,"[21] while his roof garden midnight cabarets served explicitly as lifestyle advertisements. The title of one in 1917, "Dance and Grow Thin," was an appeal to the body-conscious and included a "Show Window" scene (anticipating Urban's designs for actual Fifth Avenue and Chicago store windows in 1922). In addition, the living fashion plate on the stage was reinforced by the *Follies* program, handed out to the audience and frequently taken home with them. The programs were full of ads for perfume, women's accessories, and hairstyles (as worn by the stars), and included not only images of the new styles in costume photos of the "Glorified Girls"—as Ziegfeld, in a cynical but more accurate variation on Lady Duff Gordon, referred to his performers—but also mini-articles on "What the Man Will Wear" and "What the Woman Will Wear" (all lavishly endorsed by the stars).

At the time, long before television, theater was a major advertising tool. An estimated 1.6 million spectators attended shows every month in New York alone; and Urban clearly realized the potential of his theatrical productions for influencing the public. As he emphasized in an interview for *Sunday World* in 1920: "People, particularly women, see beautiful things on the stage and decide they will duplicate them in their own homes. They have come to look to the scenic stage for lessons in good taste." He goes on to say that "if only one person each night" picked up on something in his designs, "I shall be supremely happy."[22]

And Ziegfeld's patrons did besiege Urban to provide the décor and dresses for highly public events—a Gypsy Ball for Mrs. William Randolph Hearst at the Ritz-

Urban's décor for the Huttons' Japanese Ball, 1928: faint lines across the painted "sky" indicate the tent-like corners in light silk cloth that seamlessly covered all the walls and the ceiling of the ballroom. Joseph Urban Papers, Rare Book and Manuscript Library, Columbia University.

Carlton Hotel in 1925, a Paradise Ball at the Ritz-Carlton in 1927, a Japanese Ball (with Mount Fuji and blossoming cherry trees) for the Huttons in 1928, and a debutantes' Silver Ball at Madison Square Garden in 1929.

All were in many ways an extension of the *Follies*. The Gypsy Ball of October 1927 included a cabaret by *Follies* performers. Conversely, the Palm Beach Coconut Grove had featured in the 1927 *Follies* as "Joseph Urban's conception of the world famous dance resort," and the entire *Follies* of 1926 had a "Palm Beach Nights" theme.[23] The settings for these high-society balls were elaborate displays of Urban's art. For the Gypsy Ball the Crystal Room of the Ritz-Carlton Hotel was transformed into a nighttime

The main house of Mar-a-Lago, with its fanciful tower and the owners' pavilion
(the spires are in fact chimneys), as designed by Joseph Urban, 1926. Joseph Urban Papers,
Rare Book and Manuscript Library, Columbia University.

woodland encampment with four hundred real pine trees silhouetted against twinkling
blue lights, a white silk tent canopy suspended across the ceiling from their tops, and
a huge full moon shining through their branches—while Mrs. Hearst appeared in a
gypsy bridal gown designed by Urban (though decked out in her own jewels). Fashionable society had taken over the role of *Follies*' stars with a vengeance.

The importance of these events for Joseph Urban, beyond the publicity for his fashions, was the connection with wealthy patrons and the many commissions that came
from them. By far the most spectacular of these was the house he created for Marjorie
Post—one of the most powerful women in America, who had expanded her father's

The rear façade of the Palm Beach Bath and Tennis Club, with Spanish mission bells, 1926.
Joseph Urban Papers, Rare Book and Manuscript Library, Columbia University.

breakfast cereal business into a global food-processing company—whose name had also appeared in the lists of people who attended the *Follies,* and for whom Urban also designed a New York ball.

This house was Mar-a-Lago, the best known of several mansions that Urban built for the American elite who wintered in Palm Beach. Adopted by President Nixon as a "winter White House," it is now owned by Donald Trump, who has turned it into an exclusive club. Mar-a-Lago has been ranked with the Vanderbilt's Marble House in Newport and with William Randolph Hearst's San Simeon as among the grandest private residences in the country from the era. But in sharp contrast to those neoclassical and Renaissance turn-of-the-century Rhode Island and California palaces, here Urban made a conscious attempt to create a specifically American style of grand architecture based on local themes and materials: in this case an appropriately Floridian image, drawing on the history of Spanish colonists, the first Europeans to arrive in the area, combined with the Moorish background of their homeland.

Columns and beams were native cypress, sandblasted and aged to driftwood gray. The sculptures of animals and parrots, which he incorporated, were all indigenous to the semitropical Florida climate. He designed a tower, with balconies jutting out on all four sides at the top and an irregular roof, that has a feel of La Mancha, and arched-over chimneys derived from the bell arches on Spanish mission churches. Apart from a Louis XVI bedroom (almost obligatory for the super-rich), every element harmonized with this transplanted Mediterranean concept—like the salmon pink roof tiles, which came from old Cuban houses.

At the same time, in Mar-a-Lago the theatricality was explicit. Parrots and peacocks had become Urban's trademark figures in the *Ziegfeld Follies*. They also inhabit Marjorie Post's mansion, appearing in the form of gargoyles on the eaves all the way round the semicircular patio, as well as statues at the ends of staircase balustrades and around fountains. Like Urban's stage work too, Mar-a-Lago was highly colorful—vibrant yellow-orange stucco edged with rust-colored stone against the tropical greens of the landscape and the blues of lake and ocean—and openly fanciful. It expressed a sense of "holiday," which *American Architect* found "picturesque and dramatic"[24]—and these qualities carried over into all the other houses Urban built at Palm Beach, most in a somewhat less ostentatious way, forming a whole school of Florida architecture that still resonates today.

The same style marked Urban's most ambitious and most socially influential Palm Beach construction: the Bath and Tennis Club. Again the overall impression of his design evokes Florida history, topped not only by simplified Spanish church towers, but also by a central peaked façade carrying actual bells. Built in 1926, this club immediately became the social center for the elite community, and according to press reports was one of the major factors that made Palm Beach into the fashionable winter resort for American money. As *Vanity Fair* noted in February 1927, less than a year after its opening, this was "where the smartest clothes and newest fashions are to be seen," and both *Vanity Fair* and *Vogue* displayed their 1927 fashion-plate models against the backdrop of the Bath and Tennis Club.

It was almost literally a stage set for the lifestyle of the rich and famous. Along with the Oasis Club (a residence for bachelors also designed by Urban), the Bath and Tennis Club was where they acted out their fantasies at the balls Urban designed. Something of his influence can be indicated by the social calendar for a single week in March 1927, when he created the settings for three of these events. As the *New York*

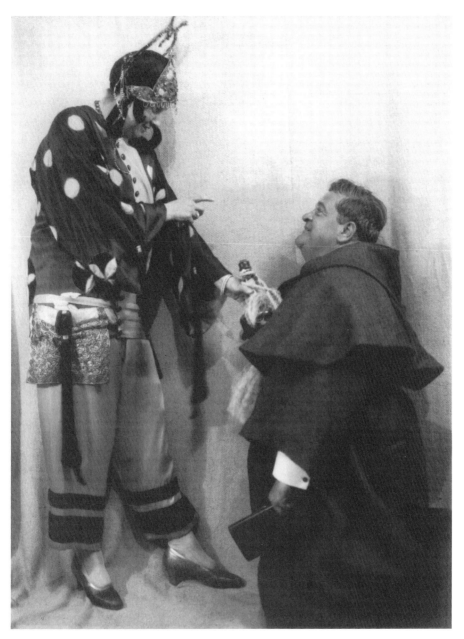

Joseph Urban with Marjorie Post at a costume ball in Palm Beach, 1927.
Joseph Urban Papers, Rare Book and Manuscript Library, Columbia University.

Evening Post reported, the Bath and Tennis Club became transformed successively into "a gorgeous panorama depicting the splendor and glory of ancient Babylon and Nineveh," and two nights later into "a street scene of Baghdad, and colorful and beautiful vistas of the orient." The third ball, at the Oasis Club, set partygoers in an idealized version of their actual surroundings, like a stage-within-a-stage, described by the *New York American* as "a cocoanut grove of exquisite beauty on the moonlit shore of an azure sea," complete with tropical moon "casting its silvery light over the picturesque and beautiful scene."[25]

The attention of New York papers to such events in Florida shows the wider public interest in this elite culture (there is no indication in these news articles of the kind of moral censure of excess so common in national reports of comparable turn-of-the-century Newport parties). The Florida scene, in particular Urban's major contribution, was even relocated to Madison Avenue. Just one month later, the Hearsts' annual costume ball transformed the Ritz roof garden into "a tropical paradise, a faithful replica of the newest and most successful of Palm Beach's fashionable institutions, the Bath and Tennis Club." This caused a minor sensation, with the *New York Herald Tribune* describing—in a long report picked up by at least two other papers—how Urban reproduced "the shimmering blue waters of Lake Worth," bordered by real palm trees imported from Florida, with beach cabanas and the clubhouse behind, and "the glistening sands with the Atlantic stretching out far to the horizon."[26]

Joseph Urban's artistic skills alone would not have been enough to give him such an influence on fashion. It was his flamboyant personality and self-assured, gregarious presence that made it possible for him to interact so successfully with the moneyed elite who set the tone for American society. There is an engaging photograph of a dainty Marjorie Post in richly decorated harem costume at the Palm Beach Persian Ball, with Urban in monk's habit as a playful "Gray Eminence," kneeling at her feet and smiling broadly up at her with bold eyes, but still with his head almost on the level of hers—a pose of social submissiveness combined with dominating influence that perfectly expresses his relationship with the social trendsetters. Although Urban's attention to detail, taste for elegance, and sensitivity to color made the lifestyle embodied in his designs attractive, it was his versatility that gave him such a broad influence.

Trained as an architect and interior designer, as well as artist and stage designer, Urban was able to operate in almost all of the most visible areas of cultural expression. Just as he sought unity in his opera productions, he reinforced the impression of the fashions in clothing inspired by his stage work through shaping the context in which they were worn. Houses and social centers, which helped to establish a specific Florida style of building, extended into stage-managing and creating the scenic ambience for major social activities, in both Palm Beach and New York. And precisely those aspects of the lives of the rich and famous were reported in newspapers and illustrated in magazines of the time—and so emulated or aspired to by the general public. Theater had merged with the outside world.

4

Stage and Screen

THE MOST OPENLY THEATRICAL of all public spaces were the theater buildings themselves, which Urban and Bel Geddes created and in which design, architecture, and fashion come together. The spectators, many of whom might well have been wearing dresses inspired by Urban, gathered to watch his shows, which promoted the new lifestyle he was defining, surrounded by the décor and even architecture he had created—total immersion in a flattering and deeply scenic ambience. And by far the most striking of these buildings was the new theater Florenz Ziegfeld commissioned Urban to build in 1927. As Urban explained in his book *Theatres,* the project expressed "in every detail the fact that here was a modern playhouse for . . . the most successful form of theatrical production in the busiest and gayest city in the world."

Along one side of the exterior, glass galleries allowed promenading members of the audience to be visible on the street. The front curved out like a swelling curtain above the entrance from a proscenium-shaped frame, topped by female figures holding gigantic masks of Comedy (which were purchased by the architect Evan Frankel when the theater was finally demolished in 1966), with stone fountains rising above the roofline. Right at the top shone a vertical neon sign, spelling out SHOWZ—ZIEGFELD—GIRLZ arranged so that reading across the main line of letters also formed a lighthearted label for the audience: ZWELZ (or "swells"). Brilliantly floodlit at night, this highly decorative façade was, as Urban claimed, "a poster for the theater."[1]

Inside he created an oval auditorium, walls curving seamlessly into a domed ceiling like the inside of an eggshell. Gold carpets and seats extended up the walls to merge with a single gigantic mural—claimed by publicity releases to be the largest oil painting in the world, larger even than the ceiling of the Sistine Chapel—crowded with figures swirling like fireworks against a dark background. Brilliantly multicolored pirouetting dancers, musicians, and leaping gazelles formed a gorgeously frivolous mosaic designed so that the audience would always be aware of it, even during performances, sensed rather than seen in the reflected light from the stage, as well as dazzling them during the intervals. Titled "The Joy of Life," it communicated an atmosphere of brightly vibrant childlike playfulness and carefree vitality. As well as enfolding the spectators, the mural flowed right up to the stage (with no proscenium to separate it from the scenery of a play) and the acting area projected out into the audience, all creating the greatest possible intimacy with the actors.

When the Ziegfeld Theatre first opened it was the building itself that received the reviews, rather than the shows mounted there—even though the second production was a musical that became an instant classic: Oscar Hammerstein and Jerome Kern's *Show Boat* (with Urban's spectacular design for an added scene at the 1893 Chicago World's Fair that was much admired). Ziegfeld's own response on first seeing the completed theater was to sweep Urban's daughter Gretl into his arms, exclaiming,

The exterior façade of the Ziegfeld Theatre, as illustrated in *Architectural Record,* May 1927. Joseph Urban Papers, Rare Book and Manuscript Library, Columbia University.

"Your father sure hit the jackpot this time." The newspapers agreed. So did all the leading architectural journals, with Ely Jacques Kahn (one of the leading architects of the period) enthusing over the way Urban had made "a break with the classic tradition" and "expressed his own version of what a theater might be."[2] A retrospective in *The Decorator,* looking back in March 1930 at all the new theaters and cinemas constructed across America during the 1920s, declared that there was not "anything quite so remarkable as is to be seen in the famous Ziegfeld Theatre."[3]

The interior of the Ziegfeld Theatre auditorium with the curving egg-shaped ceiling and
the decorative mural, 1927 (*above*); the rooftop dining room with its cabaret stage (closed)
at the Hotel Gibson in Cincinnati, Ohio, 1929 (*opposite*). Joseph Urban Papers,
Rare Book and Manuscript Library, Columbia University.

Urban also used this highly theatrical décor beyond Broadway in the wider world of social entertainment. Exactly the same multiplicity of intricately interwoven and brilliantly colored figures on a deep blue or gold ground recurs in the dining rooms of some of the hotels Urban designed. In the Hotel Gibson in Cincinnati, where he supplied a lobby with modern simplicity in its geometric layout and strong verticals in gleaming three-story columns, both the ballroom and—above at the roof level—the cabaret-dining room were decorated in variations of the Ziegfeld Theatre murals. If the Ziegfeld "egg" was designed to suck the spectators irresistibly into theatrical high spirits, in these hotels Urban was consciously transferring this theatricality out into everyday life.

Even more spectacular would have been a theater designed for the great Austrian impresario Max Reinhardt, who in 1927 was seriously considering expanding his theatrical empire to Broadway. In various newspaper interviews Urban described his

Joseph Urban's design for the façade of the Reinhardt Theatre, 1927.
Joseph Urban Papers, Rare Book and Manuscript Library, Columbia University.

design as a fusion of architecture and advertising—in his view the two outstanding practical arts of America—and, in contrast to his previous, more purely decorative work, with the Reinhardt Theatre Urban set out to create a specifically New York idiom.

Instead of the floodlit brilliance of his Ziegfeld Theatre, with its exuberant curves and playful statues, the façade for the Reinhardt Theatre was to be a flat wall of un-relieved vitrolite, a new type of gleaming black glass never used before in exterior construction and positively shouting "modernity."[4] Across that stretched a triangle of brightly lighted, clear glass galleries: one for each level of seating—again show-casing the audience to public view—with the one on the lowest level running the full width of the building to form the marquee over the entry. Picked out in golden metal tracery, these galleries served as a base for continuous lines of neon advertising, and up through the center (making an elegant feature of the fire-escape stairs required by city regulations) a gold filigree tower soared to a delicate spire high above the roofline. Urban described it as a "flaming golden pinnacle."[5]

The proposed Reinhardt Theatre would have been a miniature precursor to the modern skyscraper. At the time, the buildings of Manhattan were almost all square-topped, relatively wide in comparison to their height, and built of granite. This slim, elongated tower with its strong vertical lines narrowing at the top to a needle in the sky anticipated the design of the Chrysler and Empire State buildings, more than two years before either was constructed—while the shining black glass walls forecast the wave of the future, Mies van der Rohe's black cubes in the 1950s and the glass towers of the present.

As it happened, Reinhardt was forced to shelve these plans following the stock market crash in 1929. Urban's designs for the building were given wide exposure and featured in the *New York Times* and *American Architect,* but the Reinhardt Theatre was never constructed. The same fate befell two other theaters Urban worked on—a new Metropolitan Opera House to replace its cramped original building on Broadway at 39th Street, and an imaginative structure echoing the shape of a stylized tent that he planned as a Jewish cultural center on Long Island. But the Ziegfeld Theatre, like Urban's roof-garden cabarets, continued to set the standard for places of entertain-ment in New York.

Norman Bel Geddes, too, had close connections with Max Reinhardt, and his de-signs for Reinhardt's immensely popular shows amounted to constructing completely new theaters inside existing buildings. In staging the New York production of Max Reinhardt's mammoth religious spectacle, Vollmoeller's almost wordless pageant

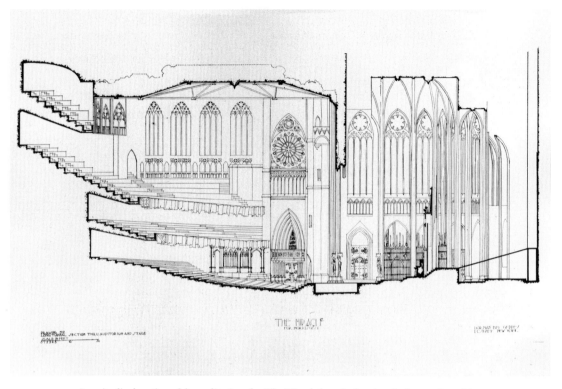

Longitudinal section of the auditorium for *The Miracle* (1924), showing the integration of the auditorium into the setting. Estate of Edith Lutyens Bel Geddes, Norman Bel Geddes Collection, Courtesy of the Harry Ransom Humanities Research Center.

The Miracle, in 1924, Bel Geddes gutted the Century Theatre to set the audience physically inside a medieval cathedral. He was to do the same with the theater for *The Eternal Road* in 1937.

For *The Miracle* he remodeled the Century's stage into a semicircular apse, with grills round the central altar, behind which could be seen eleven chapel and clerestory bays. He completely removed the proscenium, turning the side boxes into arched doorways, with a winding staircase above on one side and a pulpit on the other. This cathedral setting extended throughout the auditorium: he replaced the existing plush audience seating with wooden church pews, and all floor and wall surfaces were covered by a composite material, so as to resemble stone to the touch as well as sound. Six stories high, with the existing ceiling removed, the whole auditorium was transformed into a cathedral transept: flanked by pillared cloisters, aisles widened and paved with cracked flagstones, all arched by a vaulted Gothic roof and lit almost entirely through eighty-foot-high imitation stained-glass windows around the perimeter.

The Century Theatre, transformed into a Gothic cathedral for *The Miracle*.
Estate of Edith Lutyens Bel Geddes, Norman Bel Geddes Collection,
Courtesy of the Harry Ransom Humanities Research Center.

Even the wall behind the audience, at the back above the balcony (the front of which was hung with feudal banners), was brought into the illusion, being decorated by an enormous rose window through which colored light that changed to reflect the times of day in the piece fell across the audience. The ushers were dressed as nuns in full robes and wimples. The sound of bells tolled above. Organ music swelled to fill the space. The faint scent of incense wafted on the air. And there was the impression of a continuing life half-seen even as the spectators entered the theater—for instance, the crippled bell-ringer slowly lighting his way up the winding circular stair, his figure briefly glimpsed as he passed by lozenge-shaped openings in its wall. All this made the whole effect extraordinarily realistic, and every one of these details was commented on at length by the first-night reviews, indicating how convincing the whole atmospheric immersion was.[6]

At the same time occasional carefully selected details were exaggerated and openly fantastical—like the pulpit, which leaned whimsically to one side on a jaggedly cracked plinth, as if the stones had been worn and warped by extreme antiquity—clearly designed to inject a purely theatrical note. As Reinhardt remarked in a letter to Morris Gest (the New York producer of the show), "everybody will immediately be under the spell of this stupendous architecture, which is a miracle in itself. Every stage tradition has been eliminated here."[7]

Bel Geddes also developed a unique and complex system of tracks and hoists powered by electric motors, allowing this massive setting to be changed to a forest and various other dream locations required by the script, almost instantaneously and without visible means. As a review in *Theatre Arts Monthly* admiringly remarked, the walls of the chapel bays "located in vertical tracks . . . run up into the air out of sight above the vaulting in 35 seconds. . . . Only the altar and the ribbed columns remain, and by lighting they suggest a forest of green trees in the moonlight."[8] Even more to the point, in addition to standard theatrical reviews, and setting a precedent that was to be followed by almost all his major shows, the structure and mechanics of Bel Geddes' staging were innovative enough to be extensively analyzed and illustrated in both *Scientific American* and *Architectural Record*.[9]

With *The Miracle*, in one step Bel Geddes had equaled Urban, achieving a dominating position on Broadway that immediately brought other, nontheatrical design commissions. Thus *Vanity Fair* nominated him for "the Hall of Fame" (even though this was in fact Bel Geddes' first major production) "because he is one of the outstanding names among living scene designers; because he has achieved high distinction also as a mural and interior decorator." Bel Geddes' immediate fame was such that he gained unwanted credit and, having refused a commission to design the first Foote-MacDougal Restaurant in New York, was later forced to take legal action to stop the owners from advertising that the décor for the whole chain was by him when they expanded nationally in 1926.[10]

At first glance the vast extravagance and spectacle of the production looks alien to Bel Geddes' values, as does the overt religious triumphalism of a story in which a statue of the Virgin Mary comes to life to save an erring nun who has fled the cloister to follow a handsome knight by taking her place. Yet the climax of the show—a popular uprising led by a Pied Piper figure against the emperor—could be interpreted to support Bel Geddes' socialism. In fact, under his direction the anarchic mobs of the original script (which Reinhardt had first presented in 1911, long before any Communist regime had achieved power), waved the red banners of consciously proletarian revolutionaries, and the political message carried conviction because of the hyperrealism of Bel Geddes' scenery.

The significance of Urban's Ziegfeld Theatre, and in particular Bel Geddes' remodeling of the Century Theatre into a medieval cathedral, is in their capacity of setting individual spectators inside a new and total environment. It is this quality of conceiving complete contexts that made their industrial, commercial, and architectural designs outside the theater so effective as catalysts to promote the modern lifestyle they envisaged. And even their theater plans were not simply decorative or illusionistic, but pointed toward a specifically modernist and "machine age" type of entertainment space. From the mid-1920s Bel Geddes had been creating designs for theaters incorporated into office buildings or with factory chimneys attached, in which scenes could be switched as on a production line, while Urban labeled his design for a Music Center at the 1929 Architectural League Exhibition "The Busy Factory of the Theatre," a concept directly expressed in its massive, rigidly geometric, façade.

Bel Geddes was still more closely associated with the new drama emerging in America, and with even more populist forms of entertainment. Younger and active for over two decades after Urban's death, he designed more—and more varied—theaters than Urban (though none had quite the same impact as the Ziegfeld Theatre).[11] In 1924 he designed the Harvard University Theatre for George Pierce Baker, whose pupils included Eugene O'Neill, and his plans were used (in a slightly modified form, and, to his chagrin, unacknowledged) for the Theatre Guild stage in New York in 1925. Then in 1932 he helped shape one of the most popular entertainment venues of the era, contributing designs for the Radio City Music Hall at the request of Raymond Hood, who was the architect in charge of the whole building. Later, during the postwar reconstruction boom, Bel Geddes mounted a campaign for theater stages to be built in the hotel ballrooms, which by then—with formal dancing no longer fashionable—were largely standing idle or used for trade shows. As he pointed out in a 1949 prospectus, there was a market to be filled: of the more than eighty live theaters on Broadway in

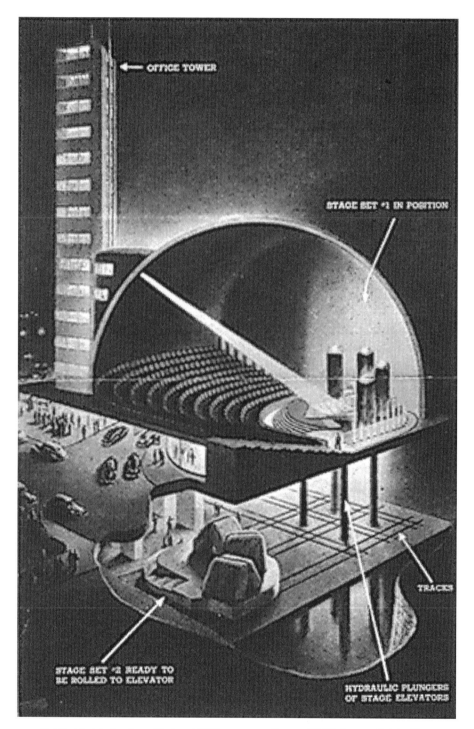

Bel Geddes' design for an "Industrial" Theater, 1947. Estate of Edith Lutyens Bel Geddes, Norman Bel Geddes Collection, Courtesy of the Harry Ransom Humanities Research Center.

the 1920s, barely thirty were still functioning.[12] The plans he published showed how a stage could be fitted diagonally into a corner, transforming any configuration of ballroom, palm court, and dance floor into an all-purpose entertainment space. He did specific designs for the Savoy Plaza, Park Lane, and Waldorf Astoria hotels, which included equipment for using the stage as a television or radio studio. His plans were picked up by others, including American Hotels Corporation, which announced in 1954 that the production of Broadway plays on the new stages in its twenty-four hotels had boosted food and drink sales by an impressive 300 percent.[13]

Although the live stage had far more importance then than now, even in the 1920s movies were beginning to attract a wider audience, and (as left-wing sociologists—and the French—like to complain) modern Hollywood was, and is, an extremely successful transmitter of cultural values and codes of behavior. Technologically, too, film represents a specifically modern way of perceiving life. And from the beginning movies helped to shape the material expectations of people across the States, promoting the new twentieth-century lifestyle on the silver screen (so-called precisely because it pictured idealized ways of living). It was just the right tool for visionaries who aimed to reshape society. So, as might be expected, both Joseph Urban and Norman Bel Geddes were very much involved in the movie industry. As these were early days, when almost everything about filming was still experimental, they were free to impose their own style.

Bel Geddes was already working for Universal Studios before he arrived in New York, writing and directing his first film, *Nathan Hale*, in 1917 (a patriotic flag-waver in response to America's entry into World War I). He went on to work for Cecil B. DeMille and Paramount in 1925, designing *Feet of Clay* and writing the scenario for *New York Story* (a film celebrating the modern city). He then collaborated with D. W. Griffith, doing the designs for his 1926 movie, *The Sorrows of Satan*. Following the success of his Broadway hit *Dead End*, Bel Geddes also made two feature films of his own: *Atlantic Crossing* in 1936 and *Hocus Pocus* (based on a 1937 story by Lester Dent). But Bel Geddes was always most interested in experimenting with new camera techniques. He developed high-magnification photography in documentary movies on *Amphibia* and *Reptilia* (as well as making a highly idiosyncratic version of *Helen of Troy* using real live ants—photographed through glass cases in his office—to represent all the classical heroic figures). He was also fascinated by stop-motion photography, using models for recording naval battles—which became the basis for the photos reconstructing World War II battles that Bel Geddes produced for *Life* magazine from 1941 on. After that he turned to industrial and advertising films, such as *Bermuda* and *Mexico Goes to Market*.

Urban's work was far more mainstream and reminds us that at one time New York rivaled Hollywood in movie production. As general production manager first for International Film Studios (later Cosmopolitan) in 1920, then in the 1930s for Fox Film Corporation, he designed and produced more than fifty films. Among these were a number of early popular classics: *Under the Red Robe, East Lynne, A Connecticut Yankee, The Man Who Came Back,* and all of Marion Davies's films up to 1925. He already knew Marion Davies from the 1916 edition of the *Ziegfeld Follies,* where she made her first breakthrough—and where she attracted the attention of William Randolph Hearst. Much smitten by her radiance and vitality (she soon became his lifelong lover), Hearst transformed the newsreel arm of his International News Service into a vehicle to make Marion Davies a star. Urban, with his *Follies* reputation, was the logical choice to head up the operation, and Hearst was prepared to pay him the extraordinary salary (for the time) of $1,440 a week.

As one might expect, there are close connections between the films Urban and Bel Geddes made and their stage work. Bel Geddes' designs for *New York Story* (which was directed by John Houseman and became the theme movie of the 1933 Chicago World's Fair) focused on the romance of Manhattan skyscrapers—in one key shot "the towering city rises as though miraculously out of the fog," and another view presents the towers as "cubist masses." From the top of one of these skyscrapers we follow people "like streams of ants" (an inversion of his *Helen of Troy* approach) on their way to work far below in the streets; at ground level we see them crowding into elevators, then the camera zooms up the elevator shaft. Steel skeletons are shown under construction; we watch massive steam shovels and derricks excavating a new tunnel under the river.[14] The sharp perspectives are very like some of Bel Geddes' Manhattan-skyline scenery for Broadway musicals. But in the film the whole effect is strikingly modernistic in its focus on movement and mechanization, speed, and flow. The same fascination with skyscraper construction reoccurred in his Broadway show *Iron Men,* glorifying the sunburned American laborers at work on steel girders high above the ground. That play had started off as a film script, developed by Bel Geddes and rewritten by Sherwood Anderson, which Bel Geddes then adapted for Broadway.

As this suggests, there was little distinction made between screen and stage. Urban too saw no problem in making King Vidor's *Big Parade* into a Broadway musical; and even though he was one of the earliest to realize that movies were a unique and different medium, his cinema techniques borrowed directly from theater. So one of his first films, *The Restless Sex,* centered around a "Ball of the Gods" scene that came straight out of the *Ziegfeld Follies,* with Marion Davies (as Woman Eternal) displaying costumes through the ages.

It was ironic that Urban should be hired on the basis of his vibrantly colorful Broadway stage settings to make movies in the era of black-and-white film. But he redesigned the lighting system in Hearst's Second Avenue studio so that with the right background and décor (as he explained to various newspapers in 1920) spectators could be made to *think* in colors, even when there was no actual color to be seen.[15] At the time, when all studio lighting was simply floodlights, creating a flat effect, this was revolutionary. Many reviews of *The Restless Sex* surprisingly mentioned "colorful" backgrounds, despite the fact that these scenes were all black and white.

In order to achieve this impression, almost all of Urban's movies—including outdoor scenes—were shot inside the studio, so that the settings were exactly like stage scenery. He insisted that the natural world be completely excluded, just as with his stage work. Once at the end of an all-night lighting rehearsal, as the first glimmer of dawn appeared, Urban is reported to have exclaimed, "There comes that damned sun again and spoils us everything."[16] Even though his insistence on complete studio production ran counter to the path Hollywood was to take, this approach gave Urban complete control of the images and effects, and most scenes looked extremely realistic. Film after film was hailed for its superior artistic quality, atmosphere, and sense of light; as a result, several of the techniques he introduced became standard in the developing movie industry.

Since his early days at the Boston Opera, Urban had based his productions on sketches indicating the moment-by-moment sequence of lighting effects, character groupings, movements, and gestures, and he carried this over into his movies, starting the Hollywood practice of using storyboards as the basis for shooting film scenes. Urban was also instrumental in developing a specific visual language for film that would take advantage of the absence of spoken words (this was still the era of silent movies) and of color. He was one of the earliest voices to insist that filmmaking had to focus on movement, creating mobile compositions, and develop its own expressive vocabulary instead of borrowing from the stage. And, as he liked to emphasize, in contrast to the aristocratic aesthetics of the fine arts, this new visual language would "express the feelings of millions." Following from that, Urban became among the first to demand a new type of story, specifically "screen dramas." Indeed, it was Urban who encouraged Charlie Chaplin to experiment with the type of purely physical action that made his comic films so memorable.

Bel Geddes' influence was more diffuse but, in a way, more direct. Although his high-magnification and stop-motion experiments may have influenced developments in technical photography, his main impact was through individuals. He had already been teaching stage design in New York through the Master School of United Artists; and during the two years he spent in Hollywood in the mid-1920s he gave a series of lectures and courses on design for the movies, which were well attended by people working for the studios.

Rather than any one film, the general movie culture of a period carries over into people's lifestyles. Still, in one or two cases a direct line can be traced.

Urban designed all the costumes for Marion Davies (a task later taken up by his daughter, Gretl), and even though many of her films were historical spectaculars, like *Janice Meredith* and *When Knighthood Was in Flower,* when the story was contemporary her costumes were widely copied. Following *The Young Diana* and *Adam and Eva,* both released in 1922, the *San Francisco Bulletin* remarked on the extraordinary number of women seen wearing "the latest fashions shown in Marion Davies' films." For films set in the present, Urban also designed all the furniture, along with distinctive décor and architecture, which carried over into everyday life in much the same way.[17] For instance *Enchantment,* the modernized version of the Sleeping Beauty story that he made in 1921, prefigures the décor he later used in the hotels he remodeled. But the clearest example is *Zander the Great,* the last Marion Davies film he made for Hearst and the only one made on location.

A melodrama about bandits and young orphans set on the Mexican border—with twenty-seven-year-old Davies (though studio publicity tried to persuade the public she was only twenty-four) obviously too mature for the part of a young teenager despite her Mary Pickford wig, particularly since she was paired with a boy of ten—*Zander the Great* was hardly a cinematic triumph. Yet it has a specific and surprisingly widespread architectural influence. Urban created a quintessential hacienda around which much of the film was shot, with arched verandas on both the ground floor and above, running around three sides of a wide patio, and its Spanish-Mexican style doors, barred windows, and elegant pillars started quite a fashion in Western buildings. The wife of a Texas millionaire, Mrs. Alex Camp, commissioned Urban to re-create the set for the new house she was planning in Dallas, while newspapers reported that three architects had copied it for houses in Los Angeles.[18] There were more indirect spin-offs as well: Hearst commissioned Urban to create an elaborate apartment for Marion Davies (his first interior design work in America), then to remodel his own New York mansion, and later to design the International Magazine Building on Eighth Avenue.

Similarly, though in a more notional way, one of the elaborate settings Bel Geddes created for *Feet of Clay* reappeared in several of his later architectural plans. This was a luxury scene of a dance in an elaborate garden: a circular dance floor under a domed canopy in the middle of a round reflecting pond, with flowerlike scalloped edges. Scaled up (in typical Bel Geddes fashion) to seat more than 1,500 people, it became an island dance restaurant for the Chicago World's Fair, and again formed part of his plans in the 1950s for a resort hotel.[19]

Perhaps just as important, Bel Geddes and Urban created some of the buildings in which the movies they made were shown. Just as the stage theaters they designed influenced the lifestyle of their audiences, their movie houses helped to define the experience of moviegoing. Again Bel Geddes was more visionary and more attuned to advancing technology, while Urban, as the consummate showman, created striking images of the time.

As early as 1914 Bel Geddes was working on plans for the very first cineplex, a "duplex movie house." Far ahead of its time, this design was shelved, but he went on to remodel the Roxy Movie Theatre in New York, which used the diagonal-axis concept he had worked out as an ideal stage form, with the screen placed across one corner, instead of in the middle of the end wall. And much later, toward the end of his life, he developed plans for introducing a seventy-foot-wide screen to standard movie houses (specifically for showing the Technicolor movie version of his earlier stage production of *The Miracle,* filmed in 1959), which he labeled "Technirama Theaters." But his activities in designing movie theaters paled beside Urban, who created an entire ambience that reinforced the images on the screen.

As well as the Paramount Theatre that anchored the Sunrise shopping center he built in Palm Beach, Urban remodeled or redecorated a significant number of New York cinemas: the Strand Theatre in 1915, followed by the Rialto, the Rivoli, the Fulton, the Criterion, among others—all of which promoted the elegance of the 1920s.[20] In the following decade his movie houses expressed the more functional modernism that was his response to the Great Depression.

At that time there was no single architectural style for movie theaters. The new technology of film was being housed in incongruous pastiches of palaces from the past like Meyer and Holler Grauman's Egyptian Theatre in Los Angeles (which won the sardonic label of "Karnak on Hollywood Boulevard"), a problem compounded by the way film screenings were merged with live theatrical performance. Silent movies had musical accompaniment, generally played on an organ, or sometimes by a small orchestra. But during the 1920s they were also preceded by jazz or classical selections that had nothing to do with the film, and frequently by live song-and-dance or cabaret acts with elaborate stage settings.

Urban was the first to attempt a unified program, insisting that a "Marion Davies Waltz" be composed as theme music for *The Restless Sex* and providing a "supplementary program" related to the most spectacular scene in the movie: a *Follies*-like Ball of

Bel Geddes' island dance restaurant, as filmed in *Feet of Clay* (*above*), and a sketch of the design for the Chicago World's Fair (*opposite*). Estate of Edith Lutyens Bel Geddes, Norman Bel Geddes Collection, Courtesy of the Harry Ransom Humanities Research Center.

the Gods. Backed by a series of elaborate cut-curtains, which exactly duplicated one of his settings for the *Follies* edition for 1917, this prologue presented a dance-mime of Eve waking up under the Tree of Knowledge, tempted by Lilith and clutching at the fatal apple. As she bit into it there was a momentary flash of light during which the curtain was whisked aside and the film began. For other openings Urban remodeled the audience space to echo the atmosphere of the movie, redecorating the Central Theatre on Broadway into a setting of European decadence for the 1923 Lionel Barrymore film *Enemies of Women,* or redoing the Criterion to suggest a Tudor environment for *When Knighthood Was in Flower.*

The high point was reached when Hearst acquired the Park Theatre (where Urban's first New York stage production, *The Garden of Paradise,* had been performed). Remodeling the old theater as the Cosmopolitan movie house, Urban transformed it into a ballroom of colonial days for *Little Old New York* and *Janice Meredith,* and this

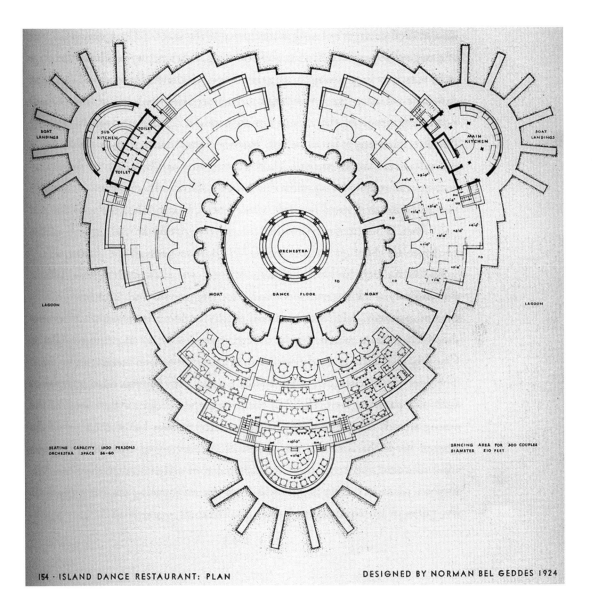

décor attracted quite as much attention as the films. The opening drew a glittering crowd of notables, including Scott Fitzgerald and the mayor of New York, and (just as with the Ziegfeld Theatre) the newspapers spent more column inches describing the redecorated theater than on *Janice Meredith,* even though it was hailed as "one of the most exquisite productions ever shown upon the screen" and broke all film records for the time.[21]

The old Park Theatre had boasted heavy imitation-marble columns, elaborately

The Cosmopolitan Theatre on Columbus Circle as designed by Joseph Urban, 1923:
the view from the stage to the balcony (*above*); the stage and orchestra pit,
with the movie screen hidden behind sliding panels (*opposite*). Joseph Urban Papers,
Rare Book and Manuscript Library, Columbia University.

carved arches, and massively ornate sculptures on the walls and ceiling round the stage: very much a nineteenth-century cliché for Culture. In their place Urban achieved a feel of elegant space and simplicity, with the movie screen set behind sliding tapestry panels in a curving wall that flowed to the back of the auditorium. On each side of the screen, flat neoclassical pillars and delicate chandeliers (along with portraits of Marion Davies in costumes from the film) gave a period atmosphere, while the boxes and projection room suggested Vieux Carré balconies from New Orleans jutting out of the rear wall. This, together with all the seats, was in light shades of gold; all the other surfaces were white or light gray. "Theater Now One of Most Beautiful in Entire World" was one headline,[22] while complete issues of *Arts and Decoration* and *Decorative Furnishing* in 1923 were devoted to the remodeling.

In sharp contrast, almost a decade after redoing the Cosmopolitan Theatre, Urban designed a cinema for suburban Westchester in 1931 that looked starkly utilitarian.

Stripped of any period atmosphere or reference to the kind of film that might be shown there—all features or details not directly related to its function as a movie theater were consciously eliminated—the interior offered a neutral space for the imagination. Instead of chandeliers, diffuse light came through a flat sheet of opaque plastic that covered the ceiling, and although there was still a suggestion of columns along the walls, these were strictly functional and concealed strip lighting.

The same extreme simplicity on the outside of the building, however, was anything but neutral. Plain white and black walls and flat roofs, opaque ultramarine glass, a rectangular façade of aluminum squares over the doors, all made it an uncompromising statement of the modern age. It was also a three-dimensional expression of the new technology of film. On the top of the gleaming metal, deep aluminum sheet letters with their edges outlined by red neon lights spelled out the name of the theater: simply CAMERA. It would still look highly contemporary today.

At first glance the two buildings seem very different. The luxurious Cosmopolitan

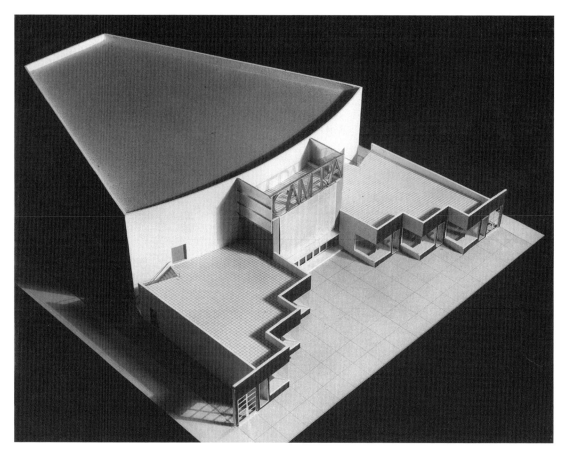

Scale model of Urban's Westchester cinema, exterior view, with stores and sign, 1931.
Joseph Urban Papers, Rare Book and Manuscript Library, Columbia University.

seems to reflect the opulence of the twenties; the later Westchester movie house has the aura of a far more scientific era. They show a clearly developing sense of what a modern lifestyle means. But the same range can be seen in some of Urban's other buildings, even several designed almost simultaneously. And indeed the same concept—one central to the architecture of the modern age—underlies this apparent eclecticism. In both of these buildings, style is determined by function. And beyond their immediate purpose as theaters, both have a similar role as cultural persuaders. One draws its audience into the imaginary (and in that specific instance, historical) world of the movie they are watching, while the other shapes their general expectations, casting spectators as people with a specifically modern consciousness. Context is all.

Urban's major belief, as he said in *Theatres,* was that "Architecture—great architecture—is always representative of its age," and he defined the aim of his stage and movie designs as being to "make a record of his own times and a prophecy of times to come." This applied still more to his work outside the theater—the office buildings, department stores, hotel interiors, and restaurants he designed for New York or Pittsburgh—as well as to Bel Geddes' projects beyond the stage or screen. The two designers both promoted an identifiably modern vision, verging at times on the futuristic, keyed to the conditions of contemporary American life.

5

Society Scenery

EXPANDING FROM CREATING artificial scenery for the stage or for movies, to designing the theaters in which they were shown, was a logical first step. Given Joseph Urban's impact on the world of fashion, it is hardly surprising that he was also extensively involved in designing other kinds of public spaces—particularly ones that attracted the beautiful people of the 1920s and 1930s. There was a close interplay between these kinds of places, where people go to see and to be seen, and the stage. He used exactly the same highly decorated "festive" style of wall and ceiling design for both the auditorium of the Ziegfeld Theatre and for hotel roof-garden cabarets (pages 60–68 and 47–48). Conversely, his scenery for Broadway shows frequently featured his own brand of Art Deco designs for restaurants (*The Love Letter,* 1921), hotel lobbies and ballrooms (*Mayflower Hotel,* 1925), nightclubs (*No Foolin',* 1926, or, most famously, *Show Boat,* 1927). Such scenes in turn brought him further commissions to remodel hotels and restaurants in New York and elsewhere, and formed the basis for his architectural layouts and décor. Sometimes too, even the way Urban created the effects was exactly the same as for his stage scenery.

His murals for the Banquet Hall of the Hotel Sherman in Chicago were painted on canvas in his Yonkers studio (where he had transferred his Swampscott workshop after leaving Boston), then transported to the location and pasted onto the walls and ceiling. As might be expected, the décor is highly dramatic. Against a bright gold background, stylized eagles soar across a huge panel suspended from the ceiling; on curving upper walls muscular black figures in Greek helmets rein in leaping panthers, flanked by strikingly patterned leopards and tigers (illustrated on pages 86 and 87). Below, the walls are covered in plain black lacquered panels, each edged in thin gold lines. Opened in 1920, the Tiger Room combines all three of the modes Urban used in his architectural work: sharply contrasting colors or tones, modified Art Deco stylization, and geometric simplicity.

In all, Urban did the architecture or the décor for more than twenty banquet halls, ballrooms, restaurants and grill rooms, hotel lobbies, cabarets, and nightclubs between 1920 and 1933—mainly in Manhattan, but also in Chicago, Pittsburgh, Detroit, Cincinnati, Palm Beach, and Brooklyn. In most cases he was redecorating existing buildings, although this frequently included adding a completely new dinner-theater for the roof, sometimes gutting and redesigning entire sections of the interior, and in at least one instance constructing a new hotel lobby. He generally designed every detail—from the shape of walls or ceilings, and the murals, to the lighting fixtures, carpets, draperies, furniture, and upholstery—creating visual unity, a total environment that made his stylistic influence still more powerful.

All these banquet halls and restaurants were for major establishments with fashionable clientele. At the luxury end of the architectural scale, like the fashions inspired by his revues, Urban's public rooms and buildings reflected the wealth and gaiety of America before the Depression. They helped to establish the hedonistic and extravagant image of the Roaring Twenties, and his reputation grew so much he was overwhelmed by requests for the same kind of work, from New York and all across the States. Even with his own architectural firm employing three other architects and as many as fifteen draftsmen, he had to turn down many projects. Indeed by 1932 his style of design was so well known that the Congress Hotel in Chicago commissioned him to create a "Joseph Urban Room" (its official title once the new space opened, which was used in the hotel's advertising).

Norman Bel Geddes followed exactly the same pattern, at about the same time: designing scenery featuring nightclubs or restaurants for successful musicals like the *Five O'Clock Girl.* These brought him similar work—a rooftop cabaret and dining room for the Century Theatre, and the Palais Royale Dance Hall—which in turn were mirrored on the Broadway stage. So just over a year after it opened, a recognizable copy of Bel Geddes' Palais Royale appeared as a setting for Ira and George Gershwin's first hit in 1924, *Lady Be Good,* starring Fred Astaire. In fact following Urban's success, this crossing between the stage and entertainment venues became quite common, with other designers like Henry Dreyfuss moving from scenery at the Strand Theatre to designing a roof-garden cabaret for Maxims and new, Arab-inspired décor for the Persian Room in the Plaza Hotel. And Norman Bel Geddes very much took on where Urban, his career cut short by his untimely death in 1933, had left off.

Bel Geddes in turn was responsible for the chrome and black Manhattan Room and Street Grill of the Hotel Pennsylvania in 1933, followed by the Barberry Dining Room for the Berkshire Hotel, and the La Rue Restaurant, all in New York; a cafeteria for the Bowman-Biltmore hotel group, which was duplicated in their chain across the country; the Palm Court and ballroom of the Savoy-Plaza Hotel in 1948–49, and the strikingly cantilevered Copa City entertainment complex in Miami the same year. His last design was for the Playbill Restaurant, which opened at the Hotel Manhattan in 1958; and he was still working on a resort hotel for Malaga, Spain, when he died.

Dancing became the latest craze in the Twenties. Dance halls sprang up catering to fashionable demand, and many of the major hotels were rebuilt to include ballrooms that formed the most formal and grandest of their public spaces. Urban specialized in these, while the Palais Royale dance hall and cabaret was Bel Geddes' first major work outside the theater.

From scene shop to public décor: (*above*) Joseph Urban (shown at far right)
directing the artists preparing the mural for the Tiger Room on a canvas spread out
across the floor of the Yonkers studio, overhead photograph from Urban's observation gallery, 1920;
(*opposite*) the completed banquet hall at the Hotel Sherman, Chicago, 1920.
Joseph Urban Papers, Rare Book and Manuscript Library, Columbia University.

To evoke the right atmosphere Urban chose deliberately exotic and fantastic
themes: Persian motifs for the William Penn Hotel in Pittsburgh, Chinese for the
Hotel Gibson in Cincinnati. For the ballroom at the Gibson, he knocked out two
stories in the middle of the building's interior to create a high-domed oval, rising
to a golden cupola thickly covered by intricately interlacing figures, with an arched
colonnade and balcony that ran all the way round the room. Polished stone facing the
pillars of the colonnade, and lozenge-shaped rosettes of beveled mirror on the wall

behind, gave fragmentary reflections of the dancers.[1] These designs set the style for hotel ballrooms all over America.

Bel Geddes' Palais Royale, one of the earliest of the new cabaret dance halls, was just as influential. For this Bel Geddes designed a ceiling of dynamic, sweeping curves with an elliptical canopy suspended from the center over the dance floor, which suggested "the petals of some gigantic ultra-modern flower" to one enthusiastic reporter, reviewing the opening for the *Boston Evening Transcript*.[2] Murals on the walls depicted couples in extremely elegant poses from the latest dances: simplified and almost faceless figures clearly promoting an ideal image for the patrons to emulate. It all gave an impression of movement and vitality that was widely praised as "extraordinary"—and in sharp contrast to the standard plaster festoons and gilded cupids of dance halls up to that time.

Bel Geddes also included a highly innovative retractable stage that slid out over the parquet dance floor, with a mechanism of his own design. As the show ended the stage slid back into the wall, the dancers flowed out to mix with the dancing patrons: murals, performers, and public merging in a highly theatrical event.

But the link with theater is most direct in the cabaret/dining rooms built on the roofs of many hotels in the 1920s, another new, highly popular fashion spawned by the success of the *Follies* under Urban's influence. These were all designed to project an atmosphere that combined elegance with joyous liveliness. The most sophisticated was the roof-garden dining room Urban built for cabarets at the St. Regis Hotel. He gave it gracefully curving ceilings and covered the whole interior with stylized Japanese cherry trees in blossom, which bore parrots (always one of his favorite images) and white cockerels with fantastically long tails in the intertwining branches (see page 12). Exotic and luxurious, Urban's rooftop cabaret-dining room vibrantly expressed the carefree 1920s.

Perhaps the most significant of the public spaces Urban or Bel Geddes designed, because of the political attention it drew, was the Central Park Casino at Fifth Avenue and 72nd Street. This rustic Victorian building by Calvert Vaux, one of the original designers of Central Park, had been a popular (and highly moral) Ladies Refreshment Salon in the 1890s. In 1926, it was chosen to become a reception center for the official entertainment of foreign notables and delegations by Mayor Jimmy Walker, always eager for prestige, who saw this as a way of asserting that New York rivaled Paris or London—where the respective mayors, of course, already had impressive historical edifices at their disposal. Joseph Urban, hired by Florenz Ziegfeld and Anthony Biddle (for whom Urban had designed his first Palm Beach mansion), was given a free hand to create "the most beautiful restaurant in the world"—as the *New York Times* observed when it reopened in June 1929.[3]

Inside the existing structure Urban created huge open spaces, adapting a new type of construction used until then solely for aircraft hangars. The five main rooms were each given a floral motif, most strikingly in the brilliant colors on the walls, carpets, and chair-covers of the semicircular pavilion with its domed ceiling of downward curving tulip petals, all (as Urban told the *New York Times*) intended to evoke "the freshness of spring flowers and joyousness of a wind among young leaves." The ballroom had multiple wall mirrors, framed to look like doorways, as well as a black mirrored ceiling, a favorite effect of Urban's, because the "dim reflections" of the dancing couples gave "space and movement in sympathy with the life of the room."[4] Urban himself designed everything for this reconstruction—the floor plan and shape of the rooms, murals and ceiling effects, light fixtures (including massive modernistic chandeliers for the ballroom), carpets and furniture, and fabrics for drapes and upholstery and

The pavilion with its tulip ceiling, as redesigned by Joseph Urban,
at the opening of the Central Park Casino, New York, 1929. Joseph Urban Papers,
Rare Book and Manuscript Library, Columbia University.

tablecloths, even the menu cards. The Casino came to be known as Jimmy Walker's
Versailles.

It was said that the mayor spent more time there than at City Hall. It was an
open secret that there were private rooms upstairs with gilded ceilings, where he
and his cronies brokered secret deals while they were entertained by scantily dressed
Broadway dancers (entire chorus lines notoriously being rushed there some nights
by motorcycle police escort as soon as the curtain fell on the show).[5]

The newly transformed casino got considerable press coverage. It was even held
up as a classroom example of decadence by William O'Shea, the superintendent of
schools, who declared that teachers should use it for lessons in arithmetic and practical
democracy by posing the question: if one hot dog at Central Park Zoo cost five cents,
while in the Casino, breast of guinea hen cost two dollars and seventy-five cents with

The ballroom at the Central Park Casino, 1929. Joseph Urban Papers,
Rare Book and Manuscript Library, Columbia University.

spinach at seventy cents, plus ten percent tip, how many schoolchildren could be fed for the price of a dinner for four? O'Shea might even have made his example more compelling by including the evidence of a (much reported) lawsuit, where a diner was taken to court for refusing to pay the Casino's eighteen-dollar cover charge on a two-dollar bottle of wine.

The prices hardly deterred the smart set. The Casino was wildly popular, attracting crowds of greater than six hundred an evening, and many more for balls—all of whom came (as even a journal like *Architectural Record* commented)[6] to be seen rather than to eat, choosing the most visible seating and particularly appreciating the doubled images of themselves in the mirrored ballroom. In more ways than one, then, Urban's Casino reflected the spirit of the 1920s and early 1930s—as well as catching the essence of the administration of a mayor popularly known as "Gentleman Jimmy."

That all this décor was specifically intended to condition people's image of themselves, and integrate the public with the world suggested by the design, is clear in Urban's frequent use of mirrors and highly reflective surfaces. These became his architectural signature; and mirrors formed the basis for Urban's design of the Park Avenue Restaurant, which—as Ed Sullivan informed the *Evening Graphic* when it opened in November 1931—was the "most gorgeous spot in New York."[7] Here, instead of murals, there were huge circular mirrors on walls painted in flat tones of black, and floor-to-ceiling mirrors surrounding the circular bar that reflected multiplying and fragmented images of the room and its occupants.

In photographs, the style of the Park Avenue Restaurant strikes us as typical of the 1930s, and of New York today—a sign of Urban's influence on the image of the city. While most of Urban's other interiors gave expression to the opulent 1920s, the apparent starkness of the Park Avenue Restaurant is equally in tune with the Depression that followed the stock market crash of 1929. In at least one case, Depression-era economics made a finished building more simplified than Urban's design: the Atlantic Beach Club on Long Island, also completed in 1931.

From its inception, this project was in sharp contrast to the Bath and Tennis Club built by Urban just four years before in Palm Beach. Where that building had been conceived to fit in with the Spanish heritage of Florida and its luxuriant foliage, the Atlantic Beach Club deliberately projected an image of a northern manufacturing state, with its industrial feel and materialistic sophistication.

As designed, the beach club suggests the rear section of a huge and highly modern ship, with its (invisible) bow afloat on the ocean. Raised boardwalks surrounding a central swimming pool and leading out on either side to a promenade on pillars along

Two views of the interior of Urban's Park Avenue Restaurant, 1931:
the circular bar (*above*); mirror and staircase (*opposite*).
Joseph Urban Papers, Rare Book and Manuscript Library, Columbia University.

the beachfront form the decks of this notional vessel, with the high white block of
dining rooms, lounges, and sun porches forming the bridge at the stern. The modular
construction speaks of the machine age. Combined with the nautical image, it was an
idealized setting for sport and the display of sun-bronzed fitness (in contemporary
photographs, muscular swimmers posed athletically against the background of the
building). It also linked the imaginative appeal of advanced technologies with the
healthy open-air life in an outside dance floor made of glass, lit from below by changing colored lights and open to the sky above.

Urban's Atlantic Beach Club was hailed in the press as "the most essentially
modern in all America" (*Evening Post,* 20 June 1930), and its influence can be seen
in the Aquatic Park Casino on the waterfront promenade in San Francisco, opened
in 1939 and now a museum. As one of the architect's press releases described this

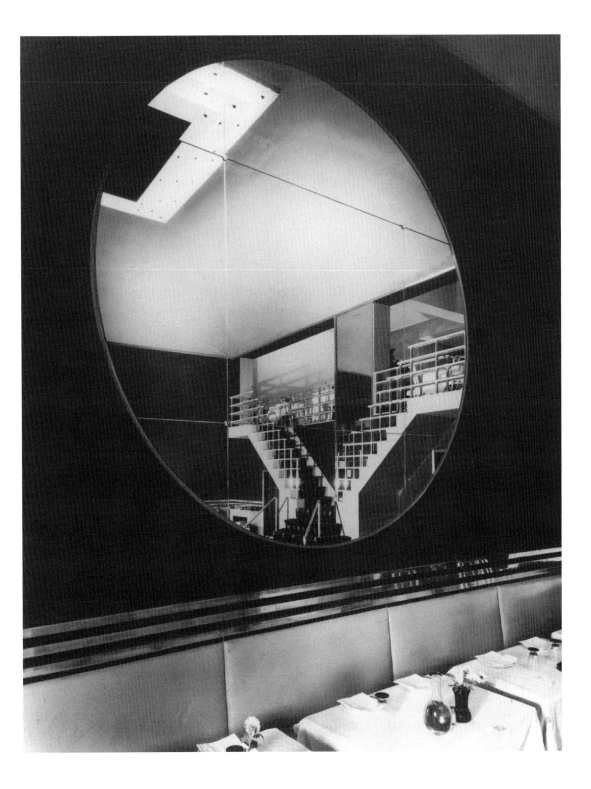

Urban's original design for the Atlantic Beach Club, Long Island, 1929.
When the project was built in 1930–31, neither the apartment complex (*left*),
nor the raised walkway along the beach (*lower left*) was constructed.
Joseph Urban Papers, Rare Book and Manuscript Library, Columbia University.

California casino, in terms that would have exactly fitted Urban's East Coast building, "its resemblance to a luxurious ocean liner is indeed startling."[8]

Urban could be said to have begun quite a fad in designing modernist buildings: even factories, like the Coca-Cola plant in Dearborn, Michigan, were streamlined as ocean liners. With these later examples the shiplike impression became still more marked, as advances in concrete construction allowed curving corners and dramatic overhangs.

The Depression and the world war that came after caused the cancellation or scaling back of many projects, so the follow-up to this theatrically modernist architecture only came with Bel Geddes' design for the Copa City complex in Miami, which opened with much public fanfare in 1948. Incorporating a theater-restaurant, television and radio studios, plus a nightclub-cocktail lounge from which singers and comedians broadcast their shows, as well as trendy boutiques, Copa City was in every sense futuristic.

All the walls curved sinuously in and out—not a single straight line marked the exterior or regularized the public areas. A row of small stores that flanked the entry had teardrop or oval floors with curving glass doors, as well as serpentine walls of floor-to-ceiling glass encircling them, which was so revolutionary that it formed the basis for a major advertising campaign for Pittsburgh Plate Glass, which had manufactured these large and geometrically complex sheets to Bel Geddes' specifications.

The building itself was equally cutting-edge in construction. The cabaret and dinner-dance theater—which seated up to 750 diners, and had only transparent glass walls separating it from the foyer with its boutiques and the lounge and bar beyond—gave an illusion of vastness, height, and lushness that *Variety* found "overwhelming."[9] Its cantilevered, movable walls could reduce this to an intimate space for smaller audiences, although there were offices and the studios on the second story, above this flexible performance area. All this could only be achieved if instead of interior partitions supporting the structure above, as was universal for construction at the time, everything hung suspended from the roof and was carried on exterior walls.

The structural techniques were so unusual that the building was discussed extensively in journals like *Engineering News.* A radio broadcast marking Copa City's opening night (23 December 1948, by Gabriel Heatter, the widely popular voice of "Mr. Mutual") called it "the only building of its kind in the whole world," noting that nobody had ever created a completely suspended structure or shaped building materials in such curves before. It was seen as combining "the magic" of the 1939 New York World's Fair and Radio City Music Hall. In a joint interview with Bel Geddes, who stressed the "revolutionary" nature of its architecture, Heatter labeled Copa City "something more than a building—an expression of the times." Praising its fluid physical rhythms at the opening, "Mr. Mutual" urged his listeners: "If this is how the future world is going to look, try and get a ticket!"[10]

All those public spaces Bel Geddes and Urban created were highly fashionable. They were specifically designed, as Urban remarked of his Mayfair Room at the Book-Cadillac Hotel in Detroit, not just to please the eye, but to "enhance the beauty of women, stimulate the appetite, and show off the people."[11] Seen and used by many thousands—even millions, if the audiences at his theaters are included—Urban's

Bel Geddes, Copa City (1948): the curving exterior and entry to Copa City (*above*);
interior with glass-walled boutiques (*opposite*). Estate of Edith Lutyens Bel Geddes,
Norman Bel Geddes Collection, Courtesy of the Harry Ransom Humanities Research Center.

social venues expressed an ideal of American culture during its formative phase in
a way that made it distinct from modernism elsewhere. And just as Urban had been
central in creating the fashions and spaces that defined so much of the lifestyle of the
1920s, so the simpler, more stripped-down designs that he increasingly developed
during the decade paved the way for the more modernistic emphasis that followed.

Still more specifically twentieth-century in emphasis, the Park Avenue Restaurant and the Atlantic Beach Club continued the dominant tone of the twenties, but
without the obvious decorative elements that characterized the rest of Urban's work.
Dispensing with external opulence, these—and as we shall see, other buildings of his
such as the New School for Social Research—highlighted the tautness of line, sleek
forms, flowing shapes, stylized simplicity, and directness that had been the hallmark of

fashion artists like Gordon Conway at the beginning of the 1920s. It was precisely these qualities, translated into architectural terms, which were promoted by Bel Geddes and dominated the next decades.

As Urban put it in a 1930 interview for the *Brooklyn Eagle,* his aim was to develop "a typical American style of architecture, fitted to meet the needs of American life and its cultural environment." In his view this meant that "Architecture should be as much part of the time and the place as the current news"[12]—and two of his public places did make headlines, although in quite unanticipated ways. In 1931, the Park Avenue Restaurant was shut down and its mirrors smashed by federal agents enforcing Prohibition. The Central Park Casino had been constantly in the news for its high prices and the goings-on of its Tammany Hall habitués. When Fiorello La Guardia was elected mayor in 1934 on a platform of cleaning up the city, the casino was demolished as a symbol of the previous corrupt administration, despite a highly public lawsuit to preserve the building. If anything, the way these two buildings were singled out for destruction is compelling evidence of how central Urban's work was in representing the lifestyle of the period.

The influence of these buildings spread far beyond those who actually visited them. In addition to all the attention they got from newspapers and architectural or home decorating journals when they opened, postcards featured the Ziegfeld Theatre, and Urban's décor for the St. Regis Hotel, the Casino, and many others, as well as Bel Geddes' Copa City. For their senders and recipients across the country, the cards served as models for what fashion should be, and the places themselves also figured as the background for many news stories about the doings of politicians and public figures.

This trickle-down effect of images of the lifestyles of the rich and famous was reinforced by the way they both helped to animate the streets. Urban created floats—including a stylishly swan-shaped boat—for the 1924 National Beauty Pageant. Similarly, Bel Geddes created floats for Macy's popular Thanksgiving parades in the 1920s.

Following on from this, in the 1940s Bel Geddes was hired to redesign the combined Ringling Brothers Barnum & Bailey Circus. The traveling circus fondly remembered from his boyhood was the great common denominator of entertainment, even a symbol of the American character. Bel Geddes saw his task as modernizing it in both taste and operating methods (for instance, by making all cages and wagons into uniform modules with fittings that allowed easy transfer between rail and truck). He turned the cages into displays for the animals—he claimed he was the first to do this—by supplying a painted backdrop for each that evoked their natural habitat, the sun-streaked darkness of an Indian jungle for the Bengal tiger, or the blue haze of eucalyptus trees for the koala bears. He also designed a completely new kind of big top. Instead of the conventional peaked tent, the canvas formed a shallow dome suspended from six high pylons that rose through it round the edges. This made it possible to create a huge, completely unobstructed space, big enough to seat 2,000 people with five circus rings as well as providing space around them for a procession of six horses abreast. (How revolutionary this was can be measured by the Millennium Dome, built for the year 2000 in London, which promoters touted as being constructed by the very latest methods. In fact, it is merely a larger version of Bel Geddes' design from sixty years earlier.)

The Ringling show was, in Bel Geddes' words, "a Circus for a Plastic World." This was by no means a negative term to him, or to his public, plastic being the latest material—and the performance rings were indeed constructed of translucent plastic, glowing from inside with flashing colored lights. He also transformed a key element of performance, the opening procession, producing mini-scenarios dramatizing children's fairy tales or (as appropriate to time of year) holiday festivals like the Mardi Gras carnival, St. Patrick's Day, and Halloween, which commentators singled out for novelty and contemporary relevance. When the circus arrived in New York in April 1941, the newspapers were full of superlatives: as the *New York Journal and American* trumpeted, "Good Old Circus Reopens in a Blaze of Color . . . conjured up for the latest streamlined version of the greatest show on earth."[13]

Big as the Ringling Brothers Barnum & Bailey Circus might have been, there was another, rather different fairground that both Urban and Bel Geddes contributed to, which was larger in every way. It was visited by more Americans and came to represent modern life on a national scale. This was the phenomenon of the World's Fair.

A Century of Progress

WHEN PLANNING FOR THE 1933 Chicago World's Fair began, it was logical for the organizers to include Joseph Urban and Norman Bel Geddes alongside businessmen and civic leaders. The overarching theme for the event had been decided, reflecting an optimistic view of the twentieth century—"A Century of Progress"—and by the end of the 1920s no one was more clearly associated with modernity and the development of a uniquely American lifestyle than these two designers. Urban, at the height of his career, was just completing the New School for Social Research, which opened in 1930. Bel Geddes had already made a name for his streamlined designs (which were gathered together in his highly influential book *Horizons* in 1932, just one year before the fair). Appointment to the architectural committee publicly recognized the central importance of their work, as well of course as boosting it still further. Far from being present simply in an advisory capacity, they were two of the key figures responsible for creating and overseeing the whole layout of the fair.

Urban was appointed director of exterior color, his job being to harmonize the appearance of the exhibition buildings over the whole site—a real challenge, because the architecture turned out to be so diverse. Bel Geddes' post was director of lighting, and he was also responsible for design of the theater buildings and organizing the stage performances envisaged for the fair. In other words it was they who would determine the tone of the whole, and the way the public perceived the experience, as well as the type of entertainment available. Beyond that, Bel Geddes and Urban were expected to showcase the central theme of the fair. The product exhibits and engineering displays might be tangible evidence of technological advance over the preceding century, but the triumphal overarching theme of "Progress" could only be realized if it was staged. That required the expertise of theater designers.

In fact their role was crucial since the most famous American World's Fair, the 1893 Columbian Exposition, had also been held at Chicago—and the 1933 event had to measure up to the famous White City constructed just forty years before, which many older members of the public would still have remembered. Back then, the display buildings of the main exhibition ground had presented a pure and gleaming urban world, as it might be if scientific principles were applied to city planning (in stark and deliberate contrast to the soot-grimed Chicago slums that had bordered the site). The whole fairground was architecturally unified, in high Beaux Arts style copied from France, with pillars and domes outdoing Imperial Rome, neoclassical figurative sculptures, and formal colonnades along geometrically laid out canals. Built of white stucco, the vista had been ephemeral—but this underlined the point that it was visionary. At the same time, the 1893 fair had demonstrated how this potential could be realized: through the power of electricity. In the early 1890s the everyday application of electricity was still a rarity. Here a dazzling electrical display created the major motif. The thousands of glittering lights that outlined the Electricity Hall, the moving sidewalks and elevated trains powered by electric motors, the bright electric lighting everywhere, and even the newly invented telephone first demonstrated at the exposition all formed one of the dominant public impressions.

The 1893 event had also broken new ground by including the first Midway, broadening the appeal of World's Fairs, which up to then had been primarily displays of manufactured goods and new technologies. The Chicago Midway, a great popular success under an associate of P. T. Barnum, included vaudevilles and comic operas, but its high point—literally—was the first Ferris wheel. The ride was invented by the engineer George Ferris in conscious rivalry to the Eiffel Tower, which had been built (by Gustave Eiffel, who also constructed the Statue of Liberty) for the 1889 Paris Exposition. The contrast between these two iron structures sums up the difference between American fairs and their European equivalents: a machine in motion that has become a common object of popular culture versus a soaring but static symbol, a unique national emblem. Although the Wild West exhibition starring Buffalo Bill formed a competing attraction outside the bounds of the fair, its Ferris wheel and other rides marked the start of amusement parks in America.

By any standards, the 1893 fair was a massive event. The site covered 633 acres, requiring the straightening of the Chicago River, and attracted well over 27 million people (a staggering 25 percent of the population of the United States at the time). More than that, the 1893 Columbian Exposition crystallized a typically American linkage of engineering, education, popular entertainment, and utopian vision. In harnessing technology to an ideal future with the official aim of "redefining" America as a cultural, commercial, and scientific world leader, the fair drew on powerful national mythologies. Harking back to the long tradition of scientifically inspired ideals that permeated the United States from early leaders like Thomas Jefferson and Benjamin Franklin (whose own experiments with electricity had attracted worldwide attention in the early nineteenth century), the exposition was harnessed to the vision of America as a land of ideal cities.[1]

The Chicago World's Columbian Exposition was widely seen as heralding the opening of a new era, American destiny made manifest. Dvořák wrote his "New World Symphony" to celebrate the fair, and a new national holiday—Columbus Day—was instituted to mark it. Major social changes also followed in the wake of the new technologies showcased there.

Less than a year afterward, Thomas Edison opened his Kinetoscope Parlor in New York. Just a few years later New York introduced electric trolleys (a more mundane equivalent to the elevated trains at the fair) as public transport; and the rapid spread of electricity into homes and cities in America was a direct result of this Columbian Exposition, as were the fairgrounds that American cities now started to build.[2] The most famous of these new entertainment centers was Coney Island in New York, where a Sea Lion Amusement Park opened in 1895, to be joined four years later by Luna Park (lit by 250,000 lights in imitation of the Electrical Hall at the fair), then by Dreamland. Coney Island was the biggest popular amusement venue in the world, not to be outdone even by later centers such as the northern English town of Blackpool.[3] The Chicago fair also entered popular culture. A childhood visit to the Columbian Exposition so inspired L. Frank Baum that, years later, he took the White City as his model for the Emerald City in *The Wizard of Oz*.

It was a high standard to match. The uniformity and symmetrical proportions, colonnades and cupolas of those grand exhibition halls in the White City expressed classically sublime principles of logic and harmony. However, designed by architects who had trained in Paris, in copying the Beaux Arts edifices of late nineteenth-century Europe they could also be seen as importing the hierarchical ideals of those old imperialist societies. In deliberate contrast, in 1933 the architecture was to be specifically American. Yet also consciously following in the footsteps of the Columbian Exposition, the 1933 official theme of "A Century of Progress" explicitly celebrated—and measured itself against—the changes ushered in by the event exactly forty years earlier. It too linked up with the traditional American myths of nation building, paralleling Herbert Hoover's *Challenge to Liberty* (published just a year later in 1934), in which science, industry, and new inventions were claimed as the new frontiers of America. Continually expanding with each fresh discovery, these areas of advancement replaced the vanished geographical frontier of the old West, in Hoover's view—and would be conquered by the same traditional frontier ideals of independence, individuality, and personal initiative.

In specific contrast to the uniformity and traditionalism of the White City, all of the 1933 exhibition buildings were to be radically modern. They physically represented Progress—like the dome of the Travel and Transportation Building, which was suspended 125 feet above the ground by cables attached to twelve external steel pylons. Instead of elevated trains, there was a futuristic Sky Ride in "rocket cars" across a bridge suspended from the top of two 600-foot metal towers. And the fair opened with a much-hyped display of up-to-the-minute technology: a graphic symbol of scientific advance converging on the exhibition from all across America. As the 1933 *Official Guide* proudly declared, "The lights were turned on with energy from the rays of the star Arcturus" through photo-electric cells in several distant astronomical observatories, "then transformed into electrical energy which was transmitted to Chicago."[4]

The 1933 display halls were consciously experimental in design and widely different in style, ranging from Art Deco to blank cubes or wildly untraditional shapes. As Urban noted in his files, they used all sorts of materials that had never before been applied to the outside of buildings—and were being deliberately used in their original manufactured form to represent "new materials turned out by the machines of the great factories of today." They were also stark and basic, a direct result of the economies forced by the Great Depression. So, quite apart from coordinating the hodgepodge of shapes and textures, Urban's aim was to provide an antidote for the prevailing economic bleakness and "to give the spirit of carnival" through color that would "transport you from your everyday life."[5]

He used a spectrum of twenty-four colors, "all of the brightest intensity" and applied in striking combinations of three or five on each building. This was not intended to be purely decorative. The colors were spatial and functional, linking the units so that the whole site became a complete composition, creating an image of modernity. So for one massive complex—a central building with a very large domed roof and tall pillars either side of its doorways, flanked on either side by multiple cubed structures of varying heights—the dome was rich orange, the pillars white, while the dominant tone for the cubes was the famous Urban blue that had been the hallmark of his theater designs. For the right-hand group that penetratingly deep color combined with yellow, green, and periwinkle blue; and with hot pink, green, and blood red on the left. All of this was reflected in the water of a pool that stretched across the whole front. Different arrangements of the same colors accentuated other buildings, like the Great Hall. Here, faced with a monolithic uniform expanse, Urban broke up each long wall into zigzag fields of solid color. On one side these ran from Urban blue through yellow (with green towers above), to blood red (with yellow and periwinkle blue towers). The opposite side of the same building was largely pink, white, and yellow, with only small areas of blue and red. Similarly, Urban decked out the exterior of the 658-foot-long Agricultural Pavilion in green and yellow, switching halfway along to black and rust red with purple highlights, while the interior had scarlet and yellow neon columns supporting the curving black roof. By contrast he gave the Hall of Science a striking blue and orange pattern.

For his part, using a new lighting technology (radiant gas) as symbol of modern life, Bel Geddes outlined these buildings with long neon tubes stretching along the tops, around perimeters, or up the sides of towers and pillars. Also multicolored, these intensified both the dazzling effect of the paint and its modernistic nature. Architectural journals praised the lighting as a "revelation" that brought out a richness and depth of color "never before attained." And the architect Raymond Hood, seeing the site in May 1933 while the color treatment was still being applied, wrote enthusiastically to Urban that "It was marvelous—swipes of pure color 40 feet high and 400 feet long. They [the architects] messed up the plan with a small exhibit building—but your color will bring back the form. It is going to save the show."[6] And indeed it did.

As the official guidebook noted, "The many colors, all tints of the rainbow, make the Fair a wonderland." Under Urban's hand the whole fair became a gigantic toy box, eye-catching and joyful, at the same time giving a vivid image of modernity with colors so dominant that they achieved a plastic value rather than being decorative additions. Dramatic both in juxtapositions and in emotion, the scene reproduced the brilliant color schemes of his stage settings in abstract form. More than 48 million people flocked to the 1933 Chicago fair, and its popularity was to a great extent due to Urban's striking contribution.

Urban's career had first intersected with America at the World's Fair held at St. Louis in 1904 to celebrate the centenary of the Louisiana Purchase. The Chicago World's Fair proved to be his swan song. Shortly after its opening he collapsed unexpectedly, dying on 10 July 1933 at the age of sixty-one. The entry on Urban in *The National Cyclopedia of American Biography* of 1936 noted in particular the striking color and lighting effects of the fair as a memorial to his genius.

The 1893 Columbian Exposition had included a World's Congress of Authors with daily presentations and lectures and a weeklong Parliament of Religions: signs of the (classical) cultural flowering, which technology would supposedly bring to inhabit the ideal city. In the original plan, theater was also a major feature, with the construction of a Spectatorium, which would have been the largest building on the site: 480 feet long, 380 feet wide, and 270 feet high. This was the last and biggest brainchild of one of New York's most innovative playwrights and actor-managers of the time, Steele MacKaye. Mirroring the fair's triumphal vision of America, it was intended to house a dramatic reconstruction of Columbus's voyage of discovery and all that sprang from that.

This production, "The World Finder," was to have been a "vast synthesis of arts"—as MacKaye's son Percy later described it in a letter to Norman Bel Geddes, who in his typically visionary way took up the challenge, doing designs for a large-scale reconstruction in the 1920s.[7] Steele MacKaye's whole concept, with its massive theater to be built for performing his own epic drama, clearly paralleled Bel Geddes' *Divine Comedy* project, which helps to explain his enthusiasm. (Both were even domed, although MacKaye's sported a classical cupola in keeping with the Beaux Arts White City, while Bel Geddes' dome encompassed the whole roof like a modern planetarium.) In an example of the close network from which American modernism emerged, Percy MacKaye, who had written the choruses for his father's "World Finder" project, was the pageant master who had provided Urban with the script for *Caliban of the Yellow Sands*.

As it happened, the economic depression that hit the United States while the 1893 fair was still being prepared caused the cancellation of the Spectatorium—which was scaled down to a very modest Scenitorium.[8] The actual theatrical performances were more along the lines of the strong-man act of the Great Sandow, who lifted a grand piano and carried three horses on a huge plank held across his chest. But even this had more significance than first appears. The show started the career of Florenz Ziegfeld (Sandow's agent), who went on to found the *Follies* revue that brought Urban his opening to the world of fashion.

In the same way, theater was intended to form a major part of the "Century of Progress"—avant-garde art on a public scale—and Norman Bel Geddes' reputation, both as a creator of spectaculars like the Reinhardt *Miracle* and as a designer of visionary new kinds of theater buildings, got him the job. Even if none of his ideal stages had been constructed yet, they corresponded well with the program envisaged for the Chicago World's Fair. "Distinctly radical and free in their form and proportions," they would "encourage new forms of dramatic writing," as he put it in a letter sent out to all the most notable experimental directors and playwrights, both in America and around the world, soliciting work from them for the fair.[9] This invitation got highly enthusiastic responses—with England's leading experimental director, Terence Gray, for example, replying that it was "the most inspiring piece of news . . . the realization of dreams," while the scene designer René Fuerst wrote from Paris that the whole project "will be of first-rate importance for the development of that theatrical art of the future we aspire to." Percy MacKaye offered to take part in any capacity "as a dramatist, or as a director, or creative associate."[10] The organizing committee of the fair approved Bel Geddes' designs, which were published in *Theatre Arts Monthly* and exhibited at the New York Architectural Show in 1930.

Some were the culmination of plans worked out over a decade, like the Divine Comedy Theatre, while others went back to designs he had published in *INWHICH,* his first journalistic foray into the theater world. Two of the most imaginative were a theater in a lake for open-air water pageants, and a Temple of Music that would have been the largest of all the structures, capable of holding over 10,000 spectators. Those in particular generated a lot of commentary and became emblems of "a new architecture." The qualities singled out—their simplicity, "organic forms," and the absence of any "impressionistic sentimentality"—can best be seen in Bel Geddes' plans for the Temple of Music.[11]

This huge building was to be completely flexible. The tower was to contain twelve

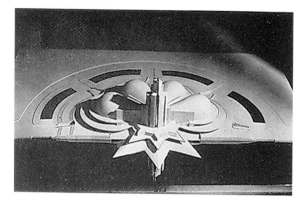

Bel Geddes' scale model for the Temple of Music
viewed from the waterside. The 120-foot tower is designed
to house a carillon of bells. Estate of Edith Lutyens Bel Geddes,
Norman Bel Geddes Collection, Courtesy of the
Harry Ransom Humanities Research Center.

floors of rehearsal and broadcasting studios. The four teardrop-shaped sections and central half moon, which together formed one huge auditorium holding an audience of 10,200 (a whole dimension larger than his planned Divine Comedy Theatre), could be divided by movable partitions and configured to hold 3,600 seats in the central portion, with the segments being transformed into smaller halls, holding 1,580 seats in each, for chamber music. The fanned-out domes (each with a fully retractable roof) and star shape of the ground plan were symbolic representations of the machine age. The first impression is one of streamlining, a key word for Bel Geddes. But characteristic of the merging of Art Deco with Art Nouveau from which a specifically American form of modernism emerged, the primary association of the whole building is with the natural world. The shape suggests the ripened seedpod of some exotic flower, just on the point of bursting into fruit.

Typical of the performances envisaged for these theaters was *The Light*—a pageant designed by Joseph Urban for Bel Geddes' Water Theatre. Light, in fact, was a major theme for both Urban and Bel Geddes, and another of Bel Geddes' designs for the fair was a Fountain of Light. This was a long narrow cascade of water, flowing from a towering fountain over a series of steps through the middle of a translucent dome (supported solely by an invisible cushion of hydrogen in the apex). Onto its curving surface, the shadows of the people walking by the water, lit from beneath in a spectrum of colors, would be projected, "a human panorama seen from the outside," as Bel Geddes noted on the sketches, adding, "In the beginning there was LIGHT."[12] The biblical phrase is a graphic illustration of his idealistic aims for using the fair as the catalyst for a new society, casting the artist as God, creating the modern world.

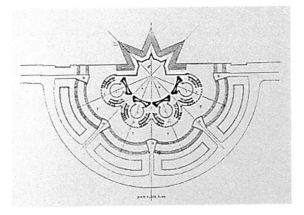

Bel Geddes, ground plans for the Temple of Music auditoriums,
1930: open configuration (*above*); configured for small groups
(*below*). From *Theatre Arts Monthly*, September 1930, p. 771.
Courtesy of the Harry Ransom Humanities Research Center.

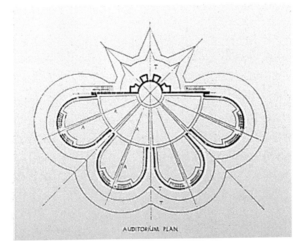

This quasi-religious glorification of the artist's cultural role may well seem over
the top; and there is a real disproportion between such grandiose notions of social engineering and the narrowly aesthetic, primarily theatrical means supposed to achieve
it here. In any case, although the vision was imaginatively compelling—Urban's set
model for *The Light* won a prize at the annual exhibition of the Architectural League
in New York—it turned out to be unrealizable, not on technical grounds but due to
global conditions far beyond the control of either Urban or Bel Geddes.

In his 1929 letter inviting new styles of performance from the international theater
world to fill his highly original designs for stage buildings, Bel Geddes had confidently

asserted, "Only an unforeseen contingency can upset the program that I am here outlining."[13] Even before the enthusiastic replies came in, the Wall Street crash occurred. And, as in 1893, among the first things to be cut back were the purely cultural aspects of the fair. Not one of Bel Geddes' theaters was built, and all of the invitations to international theater companies were cancelled. Instead the most notable performance at the 1933 Chicago World's Fair was the nude fan-dance of the notoriously curvaceous Sally Rand, which sparked journalistic outrage, led to a civil lawsuit for obscenity, and launched Rand's career as one of America's most visible nightclub and cabaret stars.

Although borrowed from Europe, as an idea the "World's Fair" became closely associated with America. More were organized in the United States over the fifty years from 1890 to 1940—fifteen in all—than in any other country; and those mounted in the States were generally larger.[14] The sheer size of a World's Fair gives it public significance. And such events offer snapshots of American culture that highlight broad changes as these occur. Equally, visited by millions of people, such events provide an unrivalled platform to spread new ideas and technologies. The earliest example is the Manhattan "Crystal Palace" Exhibition in 1853 at which William Otis demonstrated his invention, the elevator. Far from presenting a static display, Otis stood in his contraption as it rose into the air, ostensibly hauled up by ropes which were then cut, to the gasps of the immense crowd, while he continued to ascend, then came down again smoothly and safely. Brashly American in showmanship, this act signaled the start of a new architectural form that came to symbolize America and had a significant impact on modern life, since without the elevator there could have been no skyscrapers.

The 1933 Chicago fair also produced tangible effects. Urban's color schemes had a significant influence on American building design as *Architecture,* the leading journal in the field, acknowledged a year later. Commenting on the way Urban had succeeded in tying "three miles of heterogeneous architectural forms, without planned relation to each other, into one display and give unity to the entire Fair," it concluded that this "daring innovation . . . marked the beginning of a new era."[15]

The event also fed into an entire "futures industry" that emerged during the 1930s. Unlike today, these futures were in fantasy, not the stock market. In a period of economic collapse and mass unemployment like the "Dirty Thirties," one might expect escapism, and the times certainly fueled a mass market for science-fiction pulps and comic strips. But this emphasis on the future was far more than just an imaginary emigration from a depressing present. There was an observable interplay between science fiction and modernist architecture or streamlined design.[16] This relationship was particularly close in the more utopian visions of Frank Lloyd Wright's Broadacre City and Buckminster Fuller's Dymaxion Dwelling Machines and 4D Zoomobiles, which were reflected—sometimes even foreshadowed—by the fantasy worlds of comic-strip heroes like Buck Rogers and Flash Gordon. Even economists of the time saw futuristic design as a way of breaking out of the Depression. In the view of the authors of *Consumer Engineering: A New Technique for Prosperity* (1932), employment could be increased only by stimulating sales, and the way to do that was by introducing new styles for everything, from household products and appliances to cars and trains, that would attract consumers and encourage travelers. Streamlined forms were the way to go, because they symbolized the progress denied by the Depression.[17]

Another book published in 1932 was Norman Bel Geddes' *Horizons*, which made him the public apostle of streamlining. In it he forecast the future shapes of everything from theater to factories, furniture and shop-window displays in a "Changing World" (the title of his concluding chapter). Almost half the text was devoted to modes of transport: revolutionary cars, buses, railways, ships, and airplanes. Although he was already introducing the streamlining principles illustrated in his book into the industry, Bel Geddes' wider aim was to "inspire the new era" that he—together with many other Americans—saw just over the horizon.[18]

For some this meant a political revolution, given graphic expression in the theater by Clifford Odets's *Waiting for Lefty*—with its stirring call of "Strike!" which was hailed as the "birth-cry of the Thirties"—and promoted in the pamphlets that fueled the growing appeal of Communism in the period. Similarly, Franklin Roosevelt's speeches during the Depression called for a world of abundance to be ushered in through a New Deal. As Bel Geddes had put it in *Horizons*, precisely because the existing industrial system had proved so inadequate, "a new age dawned with invigorating conceptions and the horizons lifted." His streamlined designs that illustrated this had a political subtext, too, because the book held up Soviet Russia as "one of the greatest experiments the world has ever known," in part at least simply because "they try at least to look ahead and see where they are going" (a reference to Stalin's notorious Five-Year Plans, at that time much admired in the West).[19] But more important, his vision also tapped into the same widespread popular culture as the 1933 Chicago fair, with its celebration of "A Century of Progress": science fiction.

Throughout the decade futuristic pulps were wildly popular: in its heyday, *Amazing Stories* (whose editor was responsible for coining the term "science fiction" itself) sold more than 100,000 copies an issue.[20] The material within was scientifically generally spurious and unbelievably fantastic, while their stories were almost invariably set (as in George Lucas's brilliant revival of the genre) "In a galaxy far, far away." Still, the degree to which futuristic fantasy had infiltrated the American psyche can be seen in the mass panic inspired by Orson Welles's radio dramatization of *The War of the Worlds* in 1938. Hearing what seemed to be an emergency newscast, Americans jammed the roads fleeing from New York in the belief that grotesque Martians had landed and were advancing on the city, destroying everything in their path.

All this formed a receptive ground for Bel Geddes' streamlined designs, as an influential film by Alexander Korda shows. Made in 1936 and based (like Welles's *The War of the Worlds*) on a story by H. G. Wells, *Things to Come* was a serious attempt to envisage the future and a powerful plea for peace. It predicted a second world war starting in 1940—only a few months off in its forecast—that totally destroys civilization. In the first half, London (here called Everytown) is bombed back into the Middle Ages. The film is a graphic demonstration of what the scientist hero—played by a young and charismatic Raymond Massey (who had also acted the title role in Bel Geddes' *Hamlet*)—points out at the beginning, "If we don't end war, then war will end us!"

In its second half, however, the film offers a visionary alternative. The world is rescued by "engineers and mechanics" who have banded together, isolated from war in the African desert, as a "brotherhood of efficiency, the freemasonry of science" in the practical form of air pilots who impose the motto "Pax Mundi. Wings over the World." The rubble of Everytown is replaced—just one or two generations later—by a gleaming city of light. Its soaring spires, curvilinear buildings, and white circular towers overlook wide plazas inside a vast manmade cavern; and since all urban populations are underground, the countryside has been restored to pristine splendor. Everything is made possible, the script claims, simply by "exploiting all these giant possibilities of science . . . up to now squandered on war."[21] The film ends with a young couple being launched into space from a gigantic vertical cannon—just as Raymond Loewy's model rocket travelers were announced to be in the Rocketport Exhibit at the 1939 New York World's Fair—on a voyage round the moon.

The space launch by phallic cannon came from Jules Verne's classic *A Trip to the Moon,* via an 1877 operetta by Jacques Offenbach. The costumes of the "Engineers"—bulbous helmet, gleaming breastplate, and skin-tight leggings, or (in more relaxed conditions) short quasi-classical togas—echoed the Buck Rogers/Flash Gordon type. But everything else was borrowed directly from *Horizons.*

The futuristic skyscrapers of the underground city strongly resemble the designs for buildings published by Bel Geddes, specifically some of the larger structures proposed for the 1933 Chicago World's Fair. In particular the huge airplanes, in which the "Engineers" fly, exactly copy Bel Geddes' design of "what the intercontinental air liner of 1940 will be like": an enormous "flying wing" without fuselage or tail, carrying more than six hundred people inside the wings themselves and in two pods suspended beneath. (In Bel Geddes' design these doubled as pontoons for landing

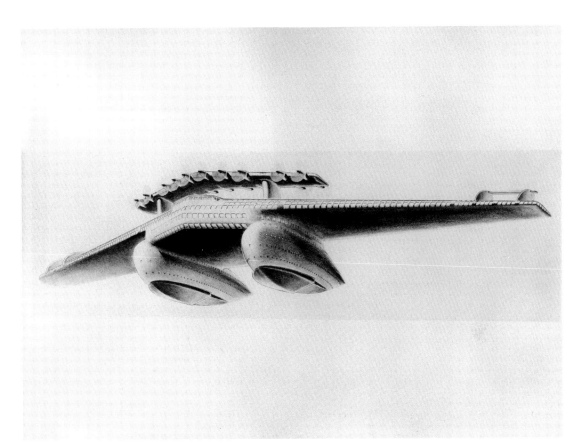

Bel Geddes' design for an "Intercontinental Air Liner," published in *Horizons* (1932),
and used as the basis for the flying wings of the United Airmen in the 1936 film *Things to Come.*
Estate of Edith Lutyens Bel Geddes, Norman Bel Geddes Collection,
Courtesy of the Harry Ransom Humanities Research Center.

on water, and the total wingspread was more than five hundred feet.) In both the film
and *Horizons,* the wing has windows all along its leading edge and great skylights
across the top in the center, while a small upper wing carries a serried rank of twenty
propeller engines.

Neither the "flying wings" of the film nor Bel Geddes' "intercontinental air liner
of 1940" was ever built, although Bel Geddes' design, developed in collaboration
with Dr. Otto Koller (the former chief engineer for the German Luftwaffe who had
designed more than two hundred planes), was certainly practical. Conceived when the
flying boat still seemed to be the most promising path for airplane design, his air liner
may well have formed part of the inspiration for Howard Hughes's famous "Spruce
Goose" (a flying boat, and by far the largest airplane the world had ever seen when

Bel Geddes' design from *Horizons:* Locomotive number 1, 1931 (*above*). The rear carriage
in this train was to be a tapering, rounded observation lounge, with wraparound windows,
a feature of the 1934 *Zephyr* and of Dreyfuss's famous train, the *Twentieth Century*;
Bel Geddes standing by the first streamliner—the Union Pacific *City of Salinas*, 1934 (*opposite*).
Estate of Edith Lutyens Bel Geddes, Norman Bel Geddes Collection,
Courtesy of the Harry Ransom Humanities Research Center.

constructed in the late 1940s). *Things to Come* undoubtedly helped to popularize Bel
Geddes' vision, not only of the future but of streamlined styling, with its title becoming a motto for anyone writing about the effect of new technology. Almost a decade
later, the U.S. Army published *Miracles Ahead!*, with designs by Bel Geddes, among
others, which illustrated how the scientific advances that were winning the war would
change the life of Americans once peace was achieved. The phrase "things to come"
is repeated throughout.[22]

• • •

Partly as a result of the film *Things to Come,* the streamlined world of sleekly curving shapes and simple, undecorated forms in buildings, cars, trains, and household furnishings that Bel Geddes was calling for—and already designing—seemed a logical extension of progressive trends. Modern styling merged with the future, particularly in transportation.

Travel was a natural symbol of change. Even though the fluidity of twentieth-century American society came from cars, it was the railways that traditionally defined the continental expansion of the United States. So it is not surprising that railway engines, in direct competition with automobile traffic and the new airlines, became the most extreme images of modern progress and the power of the machine.

So-called Zephyr shrouds—streamlined shapes of thin metal, named after the styling of the Burlington Northern Railroad's line of Zephyr trains—were bolted over the standard steam engines. And the first of these, which Union Pacific advertised as

"Tomorrow's Train Today!" (others were less enthusiastic, seeing it as a "monster airplane fuselage on wheels"),[23] was strikingly similar to designs Bel Geddes had published just over two years earlier. Capable of reaching 110 mph, it was inspected by President Roosevelt at the first stop on a 13,000-mile transcontinental tour, which ended at the Chicago "Century of Progress" fair, where it became a major attraction, toured by more than a million and a half people.

Bel Geddes clearly foresaw that the railway companies, which had been losing business throughout the 1920s, could attract passengers only by providing both speed and superior comfort, with spacious lounges, flexible seating (with telephone connections to each chair), a communication center for businessmen, and every detail custom-designed. In 1933 Union Pacific, announcing plans to develop a streamlined train, stated that "The Geddes train of 1928 is still a mark to shoot at. His plans, complete to the last detail, call for . . . a completely articulated train with lounge cars, sleepers, even a 'business car' with ticker room, offices and telephone booth; the whole streamlined without a projecting headlight, stack or door handle."[24] The earliest of these streamliners to fully follow Bel Geddes' prescription was the New York Central *Mercury* train by Henry Dreyfuss, which went into service in 1936. The layout of chairs, divans, and tables was intended to create the atmosphere of "a fine club," as he noted in his 1955 memoirs. Dreyfuss was right to call his train a "turning point in railroad design" because these were "the first streamliners done as a unit, inside and out, integrating everything from locomotives to dinner china."[25] Even the gray one-piece, zippered uniforms of the staff could be seen as costumes for machine-age travel and very much the equivalent of some of the clothing worn by the representatives of the future in *Things to Come*.

While these innovative trains were more comfortable, efficient, and (a major consideration for the rail companies) cost-effective, image was all. The mammoth engines of these classic trains of the 1930s were the embodiment of thrusting force and streamlined speed. Even stationary the steam engines looked as if they were effortlessly forging through the air, and one favorite shape was the torpedo with a single large headlight in the point of a cone that protruded over the forward-sloping shield covering the front wheels. The most famous of these was the symbolically named *Twentieth Century Limited*, which Henry Dreyfuss designed for Penn Central in 1938. By then, however, the torpedo shape had already become associated with Raymond Loewy, who had created the first of them for the Pennsylvania Railroad in 1936. Much to Bel Geddes' disgust—he claimed (correctly) that the concept for all of these modern streamliners had been "stolen" unacknowledged from his original designs—the latest of Loewy's torpedo-type engines was exhibited in a section of the Futurama at the 1939 New York World's Fair, a building that Bel Geddes looked on as his preserve. But in contrast to his largely unbuilt visions for the 1933 fair, by 1939 people were ready to accept Bel Geddes' definition of what tomorrow might look like, and his Futurama exhibit provided a concrete example of a transformed America.

Riding into the Future

IF THE CHICAGO WORLD'S FAIR six years earlier had been at least somewhat of a frustrating disappointment for Norman Bel Geddes, the 1939–40 World's Fair in New York was an unmistakable triumph. The two aspects of his double career, as scene designer and industrial designer/architect, intersect most tellingly in the exhibit he created for General Motors, Futurama (a word coined by Bel Geddes). Futurama, by far the most popular single display at the New York World's Fair, stands as a graphic demonstration of the way Broadway theatricality helped to shape the images and material objects that define modern America.

The central part of Futurama was the largest and most expensive scale model ever constructed. Together with the building housing it, also specially designed by Bel Geddes, the exhibit cost $8 million (close to $97 million today). The display dramatized a futuristic vision of everyday life so successfully that it carried over in the public imagination through World War II, ten years later being recognizable all across America and reappearing as the title of a popular television show in the 1990s.

One of the factors that made Bel Geddes' vision, and the Futurama exhibit that embodied it, so effective was the nature of the New York World's Fair. Like several previous International Expositions held in the United States, the fair marked a patriotic occasion in celebrating the 150th anniversary of George Washington's inauguration as the first president of the new republic on the steps of Federation Hall in New York. But in sharp contrast to the 1933 Chicago Fair, which had marked "A Century of Progress," this occasion six years later was in no sense retrospective. Referring back to the founding of the republic validated the vision of a made-in-America future. As H. G. Wells wrote for a special World's Fair supplement of the *New York Times* in March 1939 (his eminence as author of the influential *Outline of History* lending his views extra weight), its focus on "Building the World of Tomorrow" was qualitatively different from earlier World's Fairs. The future was at the core of the fair: the General Motors Building, with Bel Geddes' flight over America twenty years from the present, was flanked by the Ford Building, which had a "Road to Tomorrow" circling up its front wall, while the central edifice, the Perisphere, housed Henry Dreyfuss's "City of Tomorrow." One participant, interviewed for a film documenting *The World of Tomorrow*, expressed its impact perfectly: "There are moments where you can see the world turning from what it is into what it will be. For me, the New York World's Fair is such a moment. It is a compass-rose pointing in all directions."[1]

The icons of the fair, famous across America and even globally, were the rocket-like needle of the Trylon, and the Perisphere globe beside it: futuristic images, gleaming white, and brilliantly lit at night. As with most of the architecture erected for the event in Flushing Meadow, these huge geometrical shapes were made of wood, canvas,

The approach to Futurama: the GM Building with the Trylon and Perisphere at the New York
World's Fair in 1939. Estate of Edith Lutyens Bel Geddes, Norman Bel Geddes Collection,
Courtesy of the Harry Ransom Humanities Research Center.

wire, and stucco, just like theatrical scenery. They were almost literally a stage setting.
Copied on everything from paperweights and tin trays to dishcloths and postcards,
those geometrical structures represented the world of the future in purely abstract
shapes.

For H. G. Wells, however, the key to what he called this "prospectus of tomorrow"
was intensely practical. It was "new methods of communication and transport," which
he saw would create the most far-reaching changes in the distribution of population
and the nature of society, making it possible for "a score of men to sit in conference
... when bodily they are hundreds of miles apart." Long before the computer revolution, Wells was envisaging the wired world of today. More immediately, new and
faster modes of conventional transportation would lead to "an immense change in
the landscape of city and country alike"—which was precisely what Bel Geddes'
Futurama illustrated.[2]

The New York World's Fair was also distinct in being the "The People's Fair."
The "people" formed a typical 1930s theme, both in arts and politics, expressed in
government programs such as the People's Theater of the WPA and Frank Capra's
widely popular films glorifying "the little man," and perhaps most tellingly in a new
desire to consult "the people" on every aspect of public life signaled by the founding of
George Gallup's American Institute of Public Opinion in 1935. It's hardly surprising,
then, that the *Official Guide Book to the Fair* opened with the announcement: "This
is *your* Fair, built for *you*, and dedicated to *you*."[3]

Despite Gallup polls showing that most of the unemployed believed that they had
been displaced from their jobs by machines (suggesting a certain popular antagonism
to an event like the World's Fair that promised a vast extension of technology) or excluded by high ticket prices (63 percent of those who stayed away said they could not

afford it), "the people" were front and center in many of the exhibits. More than one hundred of the many quasi-documentary films shown at the fair promoted products in everyday surroundings, the most popular being *I'll Tell the World* (repeated every half hour at one publisher's exhibit) which depicted an average American family reacting to the failure of the father's business and being "restored to happiness and security when father discovers the miraculous powers of advertising."

The supposedly real-life "middle Americans" in these films were all professional actors. For the second year of the fair, however, forty "representative American families"—each comprising "a father America, a mother America, and two little Americans" (according to a press release)—were literally on daily display. Selected by local newspapers in various parts of the country, each family lived for a week in two futuristic houses erected in front of the Electrified Farm, where (in an early precursor of "reality television") they could be observed by the passing multitudes.

All this contributed to the effectiveness of the New York World's Fair as a catalyst for cultural change, and the populism led to everything being presented as entertainment. Earlier fairs maintained a sharp divide between commercial exhibits or national pavilions, and the Midway offering popular entertainment. Here the whole fair was a festival. In front of and around the exhibition buildings there were bands playing, colorful pageants, and daily parades. Brightly painted tractor trains toured the fairground to the tune of "The Sidewalks of New York"; strolling players—singers, dancers, musicians, acrobats, clowns—roamed continually through the fair; and Bel Geddes himself was also responsible for one of the most popular (in all senses) of these attractions.

Consciously emulating, indeed outdoing the notorious Sally Rand—whose teasing dances with a large ostrich-feather fan had been the high point of stage performances at the 1933 Chicago World's Fair—Bel Geddes created a high-tech nude spectacle as part of Democracity, the Theme Center inside the iconic Perisphere. What spectators crowded to watch was in fact a projected image, all the more sensuous because the naked female figures seemed close enough to touch, even though no actual dancer was on direct display. Instead, the figures of Bel Geddes' "Crystal Lassies" appeared, reflected by multiple intersecting mirrors and projected into a gigantic prism, endlessly refracted and bathed in constantly changing colored light. Even one of the period's leading intellectuals was charmed: writing in the *Nation,* Joseph Wood Krutch enthusiastically describes standing "on a platform just outside a huge crystal polygon while nude dancers, deliriously multiplied by reflection, dance on the mirror floors."[4]

Bel Geddes' "Crystal Lassies" were typical of a fair that on every level was noted for its theatricality. They competed with the show-business entrepreneur Billy Rose's

Aquacade, a fast-paced water spectacle of comic turns and swimming girls. They pirouetted alongside a whole range of equally theatrical performances at manufacturing exhibits. "Railroads on Parade" used more than two hundred live actors and dancers in historical costumes, plus trains from the early steam engines with bulbous smokestacks to the streamlined power-machines of the 1930s (the real "stars" of the show), to dramatize the romance of the railways in America. General Electric mounted technological tricks with "stroboscopes" and "thyratrons" (a vacuum tube to control high-voltage direct electrical current) in its House of Magic. The General Motors Building that housed Bel Geddes' Futurama also contained a Casino of Science Stage Show (described in the press guide as a "miracle-like stage program of exciting revelations")[5] as well as a "Research Laboratories Display." This selection of ingenious mechanical scenarios included robotics showing miniature figures of famous inventors in "authentic" settings: R. E. Olds constructing the first automobile and the Wright brothers at Kitty Hawk in 1903.

Even the central showpiece inside the Perisphere was a performance: the Democracity (designed by Bel Geddes' erstwhile pupil Henry Dreyfuss) combined film suggesting the brotherhood of man projected onto the inside of the great sphere with the spectacle of a futuristic metropolis representing progress, which was actually remarkably similar to a model city Bel Geddes had made for a Shell Oil ad campaign just the year before (compare illustration, page 176).[6] Similarly, the Focal Exhibit of the Transportation Zone (designed by Raymond Loewy) used movies, animated maps, and scale models to present a history of transport from horse-drawn chariots to a "Rocketport of the Future." Next door was Bel Geddes' Futurama, which, as newspaper reports observed and a Gallup survey clearly showed, was the most significant, and most spectacular, vision of "The World of Tomorrow" in the whole fair.[7]

Although as much a stylized representation of the future, both in concept and external shape, as the Trylon and Perisphere, Futurama was highly realistic as a display. But it was also a direct extension of Bel Geddes' stage work. Theater reviewers—such as Burns Mantle, who called Bel Geddes "the Miracle Man of the Fair" (punning on the title of Bel Geddes' recently published autobiography, *Miracle in the Evening*, which in turn played off his famous production of *The Miracle*)[8]—wrote about it as frequently as sociologists or business reporters, and the techniques he had pioneered in Broadway productions over the previous decade were precisely what made it so convincing.

The true effectiveness of Bel Geddes' theater was the way he created a total environment, which immersed spectators in the dramatic action. Much of what he staged were classics such as *Lysistrata* or *Hamlet,* and monumental spectacles set in an

Democracity. The ecstatic urbanism of Henry Dreyfuss clearly derives from the
Shell Oil advertising campaign mounted by Bel Geddes in 1937–38.
Reprinted by permission of Cooper-Hewitt, National Design Museum, Smithsonian Institution.

idealized past, like *The Miracle* or the later and still more magnificent staging of *The Eternal Road*—which would have outclassed even the modern megamusicals of Andrew Lloyd Webber with its 350 actors, singers, and dancers, fantastic setting of serpentine ramps, and 1,700 costumes based on Rembrandt's paintings. But his most effective production realistically portrayed contemporary American society. This was *Dead End,* which he staged in 1935. The play was about juvenile street crime (which first appeared as a serious problem in New York during the 1930s), and Bel Geddes' approach set the spectators in a myopically heightened mirror of their own urban surroundings.

Following what had become his usual practice, Bel Geddes both produced and directed as well as designed the scenery. He created an impression of several city blocks on the tiny stage of the Belasco Theater (just twenty-eight feet deep, with a thirty-one-foot-wide proscenium) by laying out the set with a central road: a ramp that ran diagonally back from the orchestra pit, gradually rising and narrowing in subtly exaggerated perspective, up to one corner of the theater's rear wall. Even without visual illusion, the actual length of that street—39 feet—seemed impossible in the space available. It exploded the audience's sense of reality.

In addition, Bel Geddes reversed the standard scenic conventions. The stage directions in Sidney Kingsley's script specified the East River be placed at the rear. Bel Geddes switched this around, with the edge of the wharf disappearing down into the orchestra pit, locating the audience in the river itself. Partly as a result of all these challenges to orthodoxy, the impression was extraordinarily real, with several reviewers feeling they were actually immersed "in the water." The critic of the *New York Times* enthusiastically endorsed the illusion, claiming "so real it all seemed, that I, sitting there in mid-river, found myself paddling to keep afloat!"[9]

As with his earlier hyperillusionistic *Miracle* staging, where occasional details had been exaggerated or distorted into obvious artificiality, challenging the spectators' imagination, so here in *Dead End* the reversal of perspective and extreme foreshortening of distance, together with distortions of some scenic elements, heightened the sense of realism through theatricality. Like the continuous bell, organ, and choral accompaniment to *The Miracle,* here too the crucial element in creating such an impression of reality was sound effects, which Bel Geddes exploited to a degree that had never been attempted before, wiring the auditorium to create a complete aural environment and using specially created recordings with multiple soundtracks on a continuous loop.

These recordings were not only keyed to specific moments in the action, such as the crackling of a bonfire in an ashcan, footsteps on the cinders of the wharf, and the sounds of an approaching crowd, but they also provided a continual background of

Bel Geddes, *Dead End*. The "river" in performance. Estate of Edith Lutyens Bel Geddes,
Norman Bel Geddes Collection, Courtesy of the Harry Ransom Humanities Research Center.

"River and Street." The tapes held forty-five uninterrupted minutes of water rushing
by (as recorded from a pier jutting out into the East River), boat whistles, the splash
of a boy diving off the end of a pier, all mixed with the combined sounds (as heard
from that point, and recorded on a different microphone) of traffic passing along First
Avenue. Bel Geddes had already written on the theatrical possibilities of using the new
recording technology developed for talking pictures on the stage, claiming it would
add another dimension to the theater. *Dead End* showed exactly what he meant.

As Bel Geddes gained independence, his work became more politically focused,
even with blatantly operatic spectacles. So, even more than the "Pied Piper" revolutionaries in *The Miracle, The Eternal Road*—performed in 1937, shortly after Kristallnacht when Hitler's storm troopers had smashed the windows of all Jewish shops

Backstage of *Dead End*. Note the blocking with coal hopper and steam shovel,
and the central position of the sound technician. Estate of Edith Lutyens Bel Geddes,
Norman Bel Geddes Collection, Courtesy of the Harry Ransom Humanities Research Center.

in Germany—commemorated the long history of the persecution of the Jews. *Dead End* even more directly addressed an immediate social issue: child poverty and the new phenomenon of teenage street gangs. To highlight this theme, well-known actors were deliberately avoided, throwing attention on the children in the cast, who (as the advertising emphasized) came from a charitable youth center, for which donations were solicited in the theater program: "If 'Tommy' and his gang had lived near the Madison Square Boys Club at 312 East 30th Street, they would have had a chance."

In direct response to the production, the New York Police Department opened a Community Youth Center, and the play was broadcast over the radio as part of the 1936 "Mobilization for Human Needs" campaign "to show the conditions which constantly confront health agencies in metropolitan areas." It was recommended to all members of the Greater New York Federation of Churches by the general secretary of the organization, and sixty clergymen applied for copies of the script to use in their sermons. (In contrast the Catholic Theatre Movement labeled the play "wholly objectionable" due to the use of street language, despite this being in fact considerably watered down in the script from what one might expect to have heard every day on the streets.) The mayor and the director of housing for the Federal Emergency Administration of Public Works expressed strong public support, and even the White House got involved. Eleanor Roosevelt, who was to become a strong advocate of Bel Geddes, hosted a group of the child actors at the White House, and then showcased them in her radio and newspaper appeals for her charities.[10] The play generated a series of articles in New York newspapers on the need for public housing and ways to solve street crime. *Dead End* ran for a record 368 performances. A second production opened in Chicago, then went on a road tour. The film rights were sold to Hollywood for $165,000, setting a record for the time. The movie, directed by William Wyler and starring Humphrey Bogart, was nominated for best picture in the 1937 Academy Awards.

It was a short step from creating such a totally convincing—and still more to the point, unlike *The Miracle,* highly contemporary—stage environment, as well as from exerting so powerful an influence on society (as he had in *Dead End*) to designing the physical and cultural context for society outside the theater. And all these qualities came together in Bel Geddes' work for the 1939–40 New York World's Fair: his populism, his technical innovation with stage machinery and sound-recording, and the way he challenged the spectators' sense of space, creating apparently "impossible" but convincing vistas.

Ahead of his time, like H. G. Wells, Bel Geddes correctly viewed communications as the key factor in the modern world, even though (with computers not even being imagined in science fiction, and the Internet revolution still half a century away) his vision was limited to conventional transport. This led naturally to a close association with the American automobile industry during the 1930s. He designed tires for Firestone (plus the firm's sign and trademark), exhibition displays for Goodyear and for Chrysler, revolutionary gas stations for Shell and Sunoco, spectacular advertising campaigns for Shell and General Motors—and in particular, cars for Nash, Graham-Paige, Frazer (and later Frazer-Nash), De Soto, Chrysler, and Buick.

All this made Bel Geddes a logical choice for General Motors in commissioning their display for the 1939 World's Fair. The original job description had been straight commercial advertising: "to construct . . . what might be a full size street intersection 20 years hence. . . . Adapting all of this to the immediate problem of displaying the

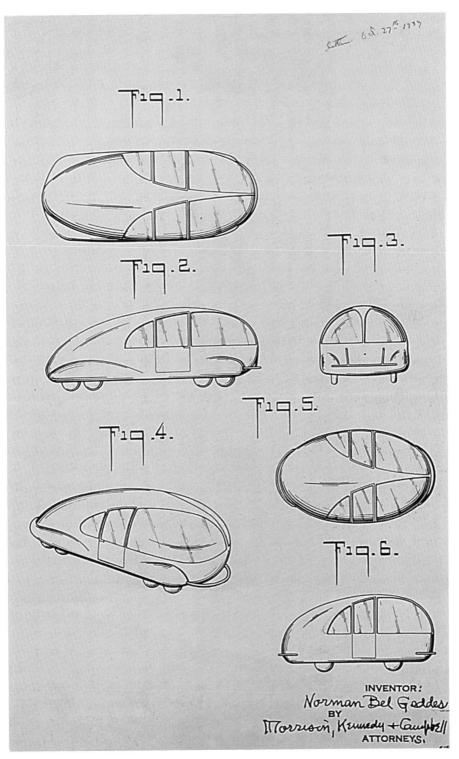

The 1939 patent for Bel Geddes' aerodynamically designed rear-engine automobile,
the cars installed in the Futurama model. Estate of Edith Lutyens Bel Geddes,
Norman Bel Geddes Collection, Courtesy of the Harry Ransom Humanities Research Center.

client's merchandise [the new range of 1939 GM cars] in their most favorable light." Bel Geddes expanded this into a far larger vision, however, suggesting he create a "continuous scale model of a national motorway system . . . and present it in *dramatic, imaginative form*."[11] He also added lighting, atmospheric effects, and spoken text—intensifying the theatricality of the whole—and persuaded GM executives that the cars had to be consistent with the futuristic buildings. Instead of advertising current vehicles, they agreed that the rear-engine, fully streamlined design Bel Geddes had presented in *Horizons* should represent the cars General Motors would be manufacturing in the 1960s.[12]

Although this display was merely a mock-up, for Bel Geddes any "model" was always a prototype. Whether designing stage sets, production cars, or buildings, his working method was to create scale models, which then became the basis for engineering or architectural blueprints. Clearly anticipating eventual manufacture, he took out a patent on the four types of cars used in the Futurama display, which had evolved into streamlined bubbles.

Bel Geddes was commissioned to design not only the GM exhibit but the whole building, as well as the landscaping around it. The simplicity of its sleek, curving shape, sweeping upward like a monumental transport machine on point of lift-off, formed a concrete expression of what Bel Geddes labeled "Futurama." It translates streamlining into the reality of bricks and mortar, while the sinuous, elevated, and multilevel ribbons of the entryways echoed what awaited the spectators inside.

On entering this building, the public funneled through a hall, illuminated only by blue light shining onto a dark cyclorama from behind. What they saw was a gigantic cutout map of the United States which seemed to float in space, covering the curving wall and arching overhead, a dark silhouette crisscrossed by intersecting lines of light representing a network of motorways. Walking under this, they took their places in pairs of seats mounted on a conveyor belt moving through semidarkness, while a disembodied voice at shoulder level explained that they are setting out on an airplane flight from one side of the States to the other. And they emerged into afternoon sunlight, apparently high in the sky. Below, through a slanting window of continuous glass, as the endless line of seats moved absolutely silently along, spread a springtime landscape. (The fair opened on 30 April.)

This rolling farmland—complete with flowering orchards, plowed fields, houses, barnyards, roads and railways, and a distant town—was all a massive but miniaturized model. Just as in *Dead End*, perspectives were accentuated, though to an even greater extreme, with the scale ranging from 1 inch representing 300 feet, to 1 inch for 10 feet, and at one point up to quarter-size of the actual objects, to achieve extraordinary effects of height and distance. The model was complete in every detail.

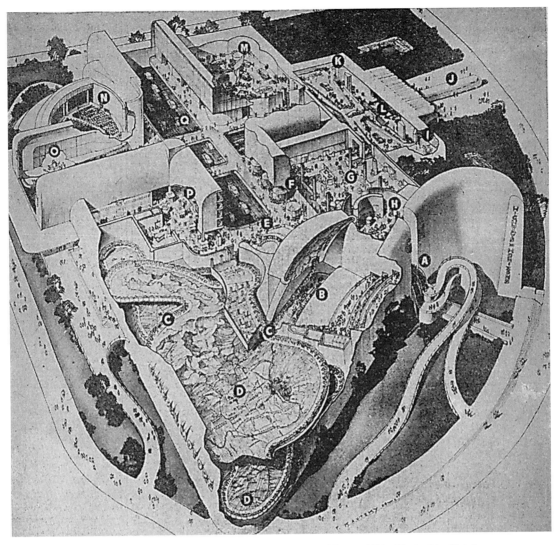

A cutaway sketch of the interior of the General Motors Building, published in the *New York Sun.*
Estate of Edith Lutyens Bel Geddes, Norman Bel Geddes Collection,
Courtesy of the Harry Ransom Humanities Research Center.

YOU RIDE IN SOUND-CHAIRS, *viewing a world in miniature — a vast world of future cities and countryside—industrial and mountainous sections — airports, lakes, rivers and waterfalls — streamlined trains, tunnels and boats — ten thousand moving cars on the superhighways of tomorrow. A spectacular and life-like "futurama" covering more than 35,000 square feet and extending for a third of a mile in and about this exhibit building of wonders.*

An artist's impression of the snaking track of the conveyor belt, 1939 press guide for the General Motors "Highways and Horizons" exhibit. The pairs of seats were separated from each other by partitions (omitted in the sketch) that curved forward at head height, blocking each couple's awareness of the long line of other spectators on either side. Estate of Edith Lutyens Bel Geddes, Norman Bel Geddes Collection, Courtesy of the Harry Ransom Humanities Research Center.

Trees were reflected in streams, miniscule people and farm animals stood in the fields, and telegraph poles and blinking signal lights marked the roads, with tiny cars and trucks actually moving along them.

Announcing that the year is 1960 and they are living in the future, a recorded voice in the spectators' ears points their attention to the flow of traffic around the entrance to a highway, which the conveyor belt swings toward and follows for the rest of the ride. Circling features of interest below, they "fly" over towns and villages, a mountain resort and observatory, industrial parks and hydroponic farms, a hydro-electric dam complete with sluiceways and canal systems. What the participants saw was a whole future world, realized in every detail, and even the notional "passenger compartment" was part of the illusion, with continuous "airplane windows" through which the spectators peered. Adding to the effect, the seats moved along the 1,600 feet of track at 2 feet per second, exactly simulating the speed of an airplane traveling at 200 miles an hour, the average flight speed for the time. Indeed, the sense of flying was crucial to making this vision of the future convincing. With passenger airlines still in their infancy, few spectators would have flown in an airplane. So looking at the country from this aerial perspective was a striking novelty—yet one they knew was already practicable.

As they traveled—carried past the changing scene and from afternoon sunlight through the night and into the dawn of a new morning—the conveyor belt on which they sat switched from one level of the display to another, built over the apparent sky of the one below, then up to a third. At each transition point the lighting and landscape changed. But the model was large enough to allow for subtle gradations within each level, and every technique of theatrical illusion was applied. Where vistas were shown, gauzes created an impression of distance. Thin wisps of cloud (specially manufactured chemical vapors) cast moving shadows on the landscape as they floated overhead or drifted across the view; when they reached a city, apparent haze misted skyscrapers on the horizon. Conventional stage lighting with nine colored filters simulated the different times of day. At night, lines of fluorescent pigment activated by pulses of ultraviolet radiation produced the effect of moving headlights on the highway, and in one town alone there were five hundred miniscule "grain of wheat" bulbs for the street lighting. The impression of realism must have been truly breathtaking.

While those at the beginning of the ride were still in bright sunlight, at the other end of the first (and lowest) level, dusk was falling. In the gathering darkness specta-tors could see the novel nighttime illumination of this motorway, where strip-lighting located in the separators between lanes automatically lighted up the road ahead of each vehicle and went out as it passed. The motorway led past an industrial city and into mountains, with the size of everything growing until (as Bel Geddes describes in

An artisan setting up. Although the lighting—standard working floodlights—
is very different from the atmospheric effects when in full operation, the mountain landscape
illustrates the changes in scale through which perspectives of height and distance were achieved.
Estate of Edith Lutyens Bel Geddes, Norman Bel Geddes Collection,
Courtesy of the Harry Ransom Humanities Research Center.

A spectator viewing the 1960s "City of the Future," with her face reflected
off the "airplane window" in the shadowed side of a skyscraper. Estate of Edith Lutyens Bel Geddes,
Norman Bel Geddes Collection, Courtesy of the Harry Ransom Humanities Research Center.

the prospectus for GM): "Great spruce trees bank the rocky ledges, tall and proud in
the moonlight," and "for an instant, huge rocks obscure the spectator's view."[13]

This is one of the transition points where the conveyor belt changes levels, disguised by the impression of an airplane climbing over a mountain ridge. A close-up
view of the motorway shows cars rushing through the night, as they emerge from a
tunnel then vanish again through a break in the cliffs. These model vehicles are corre-
spondingly larger, approximately one-quarter actual size, and "the sound of their swift
passage is heard distinctly."

The pale first light of dawn gradually grows into the soft sunshine of early morning. The motorway crosses gorges and rivers, runs through tunnels, is joined by feeder
roads—from the network of smaller, twisting secondary roads, and from a mountain-

An artisan inserting miniature cars into one of the moving belts of the roads in the model, featuring the crosswalks of the full-size intersection that visitors walked through at the end of their ride, and the model of Notre Dame, designed to give an accurate impression of scale, which Bel Geddes had developed for Shell Oil two years earlier. Estate of Edith Lutyens Bel Geddes, Norman Bel Geddes Collection, Courtesy of the Harry Ransom Humanities Research Center.

The life-size intersection in the interior of the Futurama, although with contemporary GM cars, 1939. The full-size mock-ups of Bel Geddes' streamlined patented cars were installed in 1940. The Frigidaire exhibit is in the building on the left. Estate of Edith Lutyens Bel Geddes, Norman Bel Geddes Collection, Courtesy of the Harry Ransom Humanities Research Center.

resort town—all leading the growing traffic toward a major city, apparently far in the distance, its skyscrapers rising through the haze beside a wide river.

The conveyor belt circles a high-tech bridge—allowing spectators an extended view of the four-tier highway with eight lanes of traffic on each level of the bridge—and, crossing the river, gives a panoramic view of the city itself. Illustrating Bel Geddes' ideas about urban planning, the voice at the spectator's shoulder points out the differences between the still-undeveloped 1939 sections of the city ("congested, badly planned") and the new 1960s decentralized layout with high towers allowing extensive parks and green spaces surrounding community units, and the segregation of industrial, commercial, and residential areas.[14]

The Frigidaire exhibit in the General Motors Building, echoing the futuristic shape of the Trylon
to display the appliances in an imagined 1960s context. Estate of Edith Lutyens Bel Geddes,
Norman Bel Geddes Collection, Courtesy of the Harry Ransom Humanities Research Center.

A thick cloud obscures the view for a second—masking another change in levels up to a third floor of the model—after which a closer range view of part of the city appears. The larger scale reveals a unified grid system of city blocks with elevated sidewalks separating pedestrians from the traffic below, which fills all the street area, allowing through lanes and feeders that provide exits to parking garages. Escalators link these to the sidewalks, lined by store windows, with bridges over the streets at every intersection.

A sharp turn in the conveyor belt, mimicking the dive of an aircraft, turns the spectator to a still more enlarged portion of this street scene: just six city blocks, flooded with late afternoon light. Crowds—miniature mannequins—stand on the moving sidewalks, gazing at the store windows, or lounge on the roofs of the highly modernistic department stores and apartment buildings. Cars in the same small scale stream along the streets below. A moment of darkness, and as the visitors dismount from their seats (which swing away to return to the starting point), they are faced with a single full-size street intersection of the 1960s city they had just observed. This effect was deliberately designed "to offset any dreamy impractical concept" and "to convince the visitor of the practicability of planned cities."[15] Walking out, they themselves become the crowds on the elevated sidewalks, peering into the store windows, which contain other GM displays: for instance, the futuristic Frigidaire exhibit, also designed by Bel Geddes, and even filled with kitchen appliances he designed. As Bel Geddes described the impression on the visitor: "the model he has just been looking at has come to life."[16]

Bel Geddes' Futurama for GM was drama of a high level, and the theatricality of the display was widely recognized. The *Sunday News* published its "rave review of a show staged by a huge private business corporation" as an editorial, headed "Smash Hit of the World's Fair." It was discussed in the journals of architects and town planners; it was also reviewed by theater critics. One of these was John Mason Brown, the doyen of the *New York Post,* who declared "the illusion of reality . . . in this stupendous panoramic model no less breath-taking in its details than was the background for *Dead End.*"[17] Imaginatively as well as literally he was carried away by Futurama: "There truly a new day dawns and the world of tomorrow comes to life. There an artist's logic is thrillingly imposed upon the chaos of our poorly ordered universe." And Bel Geddes certainly did draw on all his theatrical experience to express his vision of the future, as with the sight of a steel town at night described in his scenario.

Hundreds of workers' homes and lights gleaming from their windows are seen. . . . On one side of the river are rolling mills—a row of five Bessemer

The steel town of "Futurama" at night. Estate of Edith Lutyens Bel Geddes,
Norman Bel Geddes Collection, Courtesy of the Harry Ransom Humanities Research Center.

furnaces blowing and pouring steel, with the flare of lights which accompany
these processes, makes a thrilling picture.

A gaily lighted amusement park is located outside the town, with its
ferris-wheel, merry-go-round and other attractions moving . . . A wonderful
and thrilling sky-ride twists like a colored lighted pretzel amid the maze of
the other dazzlingly illuminated concessions.

A plane takes off from an enormous flood-lit airport and flies out into the
night. Railway trains are running in and out of the town . . . cars approaching
and leaving.[18]

In addition to the visual spectacle of the pulsing glow from the furnaces, those
scenic effects mirror the spectators' position, making them feel truly part of the experi-

ence. Their imaginary airplane journey is echoed by the model plane soaring up into the darkness, while—a tellingly ironic detail—the "sky ride" in the miniature amusement park duplicates the aerial conveyor belt they are sitting on in the middle of the World's Fair. Yet however spectacular the panorama, there was also a social message: the world visited on this journey into the future was specifically one of economic equality and social justice. As the voice stated in the ears of the "time travelers," a theme emphasized by being repeated in the booklet put out by GM to accompany the ride: "This 1960 drama of highway and transportation progress is but a symbol of future progress in every activity. . . . Who can say what new horizons lie before us if we but have the initiative and imagination to penetrate them—new economic horizons—new social horizons—leading to new benefits for everyone, everywhere."[19]

A month after the opening the *New York Journal and American* commented rather pompously: "I am delighted to see that Mr. Bel Geddes, who in the course of a brilliant and provocative career has moved nearly everything portable in the theater, has at last succeeded in moving the audience. I mean physically as well as emotionally."[20] Far more than such a throwaway comment suggests, both the moving system and the sound system were perhaps the most outstanding examples of futuristic technology in the fair.

The GM executives who approved the plans considered the conveyor "the most unusual thing of its kind ever constructed," which represented a "triumph in engineering."[21] It had to be flexible in every direction except the horizontal, combining the qualities of a train and an elevator, since over some sections the track was both rising and winding in corkscrew spirals. Yet the pairs of seats fixed to each of the six hundred small platforms in the chain had to remain level at all points. Compounding the problems, from time to time the seats were rotated so that the spectators' attention could be directed to particular sights, and the movement had to be completely silent.

The engineering challenge for the sound system was equally extreme, since the voice of the "guide" commenting on the sights had to be keyed to each different view along the way, yet speak simultaneously to every pair of seats moving continuously round the model landscape. This required 150 separate descriptive sound bites, each piped through a different loudspeaker and synchronized with the movement of the six hundred platforms, so that the commentary appeared almost unbroken while relating directly to what the spectators were watching at each point.

Bel Geddes' solution was a twelve-foot-high revolving steel drum, eight feet in diameter and linked to the motors pulling the seats along the track, so that the rate at which it turned would allow for possible variations in speed and precisely match the spectators' progress. Like his *Dead End* production, this audio system exploited cinematic technology, but even more directly. Round the drum were wound 150 separate ribbons of sound-film that passed in front of individual light-needles, transmitting the narrator's voice to speakers set at sixteen-foot intervals in the curved ceiling above the heads of the spectators, who thus passed from one soundtrack to the next every eight seconds.

Although the mechanics of these systems were invisible, the details had already been widely publicized in press releases, and the impression of novel technology in practical operation contributed significantly to the credibility of the whole vision of America in the future. This was reinforced by the use of unusual lighting effects, and by the sheer scale of the model itself, which covered 35,780 square feet. It extended in all over one-third of a mile, and had 500,000 individually designed buildings, multitier bridges, and a hydroelectric dam. There were also 50,000 scale-model moving automobiles; and the detail was extraordinary. Each type of vegetation was given a different texture, from pasture to wheat and alfalfa, while the larger-scale trees each had individual foliage. Waterfalls and rapids were simulated by tiny jets of water flowing over solid surfaces with air jets to create spray.

Following Bel Geddes' instructions, every detail had to be "accurate enough to photograph faithfully in a close-up, in spite of the fact that they might only be seen from 20 or 30 feet." Such visual richness intensified the attraction of this visionary future world, particularly since the glimpse of each feature was relatively brief: the total circuit of the ride lasted just fifteen minutes (which allowed five thousand people to go through every day).

Other elements further intensified the imaginative effect. The model landscape was in many ways a faithful copy of the geography of the United States, with the template following topographical geodetic survey maps and more than one thousand enlarged aerial survey photographs. It therefore contained recognizable geographical features within which Bel Geddes set his "new society" of the future. In addition, even more than with the setting for *Dead End,* the totally unexpected expanse of the model must have appeared particularly striking given the relatively small area within the building. There would have seemed to be no way of fitting in so much countryside, let alone a "ride" extending over a third of a mile. By comparison, the way Bel Geddes had expanded the audience's sense of space in staging plays like *Dead End* looks like a dress rehearsal. Futurama was greater by several orders of magnitude. It must have been almost magical—a tangible token of future science.[22]

Bel Geddes' vision of how America might look twenty years ahead was so spectacular—and popular—that in August 1939 one radio program enthusiastically declared Futurama "the high spot of the whole exhibition," while a news headline from the same month proclaimed, "Futurama: 8,307,600 Have Seen Tomorrow"—including (as a major article in the *American City* trumpeted) the Hollywood sex symbol Myrna Loy. Before it finally closed after a year and a half, in late fall of 1940, more than 15 million people had taken what the *New York Post* labeled a "fascinating journey into the land of the future."[23] Futurama also had a significant afterlife.[24]

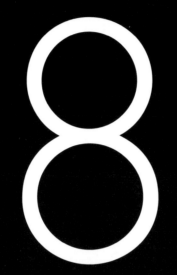

The World of Tomorrow

FUTURAMA WAS BY NO MEANS a single event. Almost a year before the 1939 World's Fair opened, highway sections of the model had been exhibited at the New York Society of Engineers, and as *Road Builder's News* commented in July 1939, its innovations and overall concept were "enthusiastically endorsed by leading highway engineers." It influenced the Pennsylvania Turnpike—America's first limited-access superhighway—which opened in October 1940 and was immediately dubbed "the magic motorway" after the title of Bel Geddes' book on highway design.

By now many aspects of Bel Geddes' motorway design have become so universal that it's hard to imagine that they came from the mind of a single person. Central barriers separating traffic moving in opposite directions are absolutely standard; the first example appeared on the Futurama highway model. We are accustomed to gently curving access ramps, interchanges, and overpasses allowing vehicles to maintain speed. These too come from Bel Geddes' model display, replacing the traffic circles and tight cloverleaf intersections of 1939 that slowed traffic to a crawl. He also developed the multiple feeder lanes on expressways in high-density areas, separating local from through traffic, for which no one else had even forecast a need.

At the time, all these were revolutionary. Enthusiastic articles appeared in leading professional journals, such as *Architectural Forum,* and the Chicago *Sales Service News Letter* advised: "Whether or not the World of Tomorrow as revealed by General Motors will come to pass . . . this trip makes you realize the great changes in styling and design that are ahead of us. No sales manager can go to the Fair without being impressed with the need of getting in step with this new thinking."[1]

The timing, of course, was hardly propitious for visionaries of the future. Even as the New York World's Fair was being put together, Hitler marched into Czechoslovakia. Just two days before it opened, a little-noticed but still more ominous announcement from Washington appeared in the *New York Herald Tribune:* Neils Bohr's discovery of "a rare form of uranium which is so unstable that it can be easily disintegrated, releasing from each atom that is smashed 200,000,000 electron volts of energy and emitting by-products that set off other atoms in a chain reaction."[2] The future was put on hold during the coming war. But then, Bel Geddes' vision had always been more far-reaching than that, peering ahead a whole generation to 1960; and the vision of Futurama was kept alive after the close of the World's Fair in 1940 right through to the postwar world.

A short film on the fair was released, partly in Technicolor (marking one of the first uses of this new film technology), and titled *To New Horizons,* which replayed the experience of the Futurama ride. Futurama also inspired textile designs and even women's clothing. When the fair was over, the model city from the display was transferred to the Saint Louis Art Museum, where it was featured in a 1941 exhibition of urban planning. Afterward large sections of the model, mounted on trucks, toured the United States as a "Parade of Progress." This traveling fairground exhibit came to an end only in 1944. So memories of Futurama were still fresh when the war ended a year later.

Perhaps the most effective source of Bel Geddes' influence in the period immediately after 1945 was through the U.S. Army, which became one of the main government vehicles for postwar renewal. During the war the army borrowed part of the Futurama model for a camouflage school, where it was used to demonstrate techniques of deceptive coloration and the effectiveness of visual illusion. More important for the future, it also kept Bel Geddes' ideas about motorways in the eyes of platoons of soldiers right up to 1945. Reinforced by his book *Magic Motorways,* which discussed the engineering and safety principles underlying the model, his views directly influenced the road-building program carried out by the U.S. Army Corps of Engineers in the decade after the war.[3]

In fact, Bel Geddes had always cultivated contacts with the army. From 1926 on he had run an elaborate weekly war game (of his own design) in his New York studio, which attracted a regular group of military officers, and in the run-up to World War II the Pentagon adopted his war games for strategic planning. During the war he syndicated maps based on topographical models, which were published in the daily papers to illustrate the fighting in Europe, and from 1942 to 1945 produced photographic strategic models for *Life* magazine, to illustrate naval battles in the Pacific. During these years his association with the army became exceptionally close. In addition to his Futurama landscape being used in the camouflage school, Bel Geddes himself designed camouflage patterns for military vehicles and aircraft. He supplied an animated tactical training model to demonstrate air-ground support for the Army Air Force School of Applied Tactics. He also designed signaling lamps for the navy.

With such frequent connections, it is hardly surprising that when the U.S. Army commissioned a book titled *Miracles Ahead!* in 1944, with victory finally in sight, the postwar America envisaged came straight from Bel Geddes. He had already put out a press release in 1942 detailing the anticipated effect of wartime technological advances on "the post-war car." His concept of flexible housing made of interchangeable prefabricated units was cited from *Horizons,* as was his airplane (here called a "super-Clipper") that would carry "one hundred and twenty passengers in the plane's wing." The cars forecast by *Miracles Ahead!*—bubble-shaped and rear-engined, wheels enclosed by a streamlined body without fenders, the driver seated right at the front for increased visibility—exactly followed the model cars he had created for Futurama. The authors also noted a clear echo of Bel Geddes' designs from *Horizons* in a Packard prototype of a car for the postwar market, which had been given vertical rear fins (so unusual at that time, the only way they could describe them was "like plane-rudders").[4]

Many aspects of Bel Geddes' vision proved accurate. While designing Futurama, he had been working on specific assumptions—"that the population in and around large cities be expected to double by 1960, and all forms of vehicular traffic would be trebled"—which, as it turned out, were to be fairly accurate estimates.[5] When the new highway between Buffalo and Toronto was opened in 1958, Bel Geddes pointed out jubilantly that it was the first to incorporate all the major elements demonstrated by his model. As also portrayed in Futurama, the redevelopment of American cities has produced downtown skyscrapers covering whole city blocks, and the segregation of commercial and industrial areas from housing, which he called for. From the design perspective of the 1930s this appeared utopian, though in many places the social results have been less than desirable, to say the least.

There was also a further—and posthumous—incarnation of Futurama at the next New York World's Fair in 1964, which repeated many of Bel Geddes' innovations from a quarter century before. Again a Futurama (borrowing the name Bel Geddes had coined) was the main exhibit in the General Motors Pavilion. This ride was in many ways a replica of the one taken by visitors in 1939 but extended to encompass a wider, though in many ways much more immediate, future. By then the highway network Bel Geddes had forecast for the 1960s indeed crisscrossed the United States from coast to coast, and the progress he predicted was, in many ways, the present. Now the voice of the "guide" at the spectator's ear pointed out: "Here before you, is man roaming the moon, exploring Antarctica, working and playing beneath the sea, stretching a highway of progress and prosperity through the jungle and over the mountains, farming the desert and creating a functional, beautiful new city."[6] Yet this 1964 city of the future was a direct extrapolation from the one Bel Geddes had designed, with multiple tiers of roadway running beneath the pedestrian sidewalks. The technology of the ride and the model world was identical—and now spread to other exhibits.

The Bell System display at the 1964 fair also featured a chain of moving chairs just like Futurama, in which spectators "glide past dramatic exhibits revealing how man's constant search for new ways to communicate has altered the complexion of our lives."[7] There was an accurate, meticulously detailed, scale model of the city of New York (still preserved today) viewed from a gondola circling the hall, as if one were flying over Manhattan in a balloon. Walt Disney, too, had an exhibit at the New York 1964 World's Fair, and this was also a variation on Bel Geddes' original Futurama: a Magic Skyride along which spectators rode in futuristic cars from a prehistoric past to "Space City." Although Bel Geddes himself had died in 1958, six years before, his vision was still very much in evidence.

The legacy of Futurama continues today. For instance, when in 1996 the Museum

Joseph Urban's scene model for the Witch's House in *Hansel and Gretel* (Metropolitan Opera, 1926). Joseph Urban Papers, Rare Book and Manuscript Library, Columbia University.

of the City of New York mounted an exhibition of "Drawing the Future: Design Drawings for the 1939 New York World's Fair," it naturally featured Bel Geddes' General Motors Building and his Futurama display. But the most obvious sign is the Disney World EPCOT Center (the Experimental Prototype Community of Tomorrow), which is built on the Magic Skyride of the 1964 World's Fair. Arguably the entire concept of Disney's theme parks can be traced to Joseph Urban and Bel Geddes.

The earliest Disneyland, which opened in California in 1955, is usually said to have been inspired by Coney Island's Dreamland—a tag very similar to Fantasyland, as Disney named his first theme park. The official Disney history, however, traces the inspiration to an educational theme park named Fairyland, founded in Oakland in 1950 and "dedicated to stimulating a child's imagination, creativity and desire to learn through fairy tales, fantasy sets, performing arts, animals and related exhibits and programs."[8] Walt Disney viewed the adult fairgrounds of Coney Island as something to be avoided, representing the corruption of modern urban life. By contrast, the fairy-tale world of his Fantasyland, centered around Sleeping Beauty's Castle, promoted the values of childhood and innocence, while he also substituted fantasy fulfillment and figures from commercial cartoons for the learning of Fairyland. Even before the

1950s numerous theme parks offered popular entertainment, but this combination of childlike naivete with commercialism distinguished Disney's Magic Kingdom from its predecessors. The nearest comparison to Disneyland was a Gingerbread Castle built by Joseph Urban for Wheatsworth Biscuits in Hamburg, New Jersey, more than a quarter century earlier.

A fantastic miniature castle crowned by an upside-down ice-cream cone of a witches' hat roofing its single turret, and much loved by children over several decades, this whimsical pie-in-the-sky was a child-sized prototype for Disney's many-turreted Sleeping Beauty Castle, though of course without its attendant cartoon characters. Just like that central building in the California Magic Kingdom, Urban's far more modest gingerbread fantasy derived from fairy tales, combining Hansel and Gretel with Cinderella, as well as Jack and Jill, whose larger-than-life-size figures were on the point of tumbling from the top of a nearby hill. Elaborately decorated and brightly colored as a toy box, it had hanging cupolas and balconies, balustrades of elephants and children marching or dancing up its winding staircases, statues of performing seals on finials, and a "birthday cake room" with seahorses and bats. In addition, there was a grotto on the grounds (complete with goblins) and a witches' cauldron (capacity: eleven children), as well as a huge storybook for children to stand in and have their pictures taken, while attendants were dressed as Hansel and Gretel or other fairy-tale characters.

F. H. Bennett, the president of Wheatsworth Mills, got the idea from Urban's Gingerbread House setting for Humperdinck's opera of *Hansel and Gretel,* which he had seen at the Met in 1926, and commissioned Urban to reproduce his scenery in stone as an advertising stunt. Immensely successful, it remained popular for generations of children—the first theme park of the kind we know today.[9] The Gingerbread Castle was completed in 1928, the same year that Walt Disney created Mickey Mouse. He certainly knew of it, if only from the publicity and photographs distributed by newspapers and magazines of the time. Even if the imagery of Disney's Magic Kingdom came from Disney cartoons (with Whirling Teacups at an Alice in Wonderland Mad Hatter's merry-go-round in place of the witches' cauldron at Urban's earlier and much simpler theme park), Sleeping Beauty's Castle itself is so similar in concept to Urban's fairy-tale park that it is hard to see how his Gingerbread Castle could not have been the catalyst for Disney's Fantasyland.

If Urban's fairy-tale theme park for Wheatsworth Biscuits helped to inspire Disneyland, the connections between Bel Geddes' forecast of the future at the New York World's Fair and the Disney World Experimental Prototype Community of Tomorrow are even more direct. The EPCOT Center—which Walt Disney began planning shortly before his death in 1966 although it opened in 1982—was a direct successor

Urban's gingerbread fantasy for Wheatsworth Biscuits: the exterior of the castle.
Joseph Urban Papers, Rare Book and Manuscript Library, Columbia University.

to the Magic Skyride of the 1964 World's Fair. Both were specifically inspired by Disney's personal memory of Futurama from more than a quarter-century before. Some EPCOT displays also echo other elements from the 1939 World's Fair, for instance, the "audio-animatronic" humanoid robots playing out scenes of middle-class life in the future. These combine the "representative American families" housed at the fair with the "life-like miniature figures" of the 1939 Research Laboratories exhibit.

Just like Futurama, EPCOT, which is also explicitly "featuring a World's Fair atmosphere," embodies the message of technology as utopian progress, and it too was conceived (in Walt Disney's words) as "the prototype of the future."[10] Among the corporate pavilions included in it are not only AT&T—a direct parallel to General Motors of 1939, with the Internet representing the contemporary form of communications just as the car did back then—but also GE, the same firm whose exhibit was displayed in Bel Geddes' "city of the future" at the 1939 New York World's Fair, and which titled its Horizons Pavilion (opened in October 1983 as "dedicated to humanity's future . . . a careful synthesis of all the wonders within EPCOT") in direct acknowledgment to Bel Geddes' book *Horizons*.[11]

Futurama was the high point in Bel Geddes' career, a nexus from which many of his ideas for modern America flowed out into society. In addition to his model city and the miniature cars that ran along his transcontinental motorway, the 1939 display contained blueprints for the kind of suburbs he went on to plan, while other parts of the exhibit contained the kitchen appliances he had designed. These aspects of his work, together with Urban's achievements in the same fields, also had immense impact.

Bel Geddes himself was quite aware of Futurama's importance and continued to see World's Fairs as the most effective way of popularizing his vision, right to the end of his life. He proposed a national exhibit for the United States pavilion at Brussels in 1958 (the first World's Fair since the 1939–40 New York event). The official theme was "man's ability to mold the atomic age to the ultimate advantage of all nations," and Bel Geddes outlined a display of "How World Peace would change the structure of living within a generation—A 'Futurama' of the results of World Peace on a global basis."[12]

This was a narrower version of plans almost exactly ten years earlier, when Europe and the Far East were still reeling from the widespread destruction of the war. Then he had proposed that the U.S. government use a decommissioned aircraft carrier (disarmed and transformed into a colorful fairground) as a traveling exhibition space—a theatrical equivalent of the Marshall Plan, which subsidized the rebuilding of Europe. The flight deck and the hangars beneath were to be filled with a scale model of the continent or country being visited by the ship, with local details substituted at different ports of call. So for instance, it would show "Europe . . . as redesigned by

Sleeping Beauty's Castle at the hub of Disneyland, c. 1960. Courtesy of John Beddington.

teams made up of American engineers, production specialists, industrial planners." What Bel Geddes envisioned was "a version of our Boulder Dam producing new power and recapturing arid wastes—an uninterrupted super-highway from Rome to Copenhagen—a decentralized Ruhr Valley—a blueprint for the rebuilding of decimated Cologne."[13]

If this 1947 proposal was a clear development of his 1939 Futurama, the final section of the proposed aircraft-carrier exhibit was still closer: a portrayal of "Main Street America" to show that it already incorporated all the advances planned for the reconstruction of countries elsewhere. America now represented the world of the future. Exhibiting "the American scene" would prove "that the 'Futurama' of Europe as conceived by our designers and engineers has a sound truthful basis in fact."[14]

Although Bel Geddes was hired by the U.S. government as a consultant for the American Building at the Brussels Fair, he died before his plans came to fruition, and with the Soviet threat appearing so closely after the end of World War II, Washington was hardly prepared to decommission and donate an aircraft carrier. Yet Bel Geddes had already done much to shape the Main Streets of America that he wanted to showcase, as had Joseph Urban. They both also helped to create the type of vehicles that drove along those Main Streets (just as Futurama had influenced the design of the highways that were built to link them)—vehicles which, perhaps more than anything else, define the mid-century golden age of American culture.

Car Culture

THE "WORLD OF TOMORROW" modeled in Bel Geddes' Futurama had been greeted with such enthusiasm at the 1939 New York World's Fair because the United States was already an automobile society. If one singles out the dominant elements in the American way of life, what come first to mind are the movies and the car. Both are based on movement (the *motion* picture, the auto*mobile*). They embody continual change, kinetic energy, progress, flux—qualities that are intrinsic to modern life in the developed world.

From the beginning, cars signified far more than just a means of transport. In 1907 Henry Ford presented the original Model T as the promise of a new social order, democratic liberation, and individual self-fulfillment: "I will build a motor car for the great multitude. . . . It will be so low in price that no man making a good salary will be unable to own one—and enjoy with his family the blessing of hours of pleasure in God's great open spaces."[1] Offering this combination of enjoyment with usefulness struck a new note in manufacturing. It was to be the basis of the coming consumer society, while the way Ford associated an industrial machine with a return to nature, and scientific progress with God, called on fundamental strands of the American cultural myth.

At the same time it was the nuts and bolts of assembly-line production, introduced by Ford in 1914, which made mass marketing—and the achievement of this grand vision—possible. This revolution in manufacturing was so notable that it came to be widely hailed as "*the* American system,"[2] and the automobile industry became synonymous with the nation. If, as President Herbert Hoover famously remarked, "the business of America is business," then what was good for Detroit (in the words of a later General Motors executive) was good for America. And, one might add, there's no business like show business.

Engineering principles require form to follow function; but for any object that has symbolic connotations—of the kind cars rapidly acquired—it is the form that matters, encapsulating the values or aspirations of the public. By 1927, when Ford finally and somewhat reluctantly responded to the market by replacing the purely utilitarian, boxy, black Model T with the Model A (which was somewhat more styled and came in various colors), other auto manufacturers had already realized that more than straight engineering was required to fulfill consumer—and cultural—demand. As a result, artists started to be brought into the engineering teams, and Joseph Urban was among the very first. His involvement with the automobile industry began in 1921, when he designed the décor for a Dodge sales event at the Waldorf-Astoria.

Soon afterward he was creating advertising campaigns, particularly for Cadillac, in which the posters and magazine ads were deliberately reminiscent of scenes he had designed for the Boston Opera and the Met. Appearing under towering arches, or standing before a sweeping façade, the cars take on a dramatic air—vehicles for an elite lifestyle. Transferring this vision from the page to manufacturing, by 1925 Urban had begun designing what came to be called the "New Era" styling for Hudson cars: color schemes for automobile bodies, the finish and setup of seats, and designs for dashboards—interior home décor applied to cars. Although this might seem superficial (and it was), a shiny individualized color on the outside did not simply make a car stand out from the puritanical black of the almost ubiquitous Model T Fords. It made automobiles into more personal possessions, indeed modes of individual expression. It helped to suggest that cars were not merely machines, but the vehicle of an ideal lifestyle.

This change is usually—but incorrectly—attributed to a California artist named Harley Earl. Starting off by custom styling Cadillacs for movie stars at the Hollywood dealership, Earl was recruited to create the color schemes and shaping of the 1927 Cadillac LaSalle, and to head up a new Art and Color Section (later called Styling) at General Motors. Before that, so the story goes, all car design had been done solely by engineers. Earl is also generally credited with producing the first "concept car," the 1938 Buick Y-Job (so called because the letter Y was used to designate experimental airplanes). However, its main claims to innovation—a "streamlined" teardrop rear, horizontal radiator-grille and wraparound bumpers, fenders extending back into the doors, and marked grooves along the sides, with no running boards—all came from Norman Bel Geddes, who had introduced precisely these features to Chrysler more than five years earlier. In terms of color schemes for a complete model line (rather than custom styling), Urban also got there slightly before Earl.

Urban's contribution to the American love affair with the automobile was a logical extension of his work as a highly decorative scene designer and vivid colorist. The same principle applies to Bel Geddes, but in contrast to Urban, Bel Geddes' scene designs were almost always black-and-white sketches, engineering blueprints, and three-dimensional models. Also, where Urban largely worked within the theater technology of the time in his *Ziegfeld Follies* stagings or his opera productions, Bel Geddes was noted for developing new forms of lighting and stage-machinery in his Broadway shows. So just as in his theater, from when he first became involved with the automobile industry, Bel Geddes focused on engineering design, instead of primarily decorative effects.

Despite his theatrical reputation for extreme realism (due to the fame of productions like *Dead End*), as a stage designer he more usually worked with three-dimensional shapes and purely utilitarian structures, and his emphasis was generally highly contemporary. For a 1925 Paris production of *Jeanne d'Arc* starring Eva Le Gallienne, Bel Geddes created a set composed solely of steps (as he also did in a different

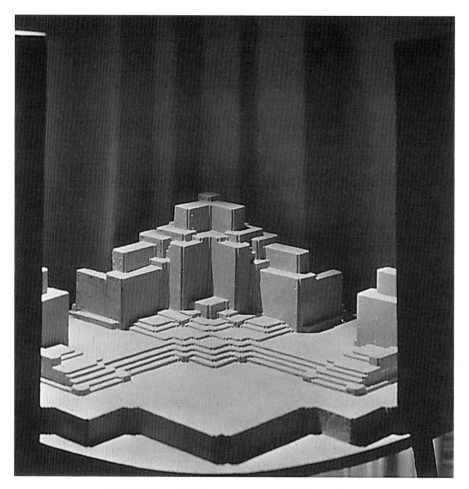

Bel Geddes' model of the stage construct for *Jeanne d'Arc.*
Estate of Edith Lutyens Bel Geddes, Norman Bel Geddes Collection,
Courtesy of the Harry Ransom Humanities Research Center.

configuration for his wildly controversial modern-dress staging of *Hamlet*—both settings being far simpler and smaller versions of his *Divine Comedy* stage), backed by plinths stacked one on top of another. All these levels were functional, and were used as acting areas. Still more to the point, even his productions of classic plays were intended (as he noted in his promptbook for *Hamlet*) "to make the audience take the play in our own terms of 1931."[3]

This radical simplification, practicality, and sensitivity to topical interests all carried over into his work for car manufacturers. So did his willingness to break out of traditional frames in his theater productions, for instance literally demolishing the proscenium arch in *The Miracle* and *Eternal Road,* where the setting in each case enveloped the audience. Although frequently disguised by sensory overload, the key qualities in Bel Geddes' theater work were simplicity, unity, and functionalism—all of which were characteristic of the modern ethos he promoted. The same kind of willingness to challenge preconceptions, to experiment (both on the "safe" arena of the stage and in his industrial designs) with solutions that seemed highly unusual at the time, but which in general became widely accepted with striking rapidity, was key to Bel Geddes' effectiveness in revolutionizing American car design. The Graham-Paige Company recruited him in 1927 precisely because the owner was an admirer of his stage work.

This transference between stage and car design is well illustrated by an interview in *Automobile Topics* about the 1929 car he designed for Graham-Paige. Bel Geddes describes its outstanding characteristics as "the absence of all accessories mounted on the surface" (such as headlights and license plates, now fitted into the "organic whole" of the body) which made the external shape "a single unit of uninterrupted, flowing lines."[4] Exactly the same adjectives were used to describe both his theatrical scenery and his car design.

Artistically, Bel Geddes' strength was as a sculptor, even an engineer. And this, together with his obsessive vision of futuristic modernity, allowed him to play a central role in designing a completely new type of car. Combined with his focus on ordinary people—as opposed to the elitism underlying much of Urban's work—these qualities made Bel Geddes a central influence on the entire American automobile industry.

The earliest automobiles had been called "horseless carriages," and even in 1932, the year Bel Geddes' book *Horizons* was published, the standard car design was still based on the horse-and-buggy. Car bodies were straight-sided boxes, fronted by a completely flat and vertical windscreen. Wheels had shrunk, but the seats were still placed above the rims, so that to get into a car you had to climb up a pair of steps, formed by a running board between the protruding mudguards. Just as the old-time coachman had sat with his torso above the level of the horse's back, a driver in the 1920s looked down on the engine in front—which was measured by "horsepower." The strength of this connection can be seen in the way people looked after their cars. As late as the 1940s it was still common to drape a blanket over a car's engine once it had been parked in the garage, just as when stabling a horse.

Working first for the Graham-Paige Motor Company, then after 1932 for Chrysler and General Motors, Bel Geddes was the first car designer to fundamentally challenge this traditional concept. Comparing a photograph of any car from the early 1930s with his first car for Chrysler—the Airflow model that went on sale in early January 1934—is enough to show how revolutionary it was. To our eyes, the standard car of

The 1932 Packard (*above*) was a standard machine of the time. Bel Geddes used this photograph to make the same comparison in his book *Horizons*. The 1934 Chrysler Airflow (*opposite*), at its launch less than two years later. Bel Geddes is one of the people standing proudly behind the car, and GM's chief engineer is holding a model of Bel Geddes' "Flying Wing" aircraft, which was to influence Korda's film *Things to Come*. Estate of Edith Lutyens Bel Geddes, Norman Bel Geddes Collection, Courtesy of the Harry Ransom Humanities Research Center.

the time looks decidedly old-fashioned, even anachronistic—while the Airflow has a clearly modern shape.

This is partly because, when he was hired to work for the Chrysler Corporation in 1932, Bel Geddes persuaded Chrysler engineers to construct a wind tunnel. Until then wind tunnels had been used only for airplane design. Unlike those, the Chrysler setup included a running belt, over which an eighth-inch scale model of a car was suspended, barely touching the surface, which Bel Geddes put in to test ground effects by simulating a road moving under the wheels. He also added a mechanism allowing the model and road assembly to be turned at an angle to the flow of air, so that the effect of side winds could be taken into account. Although these novel elements of the wind tunnel were not entirely successful (the belt flapped, distorting the airflow), the result was a radical change both in structure and styling. Chrysler named the first car to come out of that design process the Airflow model.[5]

Bel Geddes raked the windscreen of the 1934 Chrysler Airflow so that it slanted back to either side and to the top. Headlights, covered by rounded glass plates flush with the surface, were set into the curving wings over the front wheels. The rear wheels were enclosed, and the mudguards were integral with the rest of the body, instead of (as in standard designs up to that time) being separated from the engine, with headlights sticking up between. The seats were also lowered by moving the rear bench forward, so that it created a sleeker profile and was no longer perched above the back wheels. The rear end had a modified teardrop shape (to reduce drag, the vacuum effect of

eddies created by a vehicle's movement through the air). To enhance the impression of streamlining, Bel Geddes had given his eighth-inch-scale wind-tunnel model parallel grooves, flaring out from the center of the front along each side to channel the flow of air around the body. Highly theatrical, it was an impressive and immediately popular advance on car design, and within months the other major American car manufacturers had built their own wind tunnels.

An advance advertisement for the new Chrysler in 1933 proclaimed it "the first sincere and authentic streamlined car—the first REAL motorcar . . . the beginning of a new style."[6] The same ad also contained an endorsement from Bel Geddes, affirming the Airflow as the fulfillment of his vision, and Chrysler publicity brochures quoted extensively from his 1932 book *Horizons*. C. H. Breer, the executive engineer, was also cited (in *Chrysler Pictorial News,* January 1934) on the revolutionary findings of introducing air-tunnel testing. As he acknowledged, exactly paraphrasing something Bel Geddes had emphasized earlier in *Horizons,* "our cars were so poorly designed from an air resistant point of view that they would actually run faster backwards than forwards," and he proclaimed the result of Bel Geddes' improvements, the Airflow, "the ideal car shape."

Still, just one month earlier, as Chrysler Corporation minutes of December 1933 show, Bel Geddes and Chrysler's executive engineer agreed that "actually the streamline shape is poor. . . . It would seem doubtful that any great increase in aerodynamic efficiency [from previous traditional designs] could be expected." Significantly, in their view the Airflow "approaches the *appearance* of a streamline design sufficiently close to educate the public to this type of car."[7]

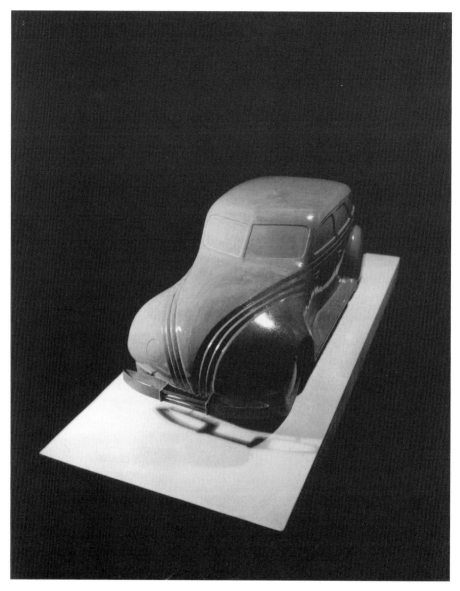

Bel Geddes' 1933 model of the Chrysler Airflow for wind-tunnel testing, highlighting
the integral body shape and the "aerodynamic" grooves. Estate of Edith Lutyens Bel Geddes,
Norman Bel Geddes Collection, Courtesy of the Harry Ransom Humanities Research Center.

Among the aerodynamic improvements proposed by Bel Geddes and rejected by Chrysler as too advanced for popular taste were rear fins, while the trunk of the car was made shorter, because it was considered too vulnerable in parking (although precisely these features were to be adopted in a still more extreme form in the 1950s when fins and elongated trunks came into vogue). The sharply indented flowing grooves were eliminated as too expensive to manufacture. Other innovations he put forward were dismissed as too mechanically complex. These included a "resilient structure at front in place of rigid front engine construction" (the "crumple zone" that was to become a standard safety feature some thirty years later). However, the same Airflow ad also repeated Bel Geddes' basic principle: "Design—style—art—all must follow reality—all must be bound up with usefulness. Gingerbread carving stuck on a building is not great architecture. Meaningless design on a motorcar is not great style."[8]

The Airflow did have a significantly cleaner look than any other car of the time, yet what was truly significant is the way the advertising associated utilitarian design with "reality." As the wording of that ad suggests, Bel Geddes' aim was more to promote a new concept than to achieve pure functionalism. Even so, the Chrysler Airflow was ahead of its time in more than just design. It had an automatic choke, as well as being the first car with automatic transmission. Engineering difficulties with these components, compounding some initial assembly-line problems due to the revolutionary styling, caused long production delays. As a consequence, many early rush orders were cancelled. Initially the design had attracted highly favorable notice and public enthusiasm. But low sales followed a reputation for mechanical unreliability, and the model was discontinued in 1937, although Bel Geddes continued to design for Chrysler until 1941. He also worked for General Motors, supplying models for the 1939 Buick Series 40, which also followed the streamlined principles that had already become standard for the industry. The Frazer-Nash line of cars he designed through the 1940s marked the next evolution, both in image and construction.

Of all objects in American culture, cars rapidly came to be symbols going far beyond usefulness, literally embodying personality—and particularly sexuality. So now it has become a commonplace to see SUVs in terms of bodybuilding masculinity, proclaiming self-confidence and dominating power. As a *New York Times* piece revealingly put it, contemplating the new Dodge Durango in 1999, "Muscles seem to ripple under its shiny sheet metal, causing its fenders to bulge. Its hood is lifted above the brawn, like the short neck of a wrestler."[9] In sharp contrast to this, the golden-age cars of the 1950s and 1960s—"Dagmar" Cadillacs with breast-like cone bumper guards protruding at the front and eyelash-like rims over the headlights, or the sinuous curves (and the highly suggestive hourglass silhouette on the side) of Chevrolet Corvettes—were

An advertising photo for the 1941 Nash designed by Bel Geddes, emphasizing width, streamlining curves, and femininity. Estate of Edith Lutyens Bel Geddes, Norman Bel Geddes Collection, Courtesy of the Harry Ransom Humanities Research Center.

clearly feminine. Doubling for the sex objects of male fantasies, such cars were presented together with well-endowed and revealingly clothed female models in 1950s television ads, making a scarcely subliminal connection between the curvaceous woman and the lines of the car's body. This was a practice that had already been introduced (if with somewhat more modesty) almost two decades earlier with ads for the 1941 Nash—which, like the car itself, were designed by Bel Geddes.

The Nash car extended the style Bel Geddes had introduced at Chrysler a decade earlier. Advertised as "the first American car designed with flowing front-to-rear fender lines" which accentuated the "extreme width" of the body, it had side panels that covered the back wheels and a wraparound grill under the headlamps. It also

The 1958 Oldsmobile featured in Motorama. Billy Rose Theatre Collection,
Courtesy of the New York Public Library for the Performing Arts,
Astor, Lenox and Tilden Foundations.

introduced new construction techniques—confirming the association between Bel Geddes' styling and technical innovation. The car body was welded as a single unit, which allowed a significantly larger area for glass versus metal, increasing the relative size of windscreen and windows.[10]

This became the standard design for the decade, with the general outline and details reappearing in other cars, such as the 1947 Frazer. It was a short step from the wide, low profile advertised in the photo of the 1941 Nash to the classic cars of the 1950s. In fact when Chrysler introduced "The Forward Look" in 1955 as a way of reversing their slide in market share—which dropped from 25 percent in 1946 to 12 percent in 1954—the qualities they singled out were "new fin-like rear fenders and a longer rear end": precisely those aspects of Bel Geddes' Airflow design that Chrysler management had found too advanced in 1933.[11] Indeed, his ideas even became exaggerated: cars being associated with the space race, like the Oldsmobile premiered at the 1958 Motorama (GM's annual sales show, named after Futurama and managed by yet another theater man, Maurice Evans, the leading Shakespearean actor of the time).[12] As the October 1958 issue of *Where* enthusiastically noted, this year's model was given highly marked chrome "booms that start at the rocket emblem on each fender [thrusting forward above the headlights] and flare backward like a rocket trail to the modern tail-light assemblies."

Just as in theater, the impression was more important than reality, and an image of futuristic modernity itself always trumped aerodynamic efficiency. This was true to some extent even with Bel Geddes' Chrysler Airflow. By the time of the GM Motorama in 1958, image trumped all utilitarian considerations; advertising was everything, and the car business had become pure show business.

In the hands of Maurice Evans (briefed to show the new range of cars as "high fashion," with the "star" of the show, the new Firebird III, being explicitly described by GM executives as "generally feminine"), this event became an extravagant multimedia spectacle: dancers, singers, "specialty" performers, a circus acrobat, and a narrator (Evans with his beautifully modulated voice), plus the very latest technology in film sequences and closed-circuit television. Hyped as a "multimillion dollar production" (though the actual budget totaled a far more modest $370,000) and presented at the Waldorf-Astoria for forty-six performances, the 1958 Motorama was hailed by *Advertising Age* (ignoring the Waldorf-Astoria's distance from the theater district) as the "Biggest Show on Broadway."[13]

Singers and showgirls twirled across the floor on circular platforms mounted on casters (illustrating streamlined mobility); even the cars were integrated in the action, swinging out, rising and falling, spinning and pirouetting on rotating platforms mounted at the ends of long extending and retracting mechanical arms with tubular lifts. Everything sparkled and glittered (to epitomize elegant styling): sequins on glistening metallic cloaks and glass beads on high-pointed headdresses, the chrome on car fins and grills.

The climax of this dance spectacular was a film showcasing the new Firebird. "The horizon extends as far as man's imagination," as Evans's script exclaimed: "Tomorrow's Firebird will take you to the launching site for your trip to the moon."[14] (This was to become a cliché, with Raymond Loewy's advertising posters for his 1961 Avanti combining images of the car, a Saturn rocket on lift-off, and the earth seen from space.) The year 1958 was when the United States launched its first satellite into orbit, racing to catch the USSR, whose Sputnik satellite shocked the nation by orbiting the earth a whole year earlier. This drive to conquer space helps to explain the exaggerated fins and rocket emblems introduced on the cars: purchasing one was buying into the strong subliminal patriotic appeal of space imagery. Streamlining had

An advertisement for Motorama, 1958. Billy Rose Theatre Collection, Courtesy of the New York Public Library for the Performing Arts, Astor, Lenox and Tilden Foundations.

become simply styling. A headline about Motorama—"Now—There's No Business Without Show Business"—neatly encapsulates the relationship between Broadway and the industrial design of American modernity.[15]

By the 1950s Bel Geddes had withdrawn from car design, and it was left to another industrial designer, Raymond Loewy, to follow through on his more functional concept of streamlining. Loewy's most famous car was the 1962 Studebaker Avanti, which returned to Bel Geddes' principles and was so striking for its time in its simplified shape and absence of decorative chrome that it drew crowds in the streets. In other ways, too, the Avanti picked up on major elements from the cars Bel Geddes had designed for Nash almost a decade earlier: the wide frame, wings integrated with the body, panels covering the rear wheels, and a sloping semiteardrop trunk.

Loewy's contribution has been rightly celebrated, and his debt to Bel Geddes forgotten, because his car designs anticipated the simplified shapes that came into vogue after the 1960s and have remained the basis for contemporary automobiles. Still, if any one person could be said to have determined the classic design of the American car, it is Bel Geddes. True, his patent for the rear-engine bubble-car of Futurama gathered dust in his files. But mock-ups for the "fish-tail" Cadillac of 1949, created by the General Motors styling studio, directly echoed Bel Geddes' designs.[16]

He can also be indirectly credited with another type of car that later became an American favorite, and is with us still. It's highly probable that he influenced the German engineers who produced a modified, but strikingly similar version to his concept of a small, rear-engine car in the Volkswagen.[17] Bel Geddes had published his designs in 1932 in *Horizons;* and given the widespread interest his book attracted, it would be surprising if Volkswagen engineers had not come across it. And there was an even more direct link, since the first production-line model of the Volkswagen (limited because of the war to fourteen cars, which were used for publicity purposes) appeared in 1941, less than two years after the opening of the New York World's Fair. Some of the Volkswagen designers might even have had opportunity to take Bel Geddes' "Ride into the Future," since when it opened in 1939 the fair included a German Pavilion (though in reaction to the war this was demolished before the 1940 re-opening of the fair). When the Volkswagen Beetle became a favorite American car—the "Love Bug" of the 1960s—this could in a sense be seen as a fulfillment of Bel Geddes' vision.

However, the "Linear Look" Oldsmobiles and "Dagmar" Cadillacs, extended from his designs, most evoke the period. The elongated, low-slung bodies of the 1950s car, those prominent grills and flaring fins—which even when motionless, suggested the speed of a slipstream—expressed the self-confidence of America after the war.

The exaggerated appearance of streamlining captured the public imagination, as Bel Geddes with his theatrical experience had realized it would. The iconic styling of these cars, their wide bench seats and boldly curving windshields, all evolved directly out of his designs. But by the time these models appeared, Bel Geddes had already turned to bigger things—cities.

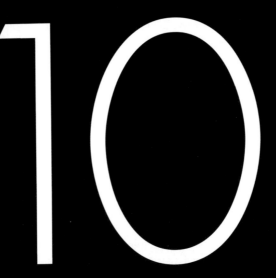

10

Street Scenes

THE AMERICAN CITY, WITH its skyscrapers and arterial expressways funneling traffic into the downtown core, is the dominating symbol of modern life, and during the twentieth century Manhattan has become its most powerful image. Highways, as Bel Geddes' 1939 Futurama predicted, have carved through the continental landscape, but nowhere is the impact of cars more obvious than in the modern metropolis. Bel Geddes' involvement in automobile design made him from the beginning particularly sensitive to the kind of urban planning cities required. Even if he never drew up specific layouts for New York, Bel Geddes was extraordinarily influential in shaping its development. He may not have been personally involved in its development plans; yet the way Manhattan looks today is a direct reflection of his ideas.

In the 1920s both he and Joseph Urban enthusiastically took up the challenge of designing core aspects of the modern city, although they were hardly alone in this. One could say that America has been fixated by the notion of ideal cities at least since the 1893 Columbian Exposition in Chicago. The heavily symbolic White City of its main exhibition ground inspired a popular preacher of the time, Josiah Strong, to proclaim "the city redeemed . . . a vision of the revelation, the symbol itself of *Heaven*—Heaven on earth," in a book with the typically futuristic title of *The Twentieth Century City*.[1] Strong also sounded a familiar theme in linking civic progress to the religious imperative that had been a founding principle of America.

This White City started the City Beautiful movement, promoting ideal solutions to the widespread social problems at the turn of the century, which became widely influential in the early decades; while the continuing flood of new immigrants spawned slums rivaling the squalor of old Europe, intensifying the demand for novel housing solutions. So designing cities of the future became almost obligatory for twentieth-century American architects. From the most famous, like Frank Lloyd Wright, to visionaries such as Buckminster Fuller with his floating Tetrahedronal City and geodesic spheres (exactly anticipating the molecular structure of the sixty-carbon atom, discovered in 1980, which was named a fullerine in his honor), plans for ideal cities proliferated—continuing through the 1970s and 1980s, in proposals like Conklin and Rossant's 1973 Future City, where all the buildings were to be interconnected by huge communication and circulatory pipes.[2] The stage contributed, too, spreading images of high-tech (and high-rise) urban life, as in a backdrop for the 1930 Broadway musical *Just Imagine*. Set fifty years in the future, in Manhattan of the 1980s, this portrayed skyscrapers more than 250 floors high, linked by bridges carrying nine levels of traffic—all in ultrarealistic detail. Architectural firms still publish designs for future-perfect cities today.[3]

Perhaps not surprisingly, almost from the beginning most of these utopian plans focused on transportation. Roadtown, proposed by Edgar Chambless in various multiplying versions from 1910 through 1931 to 1953, is representative. Like a skyscraper lying on its side, Roadtown was to extend indefinitely through the countryside from one hub to another, as a single continuous structure with railways running along the roof and subways beneath the basement. An automobile variation was Rush City Reformed, a 1953 concept by Richard Neutra, which was a flexible and expandable format for a narrow ribbon of high-density blocks, flanked by bands of suburban houses, running along a central sunken speedway.

None of these utopian cities was ever built. Neutra abandoned such grandiose visions, reverting to the more pedestrian task of designing schools and U.S. embassies. But however fantastic, almost all of these plans were serious proposals. Chambless was so committed to his vision that when his 1953 version was turned down by yet another Washington official in the mid-1950s, he leapt from a Manhattan skyscraper (the classic mode of suicide for modern America) in despair.

Utopia, repeatedly envisaged, was continually postponed. By contrast, Joseph Urban and Norman Bel Geddes had tangible and immediate influence. In some ways they were associated with this idealist aspect of the modern movement. Richard Neutra, for instance, was (like Urban) an emigrant from Austria where he had been a member of Urban's artists' group the Secessionists. Although hardly less visionary, the designs produced by Urban, followed by Bel Geddes, were more in tune with the times. As early as 1919, for example, Urban was proposing new and more effective ways for lighting city streets. Refinements or extensions of what already existed, their plans were more accessible and served as models for others. Bel Geddes' urban planning reached the eyes of government and the White House—as well as, perhaps even more important, the attention of an empire-building bureaucrat like Robert Moses—because Bel Geddes managed to gain wide exposure through commercial publicity.

The most striking example of this was a Shell Oil advertising campaign, which Bel Geddes organized, designed, and executed in 1937. This was so successful that the company reused it for 1938, and it became the starting point for the General Motors Futurama exhibit at the New York World's Fair.[4] Bel Geddes' overriding priority was (as he noted in a case history of the Shell Oil project) to demonstrate the novel traffic system "to be absolutely practical and not merely the dream of a visionary." At an initial meeting with Shell executives, the year 1957—exactly one generation away—was set as the date on which this picture of "Traffic of the Future" was to be based.[5] To achieve this, Bel Geddes not only provided a series of striking images for newspaper and billboard ads, but also created a short movie, exploiting the verisimilitude of film, which was accompanied by illustrated ads in the press. But where was he to find the "City of Tomorrow" to photograph?

Bel Geddes with the plans and miniature model for the Shell Oil city layout.
Estate of Edith Lutyens Bel Geddes, Norman Bel Geddes Collection,
Courtesy of the Harry Ransom Humanities Research Center.

Drawing on his experience of three-dimensional stage sets, Bel Geddes built a
model of 144 city blocks, on a scale of one inch to one hundred feet, with the tallest
model building being fifteen inches high. The triangular shape of the base allowed
long perspectives, and with powerful lighting throwing shadows from the towers of
the skyscrapers, plus sulfur-bombs to create haze and cloud effects, the apparent size
was so impressive that more than one newspaper review of the film estimated the
size of the model to be over 125,000 square feet—more than 250 times larger than it

really was. Photographed mainly from above, it looked like a view from an airplane, swooping down when the camera focused on close-up shots of city details, complete with traffic (Bel Geddes' trademark raindrop-shaped cars and trucks all less than one-quarter-inch long), though there were also shots showing structures from beneath, as through a car windshield.

The details of the construction were all published in the *New York Times,* which reported that there were more than 10,000 model automobiles, and 110,000 "people," represented by tiny short pieces of wire stuck up through the metal strips of the "pavement." The theatrical illusion of the whole was so convincing that even a professional journal like *Architectural Forum* extrapolated an elaborate, highly anthropomorphized, and completely imaginary scenario, enthusing: "It is at sunset that Mr. Bel Geddes' brave new city appears at its most romantic, with the last rays of the afternoon sun creating a vast patchwork of black and white. On the highways the crowds stream out to the vast suburbs. By midnight, save for the hotels, watchmen and late night revelers, the city is deserted."[6]

Among the gigantic and gleaming towers of the new architecture, some model buildings retained a recognizably 1930s character, realistically mirroring the piecemeal nature of urban renovation. There were also two specific structures, the Woolworth Building in New York, and Notre Dame Cathedral from Paris, selected because they were so well known, although bringing them together in the same urban context was a typically unrealistic detail, characteristic of the way Bel Geddes had emphasized the theatricality of stage productions such as *The Miracle* or *Dead End.* These were intended as reference points to give a sense of the scale of the new: a feature he also incorporated into the "City of the Future" two years later in Futurama. Beside these iconic edifices rose huge skyscrapers, six to ten times higher than the towers of Notre Dame, each filling a whole block to form "a city in itself—self-contained," as Bel Geddes' film script declared, leaving space in surrounding blocks for parks.[7]

The point was elaborated in a slide lecture to a National Planning Conference of 1937 by the head of the prestigious Harvard Traffic Research Group. Dr. Miller McClintock described the way "improved facilities for mobility" allowed the achievement of "maximum efficiency in human relations through even greater concentrations of building mass than would be dreamed of for today," forecasting "buildings of 1,500 feet in height . . . each accommodates entire economic or professional units."[8] Arterial highways through the city were shown as built above ground on "concrete" pylons, just like the highway network through the center of Boston used to be (perhaps a direct result of Bel Geddes' model, in which Shell executives insisted traffic should take precedence over pedestrians, who were relegated to ground level, so that the camera could focus on traffic flows in plain view overhead).[9] By contrast the recent repositioning

Aerial view of the Shell Oil model from a distance in the morning mist, 1937.
Estate of Edith Lutyens Bel Geddes, Norman Bel Geddes Collection,
Courtesy of the Harry Ransom Humanities Research Center.

of Boston's suburban highways in underground tunnels in fact corresponds more with Bel Geddes' initial concept for the central shopping and business area of this urban landscape, where pedestrian sidewalks were to have been elevated, connected by escalators to the streets below. This was eventually realized in the Futurama model for the World's Fair, which indeed put people on elevated walkways, beneath which ran unloading and parking strips, which could now be completely separated from the traffic flow, thanks to the additional space from removing the pedestrians to the light and the unpolluted air.

In the Shell "City of the Future" public transport and taxis occupied their own lanes. Main intersections had overpasses, while ramps permitted changes of direction without crossing the traffic stream, making traffic lights (which had first been introduced by the Harvard Group) redundant. A highway bypass routed through traffic around the city center. Housing, the business center, and the industrial section were all segregated, with trees and green space between.

Although several of these elements had been already subjects of discussion among urban planners, this was the first time they had all been brought together and presented in a tangible form. Adding to its cinematic realism, the deliberate simplification of building details gave what was filmed the status of a blueprint, emphasizing the credibility of the concept in engineering terms. In addition, Bel Geddes always worked out his architectural plans exactly as he did for his stage sets, starting with abstract "blocks" of varying sizes and shapes to form exteriors of the buildings. Such a method automatically tends to focus attention on the relationship between masses in proportion and balance, curves and outlines; and this gave his urban model a strong aesthetic appeal.

McClintock, who hailed Bel Geddes as "that master of functional shape and form," pointed out that the core of his vision was providing "maximum facility for intercommunication."[10] Anticipating today's computerized vehicles and traffic cameras, Bel Geddes forecast "automatic in-car traffic control" and television feeds of traffic conditions broadcast from cameras on surrounding streets. More immediately relevant for developments were his "city fringe parking terminals" linked to public transport, and his "trailer park village" outside the city (combining mobility with community), both of which became standard features in the 1950s and 1960s. He was also the first to propose building a central barrier on highways to separate opposite flows of traffic. Most relevant of all was Bel Geddes' proposal to McClintock that the rate of travel in New York could be doubled "by making north and south avenues one-way streets" to form "a gridiron"—which was not the case at the time.[11]

Combined, these effects made the whole seem convincingly realizable, and it caused something of a sensation. The "Future City" was given added credibility by

McClintock, who became its chief presenter on a national tour and provided the voiceover on the film. He liked to close his speech by making claims like, "Inevitably in our development of a better civilization, the prophecy we have seen here today will become reality."[12] Newspapers enthused over this "prediction made by Norman Bel Geddes, the famous designer of the future," and a multipage advertisement in a September issue of *Life* announced: "In the thirty days since Shell's new and startling 'City of Tomorrow' campaign broke in the country's leading magazines and newspapers, editorial writers, public officials, automobile manufacturers, traffic experts, city planning commissions, and the public in general, intensely interested, have acclaimed it as one of the year's outstanding contributions to traffic research and sound civic planning for the future."[13] The film was shown all across the country. The scale model of the city was exhibited at the Cleveland Auto Show in November 1937, and in New York, as well as being discussed in city planning conferences nationwide. Photographs and background material on the model and on Bel Geddes himself were released and found their way into literally hundreds of American newspapers. In addition most of the predictions raised in the brainstorming sessions between Bel Geddes and the Shell executives were repeated and expanded in his 1940 book, *Magic Motorways*.

By any standard, this was a landmark advertising campaign, reported in the "Advertising News" section of the *New York Sun*. Extensively illustrated pieces were published twice by *Life*, and it was reported in towns big and small, by the *Christian Science Monitor*, the Detroit *Saturday Evening Post*, the *Louisiana Chronicle*, and the *Baltimore American*, as well as by the *Cohoes American* (the upstate New York textile town), the *Plainfield Courier-News* (New Jersey), and the *Elyria Chronicle-Telegram* (Ohio), all of which were uniformly enthusiastic. The tone of the *Cleveland Plain Dealer*, lauding "this revolutionary exhibit" in superlatives, was typical. And the New York *Journal of Commerce and Commercial* as well as *Architectural Forum* (which was to become one of Bel Geddes' strongest supporters) singled it out as of particular interest.[14] It certainly attracted the attention of a power figure, now notorious, who had taken it upon himself to revitalize New York.

Even through the bleak decades of depression and world war, the American city continued to develop in ways that significantly conditioned how individuals lived. As on so many other levels, here too New York led the way. And just as Urban and Bel Geddes effectively shaped the lifestyle of the period, a single person was responsible for creating much of the modern geography of New York.

This was Robert Moses, who shared the same entrepreneurial spirit. Even people who disliked him intensely (and there were many who hated Moses for his arrogance and the often brutal way he shoved through his grandiose civic plans) acknowledged that he did more to shape modern American cities than anyone else in the twentieth century.[15] Moses was no designer, however. Nor did he have the versatility that gave Urban and Bel Geddes something approaching a continentwide influence over multiple fields that reinforced each other. The impact of Moses, who was a Napoleonic manipulator of bureaucracy, was practical and organizational, rather than through design.

His appointment as special assistant to Governor Al Smith in Albany in 1923 got him his first break, heading the apparently insignificant Long Island State Park Commission. When he took up the reins in 1924 there was little for the commission to be responsible for, apart from the ash heaps of Flushing Meadow (later to be transformed into the site of the 1939 World's Fair), the rundown Coney Island fairgrounds, and Prospect Park in Brooklyn. But by the end of the 1920s Moses had opened up miles of seashore and engineered 10,000 acres of parks, fourteen in all, as well as the parkways that connected them to the city. His vision of a nature playground for the masses of New York was heroic, even if it required bully tactics, forced sales, and expropriations. This achievement gained Moses an unchallengeable reputation, which he was able to parlay into a power base to dominate the physical development of New York City itself. He became known (not always admiringly) as the Construction Czar.

In many people's eyes, Moses was an incorruptible giant who moved mountains to make the city a better place to live. Despite this, he failed in attempts to become mayor in 1934 (just before the election La Guardia was chosen as the reform candidate, instead) or, later, governor of New York State. Moses, the Republican challenger, ran the most disastrous gubernatorial campaign on record—one that revealed his personality all too clearly. His mudslinging personal attacks on the incumbent were so outrageous that one radio station refused to broadcast his speeches unless the Republican Party first took out an insurance policy against libel suits.

Such ruthlessness, deliberate abandonment of social niceties, and ambition helped Moses to gain complete control of the New York bureaucracy. Under La Guardia he was appointed City Parks Commissioner (in which capacity he was personally responsible for demolishing Urban's landmark Central Park Casino). In quick succession he served as City Planning Commissioner, City Construction Coordinator, chairman of the Slum Clearance Committee, chairman of the Triborough Bridge and Tunnels Authority, and chairman of the State Power Authority. Holding all these posts, as well as seats on other boards, simultaneously, together with the detailed files he kept as potential blackmail material on all the major local and state politicians, allowed Moses to reshape the urban landscape as nobody else, before or since.

For more than forty years, from the mid-1930s up to his forced retirement in 1968, he wielded this authority to the full, in a highly personal exercise of power. He could—and repeatedly did—outface any civic body, even defying a direct order from

Mayor La Guardia as he did when he had the East River ferry terminal demolished in 1936. He compounded the insult by closing it down while a ferry laden with passengers was still crossing the river. He rode roughshod over any opposition from citizens' groups, demolishing more than 1,500 apartment buildings and evicting some 60,000 people in constructing the Cross-Bronx Expressway, as well as dislocating many more in replacing the slum neighborhoods of the Lower East Side with blocks of public housing. In all, between his first appointment as La Guardia's City Parks Commissioner and his forced retirement, Moses personally conceived and executed $27 billion worth of public works. He created seven bridges, including the Triborough, Bronx-Whitestone, Cross Bay, and Henry Hudson; engineered more than six hundred miles of expressways in and around the city; built Lincoln Center, as well as extensive public housing projects; and not least, by any means, oversaw two World's Fairs.

At the beginning he was helped by the sheer romance of building Manhattan's soaring towers in its first grand construction boom from the mid-1920s to the early 1930s. But paradoxically it was the Great Depression that made his plans possible. The financial crisis was already biting hard when the Empire State Building was completed in 1931. Begun just before the Wall Street crash, there were now simply no takers for its 102 floors of empty offices, and the developers managed to stave off bankruptcy only by persuading the federal government to relocate government agencies there. With the disastrous drop in commercial activity, public works alone offered employment.

At its most obvious this meant public housing as well as new roads and bridges, and the scale of government projects sometimes rivaled those ideal visions sketched out by the architects of American utopia. The Tennessee Valley Authority undertook a massive experiment in regional planning during the 1930s, while President Roosevelt's New Deal, announced in the 1932 election campaign, included the redevelopment of ninety-nine communities and ultimately led to new towns like Columbia, Maryland. The New Deal also funneled millions to New York City, which at the time was the largest manufacturing center in the United States. And Robert Moses was there to spend it.

In New York, with Moses at the helm, reconstruction could be carried out more swiftly and thoroughly than anywhere else, which in turn encouraged further federal investment. Not surprisingly, Moses took personal credit. There is a well-known photo that vividly captures his image of himself as the great urban visionary and city builder, commanding the future. Legs braced apart, hands on hips, he poses heroically on a steel girder stretching out over the river with the skyscrapers of midtown Manhattan behind, staring out into the distance and gripping a roll of blueprints. But where did his vision come from?

Moses's strengths were political. He was the organization man, not an engineer. He had no training in architecture, or even city planning. While he liked to see himself as a modern Baron Haussmann (the nineteenth-century engineer who had demolished much of the remaining medieval Paris to create the wide, sweeping boulevards of the most elegant city in Europe) and publicly compared his Brooklyn civic center to the Place de la Concorde, the actual type of city he envisaged was very different. Moses's grid of underpasses, overpasses, and expressways, which carried volumes of traffic through New York and linked towers of high-density housing, were conceived for the efficient movement of masses of commuters. Haussmann's Parisian boulevards converged on symbols of French national pride—the Eiffel Tower, the Arc de Triomphe—and encouraged leisurely pedestrians.

The contrast cannot be explained simply as the result of a democratic and economic society versus an imperial, centralizing ethos. Moses's vision was futuristic—in the 1920s there were barely 200,000 cars in New York (compared to 1.9 million in the 1980s), and, while Moses had an engineering and architectural staff reporting to him, his concepts came directly from Norman Bel Geddes.

Bel Geddes devoted a significant portion of his career to redesigning city layouts, and Moses was well aware of his work. As parks commissioner he had overseen the 1939 New York World's Fair and been particularly impressed by Bel Geddes' GM Building and its Futurama exhibit. Moses, and his departmental officials, were also familiar with the "City of the Future" that Bel Geddes had constructed for Shell Oil's advertising campaign. As well as receiving wide publicity, this had been officially approved by a 1937 National Planning Conference; and the head of the Traffic Research Bureau at Harvard University told the *New York Sun* that Bel Geddes' models embodied "an inevitable development of the automobile revolution."[16]

Furthermore, in April 1938 the Shell model had been presented at a public meeting over a rezoning proposal for Harlem to the New York City Planning Group, as well as at an Uptown Chamber of Commerce meeting, both of which Mayor La Guardia attended. In fact, when the model of the city was on display at the offices of the J. Walter Thompson advertising agency (which had brought Bel Geddes and Shell Oil together), Moses sent his managerial staff: the chief engineer of the Long Island State Park Commission (A. E. Howland), the district engineer of the Department of Public Works (J. J. Darcy), the consulting engineer for New York City (M. J. Madigan, who was particularly influential, being a personal appointment by Moses as his chief assistant). Together with representatives from the Port Authority and the New Jersey Highway Commission, they had a daylong private view. Others who also had private views were the general manager and chief engineer of the upcoming 1939 New York World's Fair, as well as Henry Dreyfuss (the designer of the future Democracity in the Perisphere), the director of the Museum of Modern Art, and a reporting crew from Pathé Film News. Another influential visitor was the managing editor of *Architectural Forum,* which continued to keep the "City of the Future" in the public eye with a series of articles up to and including an interview with Miller McClintock (the Harvard traffic specialist) in September 1945. A New York monthly picture-paper, *The News,* ran a piece relating to the future changes being planned by Moses for Brooklyn, which was illustrated with photos of the model. Bel Geddes corresponded with Moses himself about his urban plans.[17]

In addition, Moses would have known about the Toledo city plan, designed by Bel Geddes in 1945, which sparked calls for exactly the same kind of projects to be initiated in other cities, notably by New York and Rochester newspapers.[18] In 1949, both candidates for mayor of New York campaigned on visions of redevelopment that sounded very much like aspects of Bel Geddes' plans, with the Republican, Grover Whalen, calling for "elevated arcades for pedestrians, moving sidewalks, helicopter landings on buildings in the heart of the city and greenbelt parkways." Elevated arcades had featured in the Shell Oil model; mechanized sidewalks above the traffic came straight from Futurama.

Robert Moses never directly acknowledged Bel Geddes' influence. But even if by the late 1940s such ideas had become general currency, their source was undoubtedly Bel Geddes' theories, and the plans and scale models he had created a decade before, which showed their practical application.

The 1945 city plan for Toledo, Ohio, was a direct follow-up on the Shell Oil advertising campaign from twelve years before. Bel Geddes had special affection for the place, having grown up in a nearby Michigan town (sometimes he even claimed to come from Toledo). He had already made his mark there, one of his earliest commercial jobs being to design a new line of products for the Toledo Scale Company, and (in 1929–31) its factory. Now, in anticipation of victory in the war against Germany and Japan, and the rebuilding that would follow, Paul Block, the publisher of the *Toledo Blade,* sponsored Bel Geddes to design a comprehensive plan for redevelopment. "Toledo Tomorrow" opened one month before the bombing of Hiroshima on 6 August 1945, finally brought World War II to a rapid end.

Toledo—the third biggest port on the Great Lakes, a major automotive and aircraft manufacturing center and the world's largest coal shipper—was suffering the all-too-familiar symptoms of urban blight in an extreme form. The twenty-four rail lines that converged there and made it a transport hub were strangling the city. Heavy industry blocked access to the Maumee River and covered surrounding neighborhoods with smoke and grime. In addition, since factories and warehouses were located upstream of the center, traffic across the river was continually stalled when bridges opened for ships to pass through, while the current carried all the smelly and dangerous chemical effluents down into the heart of the city. Homeowners and businesses had fled to the suburbs, leaving the city center in decay and crowded by low-income apartments. Bringing together city officials and members of the council, Paul Block commissioned Bel Geddes to create a scale model representing his solution to the problems, which could serve as a focus for a public campaign.

Transport and traffic flow therefore formed the foundation of Bel Geddes' plan. Working on case studies with two experts whose national reputations in their specialized fields lent authority to his proposals—Colonel Henry Waite, a railroad expert who had already reorganized the rail lines in Cincinnati, and W. Earle Andrews, a highway engineer—Bel Geddes planned a wholesale reorganization of the city. Industry, with its coal and ore docks, oil refineries, and grain storage, was to be moved downstream, solving the bridge problem and freeing space for a riverside park and small marina in the central core. In their new location on the outskirts, factories were segregated from housing by a broad greenbelt. There were blocks of modernistic buildings with open green spaces between, and self-contained residential communities built on curving streets.

Perhaps most strikingly, an integrated passenger terminal, linked to expressways and bringing together rail, buses, and cars with an airport, was envisaged on reclaimed marshland within walking distance of downtown. Bel Geddes was already contemplating problems that still confront airport designers today. Using detailed schemes for traffic movement, he envisaged mass air transit at a time when regular air services had only recently been established. This terminal is a striking example of his prescience.

Bel Geddes was already working in a practical way to realize the new potential of air travel that he had forecast in the 1939–40 Futurama. Even if the huge aircraft he designed were realized only in film, Bel Geddes was involved on the nuts-and-bolts level of passenger terminals. He had been hired by Texaco to create the trademark and logo for their new Skychief gasoline and pumps in 1938 ("design desired . . . implying speed in the air," as his notes laconically stated). In 1945, Texaco commissioned Bel Geddes to design a "Service Air Station" for commercial airports, initially intended solely for flight servicing, with stock and "field equipment" rooms, oil and grease storage, mechanics' rest room, and pilots' ready room. To this Bel Geddes added a lounge for passengers and, in yet another demonstration of his focus on communications of all kinds, a soundproof phone booth. Commissioned to devise a standardized design that would be reproduced at airports throughout the country, Bel Geddes' metal building had rounded corners and a flat roof. As he noted for his job file just after the prototype had been constructed, it was "the *first* airport station."[19] If this

"Toledo Tomorrow": the present reality versus the planned future. "Air view of Toledo as it is today [1945, *above*] shows concentration of railroads on river, overcrowded city blocks. Model of Future City [*opposite*] reveals shoreline park, open block plan, highly efficient expressway system." Photos supplied by Bel Geddes for *Architectural Forum*, August 1945, with his own captions. Estate of Edith Lutyens Bel Geddes, Norman Bel Geddes Collection, Courtesy of the Harry Ransom Humanities Research Center.

sort of terminal, with passengers walking out to the planes on the tarmac, was soon outdated by rapid increases in passenger volume and aircraft size, Bel Geddes' multi-transport terminus envisaged in the Toledo plan was already far more sophisticated in concept, separating the passengers from the planes.

By any standard, "Toledo Tomorrow" was a major project, with all Bel Geddes' preliminary studies, as well as the construction of the model, costing a reported $150,000 ($1.4 million in today's money).[20] Even so, the model was considerably

smaller than the one Bel Geddes had built for Shell Oil—a mere sixty-one feet in diameter—and, outlying areas being simply sketched in by a grid of streets without buildings, it was intended to be inspirational. Taking account of the sheer scale of the changes proposed, Bel Geddes specified that it represented Toledo fifty years in the future, in 1995.

Bel Geddes' plan was a statement of faith in the "future great city of the world" (as Toledo had once liked to proclaim itself), and the model was put on display in the Natural History Museum of the Toledo Zoo, remaining there until 1955. As with the Futurama exhibit, Bel Geddes provided an audiotape for the viewers which emphasized his point: "What you have seen is a possible long-range plan . . . intended to demonstrate what can be done. . . . We, as a community, proceeding on this great idea—will have pioneered the most important phase of the post-war world."[21]

A sketch by Bel Geddes for the transport terminal of "Toledo Tomorrow,"
with cutaway sections showing the underground rail station and passenger walkways
beneath the runways. Estate of Edith Lutyens Bel Geddes, Norman Bel Geddes Collection,
Courtesy of the Harry Ransom Humanities Research Center.

"Toledo Tomorrow" was widely hailed as spectacular. *Life* published a long, extensively illustrated piece on "Future Toledo." So did *Architectural Forum*, concluding with the statement that the city planning commissioners "will eventually work out a detailed program from this spectacular beginning." The local reaction, reflected in an October issue of the *Toledo Blade*, was nothing less than ecstatic:

">. . . a remarkably bold concept, instructive and provocative in offering a tangible goal for Toledo" (President of Libby-Owens-Ford Glass Co.).

">. . . not only an inspiration—it is a challenge to start now and redevelop Toledo along a definite long range master plan" (Chairman of the City Council Planning Commission).

"More favorable publicity and attention came to Toledo because of 'Toledo Tomorrow' than from anything else in recent years" (President of Owens-Corning Fiberglass Co.).[22]

Visited by more than three thousand people a day throughout the first month and with a thirty-minute color movie that opened in New York in July 1945 and then was distributed across the country, Bel Geddes' plans retained major public interest for the rest of the decade. The Toledo chamber of commerce adopted the model as the basis for a redevelopment fund-raising campaign that produced about $126 million ($2.5 billion today) in subscriptions to put Bel Geddes' plan into operation. The city and county planning agencies were combined in 1947, precisely to enable the creation of the kind of road and rail network he was proposing. Sections of the riverfront were turned into parkland, and a new Union Station, uniting and centralizing rail lines, was built in 1956, although it was never integrated with other forms of transport.

That was it. "Toledo Tomorrow" remained for the most part inspirational. Although widely hailed as the most practical example of urban planning by both major newspapers and trade journals, Bel Geddes' model became only a partial blueprint for Toledo's future.[23] Instead, it was in New York that the Ohio exhibit had the most tangible effect.

Life, with its circulation in 1945 approaching five million, was everywhere on the coffee tables and waiting rooms of North America. The same issue that featured "Toledo Tomorrow" (headlined "Scale Model Gives Citizens Prophetic Look at Wonderful City They Could Have in 50 Years") set it side-by-side with "Japan Signs Surrender" and "Effects of Atomic Bomb."[24] Bel Geddes' plans could hardly have had wider public exposure. Eleanor Roosevelt, writing in her nationally syndicated column, predicted that the kind of foresight shown in "Toledo Tomorrow" would inspire other cities, repeating a point she had made about Shell's futuristic advertising campaign.[25] The *Rochester Democrat and Chronicle* duly urged that "the principles of some of its main features are worthy of study by other cities, particularly by Rochester."

More to the point, the *New York World Telegram* ran a major article when the Toledo display opened, reporting that "New York bankers, realtors and city planners were generally agreed that many phases of the Toledo Plan should be applied to the five boroughs here—particularly in Manhattan and Brooklyn." Significantly, it concluded: "The New York Planning Commission have formulated tentative plans for this area along the lines of the Toledo plan."[26] The New York Planning Commission, of course, meant Robert Moses.

The surge of national self-confidence that followed victory in World War II propelled Moses into even bigger rebuilding programs. The same sense of mission that had mobilized the population for "the people's war" fueled support for reclaiming the cities from social disaster. In addition, New York and Washington, as well as Philadelphia and San Francisco, harbored ambitions to become world capitals—all

Spectators viewing "Toledo Tomorrow" on exhibit at Toledo's Natural History Museum, 1945.
Estate of Edith Lutyens Bel Geddes, Norman Bel Geddes Collection,
Courtesy of the Harry Ransom Humanities Research Center.

were competing to be the site of the new United Nations. And modernization was the key. Business groups and organized labor agreed with city planners in replacing slums and manufacturing industries by university and hospital complexes, corporate offices, as well as downtown housing for the professionals who worked in them and the expressways that gave access to them.

With the benefit of hindsight, we see Moses's wholesale destruction of neighborhoods, together with the creation of expressways and concrete blocks of public housing that replaced them, as disastrous. It was city planning at the expense of people. But despite scattered protests, the social costs did not become clear until the Bronx burned in the 1970s. The changes Moses introduced, which replaced blue-collar trades with white-collar services, turned New York into the first postindustrial metropolis. It was through him New York earned its title as the "Imperial City."[27]

When Robert Moses built his expressways and cleared the slums for the high-rise towers of public housing and the projects surrounded by green space, he was following principles promoted by Bel Geddes. Moses's redevelopment of Brooklyn's retail and factory zone into a new civic center in 1952 placed public buildings on tree-lined malls running from the Brooklyn Bridge, and relocated Long Island University and the Brooklyn Hospital there. The plan looks a lot like the downtown section of "Toledo Tomorrow" near the approaches to the new bridge Bel Geddes envisaged over the Maumee River. Bel Geddes' model might have been intended as a projection of what could be achieved by the millennium. In the hands of Robert Moses, "Toledo Tomorrow" became "New York Today."

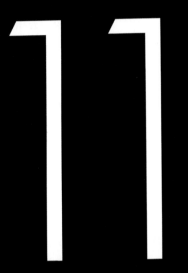

11

Reaching for the Sky

IF THERE IS ONE UNIQUELY modern and characteristically American kind of building, it is the skyscraper. Forget local landmarks like the Golden Gate, even the Statue of Liberty; in American cities, it is the towering structures of steel and glass that catch the eye. Le Corbusier's notion was that contemporary architecture should create "machines for living," and skyscrapers have been called, in typically American fashion, "machines for making money."[1] The twin towers of the World Trade Center, reaching above the Manhattan skyline as well as being at the core of the global economy, were an ideal target for terrorists bent on destroying a symbol of American financial power.

One New York builder famously declared, "Our civilization is progressing wonderfully . . . we must keep building and we must build upwards."[2] That observation was made in 1906, already emphatically marking the link between social aspiration and altitude that America has given the world. In 1911 the cover of a popular guidebook, *King's Views of New York,* showed Manhattan as a city of towering blocks with airplanes flying through the canyons between, and elevated road-bridges and tramways crisscrossing on every level. This was highly misleading advertising: even the sixty-floor Woolworth Building—the first recognizable skyscraper, which proclaimed its status as a product of up-to-the-minute science by having the lights turned on by President Woodrow Wilson pressing a button more than two hundred miles away in Washington—appeared two years after *King's* cover picture. But it speaks to the sheer romance of building Manhattan's soaring towers, which peaked in the construction boom from the mid-1920s to the early 1930s.

The public imagination was caught by the race to the top, as much as by the riggers and welders nonchalantly doing their jobs so high above the ground. For instance, there was the still-famous competition between the bank tower at 40 Wall Street and the Chrysler Building. Even the way this was won had immense appeal. In a bravura display Van Alen, the Chrysler architect, surreptitiously had a 185-foot spire fabricated inside the gleaming steel ellipses that apparently formed the crown. As soon as the top of the bank was finished, triumphantly outdoing its rival by just two floors, the spire (all seven tons of it) was shoved up through the peak to make the Chrysler the tallest building in the world—a title it held only briefly, being overtopped by the Empire State Building less than a year later. All this was reinforced by breathtakingly dramatic photos in the daily newspapers, showing the steelworkers laboring on the top floors of these and other skyscrapers. No safety-lines, not even hard hats: ordinary men in caps balancing (as in a famous *New York Times* photo) without any sign of concern on precariously thin girders way above the peaks of the surrounding skyscrapers, and with nothing but empty air below.

This aura of romance, so clearly associated with modern progress, was vibrantly expressed in the 1933 Chicago World's Fair. The New York State Pavilion mounted a "Man Power Panorama," showcasing huge photographs of the Brooklyn Bridge as a "Climax in Steel." It also found its way onto Broadway in theatrical productions, particularly in Norman Bel Geddes' work. His settings for the Guy Bolton musical *Five O'Clock Girl* showed elongated silhouettes of skyscrapers and a romantically exaggerated city skyline. In one highly effective scene of his *Seven Lively Arts* revue, the audience found themselves looking at a worm's-eye view of Manhattan skyscrapers towering around their circle of vision in a vertiginously receding perspective.

Still more directly it was reflected in a 1935 production, *Iron Men*. This was an event where Bel Geddes was almost the sole creative artist—a sign of his deep commitment to the vision of urban renewal. Originally intending it to be a movie, Bel Geddes drafted the scenario (then commissioned Sherwood Anderson to adapt it for the stage). In addition he produced and directed the play, as well as designing the scenery. And he turned the stage into an actual building site. His set design was an engineering blueprint. Steel posts and girders formed the acting area, each labeled by numbers (C1–60 or S4–59, and so on) with notes—not, as you would usually expect, on the visual impression—but solely on structural requirements such as "Girder D must be designed to take LL [live load] of 3,000 lbs."[3] Diagonally through the middle rose the top section of a crane on which the girders were swung up. The main dramatic action was the actual construction, in full view of the audience, of a massive steel scaffold, representing the fifty-ninth to sixty-first floors of a midtown office tower, and the characters were all steelworkers. The actors functioned as roustabouts and welders—and underlining this blurring of theatrical illusion and real life, in a carefully planted prepublicity leak, Bel Geddes let it be known that an actual steelworker, who had never before performed on the stage, was playing the lead role.

The relationship between Broadway and the skyscraper also went the other way. Despite the technological innovations so triumphantly advertised in the presidential opening of the Woolworth Building, skyscraper styling was archaic: Gothic buttresses, tracery, and pinnacles. And elaborate mock-gothic ornament continued to appear, in paradoxical defiance of modern structures, up to the mid-1920s in buildings such as Raymond Hood's Chicago Tribune Tower. A coherent style was needed, an appearance that matched the materials and expressed the modern function, and just before the great Manhattan construction boom got under way, New York architects started to take note of what was happening in the theater. Architectural journals increasingly carried articles about the stage, while scene designs began to be included in annual exhibitions of the Architectural League of New York at the Metropolitan Museum of Art, specifically in response to Joseph Urban's arrival on Broadway. As *Architectural Review* noted in July 1921, citing the display of Urban's designs at that

Actors constructing the skyscraper "set" live, during the performance of *Iron Men*, 1935.
Estate of Edith Lutyens Bel Geddes, Norman Bel Geddes Collection,
Courtesy of the Harry Ransom Humanities Research Center.

year's exhibition as a "striking recognition" of the "relation of stage settings to architecture," the profession was "awakening to the fact that much can be learned." Given the intrinsically dramatic structure of skyscrapers, of all buildings their design had the most convergence with theater. Naturally Urban was attracted by such prominent projects. He was also acutely aware of the anachronistic look in most of what he saw rising around the city, and he was in a position to influence the development of a new style, since he knew several of the leading architects in New York.

Frank Lloyd Wright, for instance, was one of Urban's circle. They discussed architecture, corresponded, and were both members of a weekly New York lunch club that included Raymond Hood, Ely Kahn, Ralph Walker, and other leading architects of the time. Urban, always convivial, was very much the center of the group, even inventing a new cocktail—which he playfully named "Nipple Spray"—that their meetings began with.[4]

At the time Wright was in an extremely unhappy situation. After commissions for one or two houses in the early 1920s, he found himself unemployed for over a decade. In contrast to Urban, as *Architectural Review* all too discerningly noted in 1929, Wright's work seemed alien and unsympathetic to the tone of the 1920s.[5] With his usual generosity, Urban loaned Wright considerable sums of money (never repaid) to tide him over. There was also a professional connection. Edgar Kaufmann, who commissioned Urban to redesign his Pittsburgh store in 1926, was also, ten years later (and after Urban's untimely death), the person who commissioned Fallingwater, one of Wright's landmark houses and the project that ended his dry spell.

In 1927 Urban designed the International Magazine Building for William Randolph Hearst. On its opening in 1928 the *New Yorker* labeled this seven-story block with its cylindrical, purely decorative columns standing out from the walls and rising at the sides and corners, topped with pastiche imperial vases high above the roofline, "theatric architecture."[6] This seems all too accurate, but the impression would have been different if Urban's plans had been followed. The building Hearst had commissioned was to have another twenty floors, but the Wall Street crash meant these were never added. This landmark edifice is now being completed with an imaginative thirty-six-story rhomboid tower of intersecting mirror-glass diamonds, each divided by lines of black glass into double pyramids, designed by the British architect Norman Foster. While Urban's original concept was not as radical, in his design the missing tower had also contrasted with the monumental stone base (the building takes up the entire block of Eighth Avenue between 56th and 57th Streets). It would have used new industrial materials (metal cladding, smooth-glazed and colored synthetics) as in the style of architecture Urban was calling for at the time: walls of windows with the narrowest steel strips in-between to emphasize the effect of height. His plans for the Reinhardt Theatre, with its shining black façade and gold spire, were one example.

Another was his design for a new Metropolitan Opera. A site for this had been acquired at 57th and 58th Streets between Eighth and Ninth Avenues, funds raised, and Urban was hired to design a larger and more up-to-date home for the Met together with Benjamin Morris, the architect of the Cunard Building on lower Broadway. But this collaboration, with Urban supported by the artistic side of the organization and Morris nominated by the box-holders (who were also shareholders), was a disaster. Urban, ebullient and fresh from designing the spectacularly successful Ziegfeld Theatre, almost immediately found himself at loggerheads with Morris, who up to then had never had anything to do with theater buildings but dourly insisted that he was the professional, dismissing Urban as a dilettante artist.

Both drew up competing and quite different plans (Urban preparing nine successive versions, each with detailed blueprints and full elevations). Occupying a whole city block, his design included a tower of studio apartments at one end, an office tower

The truncated edifice of the International Magazine Building,
with its eccentrically playful columns and "imperial" vases. Joseph Urban Papers,
Rare Book and Manuscript Library, Columbia University.

at the other, as well as a five-thousand-seat auditorium in the middle. The soaring pinnacle containing the offices was specifically intended, Urban informed the press, "as a symbol of the athletic eagerness and vitality" of the young American culture, while the theater itself would "set free every modern impulse," with "democratic" seating giving everyone in the audience an almost equal view of the stage. Morris's plans, after a bare month studying theaters in Europe over the summer, were extremely conservative and traditional. When they met, they quarreled; and when both appeared to present their separate plans to the chairman of the Met board Otto Kahn, their personal antagonism became all too public. Going behind Urban's back, Morris persuaded a number of box-holders that Urban's "democratic" auditorium would rob them of their privileged status. Not content with that, he referred insultingly to Urban's design in the press, and incited the financier and architectural critic Kenneth Murchison to dismiss Urban as a mere "scene painter" and announce to the *New Yorker*, "we will see that he is kept well behind the footlights."[7]

In outraged self-defense, Urban arranged for his plans to be published (without permission from the Met) along with an interview by *Musical America* in October 1927. This ploy backfired. Some of the New York daily papers picked up the story, implying that Urban's design had been adopted and forcing Kahn to issue a statement denying it had been authorized. The headline in the following issue of *Musical America* read, "Publication of Urban Plans for Metropolitan Crystallizes Conflict Between Democratic and Conservative Elements"—provoking precisely this result. Raymond Hood, one of the leading New York architects of the time, weighed in on Urban's side. Otto Kahn, who up to then had strongly supported Urban, was forced into neutrality. Morris, who had also built the annex to the Morgan Library, was backed by one of the most powerful box-holders: J. P. Morgan. Nothing could be decided, and with the stock market crash of 1929 (which also truncated Urban's International Magazine Building), the whole project was dropped. It was the first time Urban's jovial diplomatic skills had failed.

Even so, his design still had indirect influence, with the shape of his double towers being echoed in the much higher towers of Raymond Hood's Rockefeller Center, built in 1930, as well as (according to Urban) in the Louisiana State Capitol, completed two years later.[8] Urban stuck to his guns, continuing his campaign in the press. Declaring that "too large a volume of American architecture is still imitating obsolete European models," he used interviews in the *New York Post* and *Evening Post* to announce his ambition to design a skyscraper along the lines he had pioneered in the Met designs.[9] This was to be entirely steel and glass, completely without decorative features. Its function as an office would be clear from its structure alone.

Nothing came of this aspiration. After the Chrysler and Empire State buildings

Urban's elevation for the new Metropolitan Opera House, 1927. Although the
main façade is stone, in keeping with its public function, the metal upper frames of the towers
together with the strong verticals and simplicity of the whole express its modernity.
Joseph Urban Papers, Rare Book and Manuscript Library, Columbia University.

were completed in 1930–31, the Depression led to a twenty-year pause in reaching
for the sky. Yet Urban's plans for modernistic skyscrapers were eventually realized
by proxy, since they were almost certainly the source for Frank Lloyd Wright's first
skyscraper. This represented a sharp break with all Wright's other buildings, which
were defiantly horizontal and integrated with the landscape. Up to then Wright, notoriously opinionated and antagonistic to much of what he saw in modern American
life, identified skyscrapers with "evils" such as ruthless economic competition. Even

though he had begun his career as a draftsman for Louis Sullivan, the Chicago architect who pioneered the early skyscrapers in the 1890s, in Wright's view any vertical building promoted social inequality. In 1929, however, just at the time when he was closest to Urban, Wright designed a narrow twenty-story tower, with sheer glass walls cantilevered out from a central core, for a New York developer. His proposal echoes Urban in describing it as "a logical development of the idea of a tall building in the age of glass and steel, as logical engineering as the Brooklyn Bridge or an ocean liner."[10]

Wright's plans, like so many in the Depression, had to be shelved. His skyscraper, relocated to Oklahoma, was eventually built for the H. C. Price Company in 1956; and it was in the fifties that Urban's modernistic concept finally filtered through to become the architectural norm. The first glass slab, Gordon Bunschaft's Lever House—which would have been close to Urban's notion of thirty years before—was completed in 1952, and served as a model for office-tower design through the 1960s. Another, more immediate, example was to have significant influence on later architectural developments: Urban's strikingly modernistic designs for the New School for Social Research.

Founded in 1919, the New School was a unique venture in adult education, which declared in its brochures that the curriculum encompassed "any subject of intellectual or aesthetic interest." By 1929 it had expanded far beyond the capacity of its original site; and two architects were considered for the job of designing a new building that (as the public announcement stipulated) would be "architecturally distinctive, and down to the slightest detail fitted precisely to the ideals of the New School and to the requirements of its function."[11] Urban was one, Frank Lloyd Wright the other. Being paired in competition with the man who was already regarded as America's greatest architect, even being chosen in preference, is a measure of Urban's stature and an indication of the way he had come to dominate the New York cultural scene in the 1920s.

The New School saw itself as at the cutting edge in an age of revolutionary change, and its values were modernist and rational. As one of their bulletins stated, art for art's sake was anathema: "Everything today must establish its right to exist through the performance of a function."[12] Urban, rightly recognizing this as a project with the potential to set the cultural tone for a broad section of New York culture, and responsive to his client's nontraditional aims, was prepared to lower his usual fee to what the New School could afford.

He designed every detail of the building: the structure, interior layout, external styling and materials, as well as all the interior décor, from the bronze handrails on the stairways, through furniture, bookshelves, carpets, and all the colors of the walls,

The auditorium of Joseph Urban's New School for Social Research, opened in 1931.
Joseph Urban Papers, Rare Book and Manuscript Library, Columbia University.

down to the exit signs and clocks above the doors. What he created was not so much
a building as a complete environment, and the whole effect had a radical simplicity. It
was indeed, in the words of a fund-raising leaflet, "one of the most strikingly interesting educational buildings in the country."

The whole structure was determined by the oval two-story auditorium seating
650 people. This could double as concert hall, theater, or movie theater, and filled the
ground floor. Its domed ceiling created the sloping seating for two large lecture halls
back-to-back above, and dictated large open spaces in the center of the upper floors,
which *Architectural Record* found amazing.[13] There were two additional lecture rooms
and three other classrooms, a library and reading rooms, three studios and an art exhibition hall, dining rooms, offices, and two apartments, plus workshops for modeling
and design in the basement. Though minimalist, with no nonfunctional features, all the
interior spaces conveyed a definite sense of design. The shape of the auditorium was
emphasized by its ceiling of overlapping oval rings—installed for acoustical reasons,

but allowing indirect lighting, as well as heating and ventilation—all curving toward a half-circle arching over the stage. Its oval was echoed in the top-floor studio, surrounding a circular dance floor in the center, while the double staircase leading down from the students' lounge into the library created a sweeping triangle.

The front formed a bold statement of modernism: a flat wall, cantilevered over the entrance, with strong horizontal lines accentuated by the black and white rows of glazed brick between broad bands of windows that stretched the whole width of the building on each floor. From the outside this austerity was broken only by blocks of color that could be seen through the windows, red and purple on one floor, green and orange on another, yellow above that, hinting at the strong colors covering the interior walls—ninety shades and tones in all. The effect was captured by Edmund Wilson, the leading left-wing American intellectual of the period, who labeled it "Aladdin's Lecture Palace."[14] Large areas of high-reflective color were set against smaller blocks of color that absorbed light; cool color in shadow, warm on brightly lit surfaces to accentuate tonal contrasts. So the director's room, carpeted in dark gray and with a light gray ceiling, had black chairs and desk, set off by orange interior walls and bright purple above and below the windows as well as on the door. The large studio on the top floor was given an orange dance floor, a black ceiling, and nine contrasting colors for the walls. None of these colors were decorative, as various architectural journals noted, but presented form and volume.

The New School was prestigious. Its lecturers included America's most famous philosopher and educationalist John Dewey, the leading American historian Charles Beard, Aaron Copland, who had already become an iconic American composer, eminent anthropologists and sociologists like Franz Boas and Thorstein Veblen—as well as Urban himself, speaking on "Modern Architecture." The publicity put out by the New School had enthusiastically forecast that the uniqueness of the new building would "draw thousands of persons to examine it, and to inquire into the educational function it expresses." This turned out to be an understatement. When it was completed in February 1931, *Architectural Record* noted, "Few buildings have opened with an equal air of suspense. Few buildings have ever had so much experiment and intense conviction at stake."[15] It attracted broad press coverage, and Urban's design continued to receive attention in New York architectural journals throughout the 1930s.

He had described his aim as creating a building that would not only function in the present, but also forecast the future. One of the architects it deeply impressed was Philip Johnson, the first American exponent of what came to be called the International Style. Hailing the New School as an example of a completely new style in a long article for *Arts* magazine, Johnson analyzed the principles on which it was constructed, which would later characterize his own architecture.

Joseph Urban, façade, the New School for Social Research, 12th Street, 1930–31.
Joseph Urban Papers, Rare Book and Manuscript Library, Columbia University.

1. The function of the building is the starting point for the ultimate design, which thus develops rationally from within and determines the form of the façade.

2. This structural arrangement is the main decorative effect. Ornament is not employed.[16]

The New School building also directly influenced other New York architects. William Muschenheim renovated the Astor Hotel in the same style and came to be one of the leading modernist architects in the 1930s. Wallace Harrison, who had already worked with Urban on the Met project, went on to design Radio City Music Hall, the United Nations buildings, and Lincoln Center. Raymond Hood switched from the neo-Gothic of the Chicago Tribune and New York American Radiator buildings to a far plainer modernistic style around the time he met Urban, making the façade of his 1931 Beaux Arts Apartments in New York very similar to the New School's.

However, the extravagant curves of the oval auditorium, contrasting dramatically with the rigid rectangles in the rest of the New School building, and the brilliant, band-box colors that shone through the glass to illuminate the restrained black-and-white exterior (like the juxtapositioning of huge color areas in his work for the Chicago World's Fair) all pointed in a rather different direction. So did Urban's use of a honeycomb surface for the ceiling in the New School auditorium which, like the gleaming vitrolite that marked his façade for the Bedell store and his design for the Reinhardt Theatre, Urban promoted as a high-tech modern building material. Such elements, with their architectural playfulness, contain the seeds of the contemporary wave ushered in by Frank Gehry's Guggenheim Museum in Bilbao in 1997. Of course in the early 1930s Urban had no access to the computers, still more than seventy years away, which alone have made possible the fantastic metal shapes and floating forms of Gehry's landmark buildings, the cubes and shards of Daniel Libeskind, or the curvilinear glass fantasies of Norman Foster (and it is not altogether coincidental that it is Foster who was selected to put the missing upper floors on Urban's International Magazine Building). If such extreme experiments with architectural form was far beyond the technology of Urban's time, his theatrical blazoning could be seen as foreshadowing this new contemporary school.

The New School should also be recognized, not as a unique phenomenon, but as marking a distinctive 1930s modernism that signally included Bel Geddes. Bel Geddes' architectural designs for the Chicago World's Fair, published a decade before Urban's New School opened, encapsulated the same qualities as the New School displayed, and could apply almost equally to the contemporary school of Gehry and Foster. As one architectural reviewer put it, what distinguished Bel Geddes' buildings was "surfaces finished and polished and the scintillation of steel, the brilliance of paint, and the transparent openness of large window-walls of plate glass. The effect is a style disengaged from all impressionistic sentimentality, dependent on clear proportions, frank colors, plainly organic forms, divested of all that is superfluous; a new architecture."[17] Bel Geddes' designs for the Chicago fair were never built, but the comparison is still clearer in the wildly anthropomorphic curves of Copa City as well as the radically new cantilevered construction technique that Bel Geddes pioneered (see pages 95–97).

Still, as we have already seen, in effect Urban's New School for Social Research was more immediately the catalyst for International Style architecture, even if some of its intrinsic qualities were overlooked as décor instead of structural design. So after the end of the Depression and once the United States had emerged from World War II, when new skyscrapers began to be built again, this style dominated the skyline of American cities. The New School also gained significant international exposure. From 1934 until the end of the war, Urban's building became a "university in exile" for German refugees like the Nobel Prize–winner Thomas Mann, architects from the Bauhaus, and Erwin Piscator, the radical Berlin theater director whose classes were attended by Marlon Brando and Tennessee Williams. When these refugees returned to their homelands, many of them to leading positions in rebuilding the shattered cities of Europe, they carried back the image of the New School. And this was no isolated example. Urban and Bel Geddes had long been in the forefront of exporting American modernity to the international community.

Both Urban and Bel Geddes eagerly pursued opportunities on the international scene. In 1931 Bel Geddes entered an international competition to design a Ukrainian State Theatre for Kharkov—encouraged by Urban, who the same year was engaged in designing a Palace of the Soviets to be built near the Kremlin in the center of Moscow. Both were mammoth projects. They required acoustical studies, engineering calculations, full working drawings, architectural blueprints, elevations, and detailed scale models.

The specifications for the Palace of the Soviets called for a debating chamber seating three thousand delegates, an office building and a library to serve them, plus a multipurpose main hall capable of holding fifteen thousand people for mass meetings, or pageants permitting "the participation of the spectators in any of the events taking place upon the stage," as well as exhibitions of Russian industrial and technological achievements. The structure was also supposed to "correspond to the character of the epoch, expressing the will of the toiling masses [a phrase recurring several times]

Urban's designs for the Hall of the Soviets, 1931, showing one possible arrangement for
mass pageants. Urban's handwritten notes indicate a vibrant color scheme: bright orange lettering,
a purple panel behind the white stage arch, and yellow walls. Joseph Urban Papers,
Rare Book and Manuscript Library, Columbia University.

Bel Geddes' model for the Ukrainian State Theatre, 1931, showing the fan-shaped open-air
amphitheater on top of the main auditorium, the bridge-stairway linking the roofs of the
two buildings, and the circular audience space with lighting pylons, allowing the whole structure
to be used as a stage. Estate of Edith Lutyens Bel Geddes, Norman Bel Geddes Collection,
Courtesy of the Harry Ransom Humanities Research Center.

to build socialism." Ironically, the Cathedral of Christ the Redeemer was to be torn
down to accommodate it.[18]

Urban brought all he had learned in designing the New School for Social Research to create an impressive modernist complex. The centerpiece exhibition/perfor-
mance hall was to have a curved ceiling of glass panels that formed a sound-reflecting
surface and refracted light, while floor-to-ceiling louvers covered sound-absorbent
walls. "Through and between these" louvers, Urban noted on his design, "gleam
colored lights making it possible to bathe the hall in any atmosphere suitable to the
mood." The floor was divided into sections that could be raised or lowered hydrau-
lically, and large entryways could be accessed from the streets at each side "so that
demonstrations, troops, machines, vehicles can cross the stage at any time," as Urban
stated in his submission.[19]

Bel Geddes' task was no less complex. The Ukrainian State Theatre was to have
three performance spaces: an indoor auditorium holding four thousand spectators
and an open-air stage with seating for two thousand, plus an arena in which mass
meetings of up to sixty thousand people could be addressed. His solution was to

Artist's renderings of performances for a mass audience, Ukrainian State Theatre:
the main auditorium (*top*); the roof of the theater complex as a stage (*bottom*).
Estate of Edith Lutyens Bel Geddes, Norman Bel Geddes Collection,
Courtesy of the Harry Ransom Humanities Research Center.

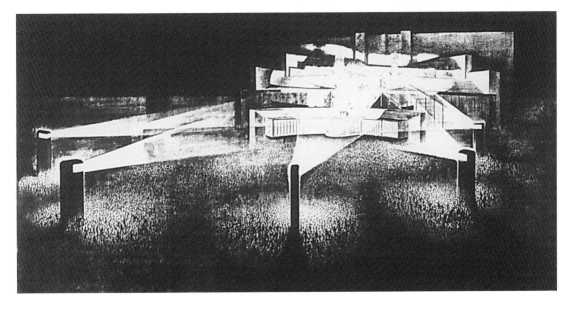

place the smaller outdoor stage on the roof of the main auditorium and create a circular amphitheater backing onto the building, surrounded by immensely tall pylons containing amplifiers and an array of spot- and floodlights. This could be used by a single politician to harangue the crowd, standing on a rostrum jutting out in front of a curving gallery, within which supporting public figures could be ranked. Or, the whole façade of the building could serve as an immense backdrop to the sort of spectacles and mass-pageants that had celebrated the Revolution in the early 1920s, using the roofs and stepped bridge joining them as a multilevel stage for up to five thousand actors. In addition, the theater building housed eight exhibition spaces, and the indoor stage was divided into three areas, each on a hydraulic lift for Bel Geddes' scene-changing system and equipped with ramps permitting actors to merge with the audience.

In some ways the designs for the Palace of the Soviets and the Ukrainian State Theater were remarkably similar. Apart from the monumental quality required by the nature of these projects, both are marked by the same kind of radical simplicity. As Urban put it in his report to the Committee for the Construction of the Palace of the Soviets, "As far as possible the attempt has been made to eliminate all forms and details which are not a part of the necessary structure."[20] The absence of decorative ornament, combined with organically curving shapes and an asymmetrical flow, is the hallmark of the image of modernity that evolved in these projects. The similarities show the extent to which Urban and Bel Geddes, while working separately, developed along parallel paths and influenced each other.

Neither of these designs was (officially) adopted by the Russians, even though both were constructed (unacknowledged). The typically jargon-filled response to Urban's plans stated that the composition was "too utilitarian" and failed to exemplify "the new structure dictated by the victorious march of the socialist upbuilding [sic]," since the right kind of "creative strength could not be attained under the bourgeois mode of life." As a sort of backhanded recognition, however, the Soviets awarded Bel Geddes a prize for his design, while blatantly stealing major elements of his plans, which were built under the names of a team of Russian architects.

The invitations to compete, and the plagiarism as well as the prize, indicate the growing reputation of Urban and Bel Geddes, in addition to the way elements of American culture were beginning to spread across the world.

In the early 1950s Bel Geddes again entered an architectural competition for a large metropolitan project, submitting plans in the international competition for the new United Nations buildings. His scheme—an avenue alongside the water flanked by a series of tall glass slabs, rising at the south end to four high towers with curving sides that jutted out from a large circular debating chamber—was to make the UN a vast cultural center. It closely followed ideas in an article entitled "Flexible Theatre" that he had written for the *New York Times Magazine* in November 1947.[21] There, anticipating (and far exceeding) the Rockefeller–Robert Moses plans for the Lincoln Center development, he had proposed a complex covering several city blocks, and comprising ten theaters, a dozen restaurants, bars, terraces, roof gardens, swimming pools, skating rinks, broadcasting studios—plus two hotels and a dozen specialty shops, as well as incorporating subway, bus, and car facilities. All this, with offices substituted for the hotels, was included in his UN plans. It was a typically grandiose vision, too ambitious to be seriously considered.

By contrast, another of Bel Geddes' plans—more focused in scope, even if much more futuristic—did bear eventual fruit. One of the structures he designed for the Chicago World's Fair was an aerial restaurant. A thin column, 280 feet high, carried elevators running up glass tubes on its exterior to three broad, glassed-in decks, cantilevered from the top and continually revolving. It was a revolutionary idea for the time: as Bel Geddes told the *Chicago Daily News,* "I wanted to build something that had never been done before."[22] He envisaged it as constructed of steel and aluminum (then the newest metal), and large enough to hold twelve hundred diners: six hundred on the lower level, which also had space for a dance floor; four hundred on the middle deck; and two hundred in an exclusive restaurant on the top.

Although never constructed, the restaurant was extensively discussed in the press ("Unique and Fantastic Architecture" was a typical headline in the *Philadelphia Public Ledger*).[23] Bel Geddes also featured the designs prominently in his book *Horizons.* Just over thirty years later, something extremely similar was constructed for another World's Fair, the Seattle Space Needle. Conceived by Edward E. Carson, this had only a single two-tier revolving deck, and the column was created out of a series of struts like a tripod. Still closer to Bel Geddes' design is Toronto's CN Tower, by the architect John Andrews, which opened in the mid-1970s. Its single pencil-like shaft carries glass-tube elevators up the outside, but it outdoes even Bel Geddes. The "Sky Pod" contains seven stories (though two are taken up with a broadcasting studio and telecommunications equipment), and is at a height of 1,100 feet—almost three times higher than Bel Geddes' design. Counting the tall spire atop the revolving restaurant, the CN Tower became the world's tallest freestanding structure: a record it continues to hold today, a quarter century later.

The Space Needle and CN Tower are symbols of their cities. Both have also become icons of modernity. Whether their architects were aware of it or not—and it's more than likely in the case of the Space Needle—the whole concept of these towers

Model for Bel Geddes' proposed aerial restaurant, 1929.
(The vertical shaft is foreshortened in this photograph.)
Estate of Edith Lutyens Bel Geddes, Norman Bel Geddes Collection,
Courtesy of the Harry Ransom Humanities Research Center.

and revolving restaurants derives directly from Bel Geddes. Of course, towers with revolving restaurants tend to be few and far between. But in another area, Bel Geddes' influence reached into the everyday life of ordinary people even more than his highway designs. This was an extension of his city planning: the layout of the suburbs, in which he designed workplaces and housing for the masses.

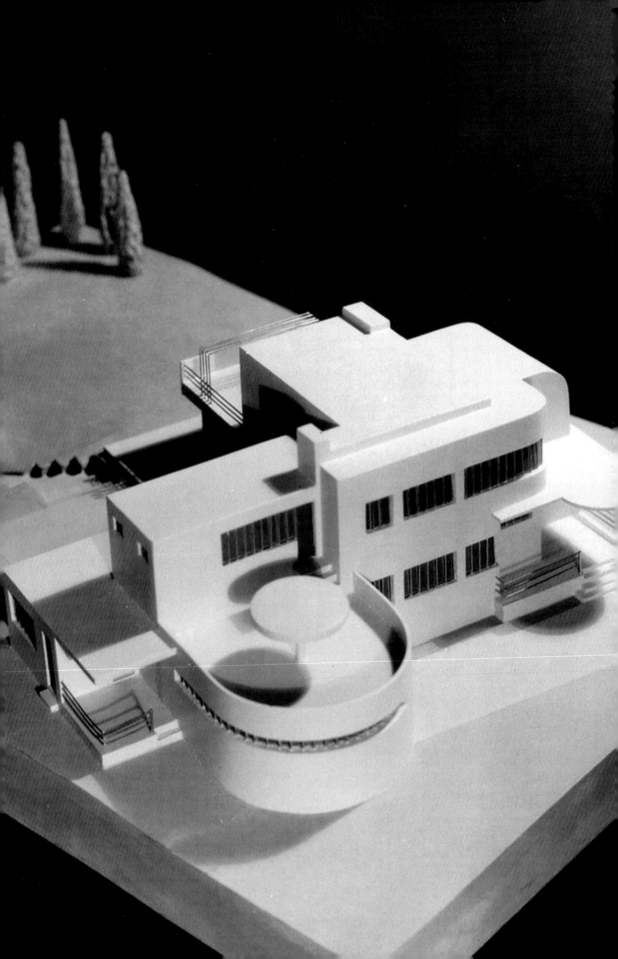

12

Suburban Heaven

SOARING SPIRES SUCH AS Seattle's Space Needle or Toronto's CN Tower may be highly visible statements of modernity. Still, Norman Bel Geddes was always more interested in functional structures than symbols, and perhaps the most functional of all buildings is the factory. In the opening chapter of *Horizons* he declared: "Just as surely as the artists of the fourteenth century are remembered for their cathedrals, so will those of the twentieth be remembered for their factories and the products of these factories."[1] One of Bel Geddes' major projects was a factory in Ohio for Toledo Scale.

Bel Geddes had already redesigned the counter scales manufactured by the company, creating slim-line, elegantly simple models of lightweight metals. Contrasting with previous bulky machines, these allowed the customer to see simultaneously what was being purchased and its weight. The utility and strikingly modern look of this new line, as Bel Geddes remarked with characteristic self-congratulation in *Horizons,* "made it the most popular and most widely used and imitated counter scale on the market."[2] Toledo Scale's management was so pleased with its success that they commissioned him to design an entire new factory complex for the expanding company.

As Bel Geddes intended, this industrial complex on the outskirts of Toledo was highly unusual for its time. The landscaping, which called for belts of trees and open green areas, a fountain, and a reflecting pool, was a prototype of the modern industrial park. The machine shop and assembly plant combined functional efficiency with an aura of cleanness and technological sophistication.

The administration building's lobby was open several floors through the center. To one side stood a rectangular laboratory building with curtain walls of floor-to-ceiling glass cantilevered from internal columns (a novel construction technique in 1930). A circular machine shop was roofed with circular "sawtooth" flanges carrying windows, again for maximum light. This had an unmistakable machine-age look, the shape symbolizing a gigantic dynamo. Concentric bands of glass in the roof and the external beams projecting from the top like spokes from the central hub created an open working space one hundred and sixty feet in diameter. On the other side of the administration building, the main factory was designed to be as well lit and dust-free as possible. The work floor was raised to create a completely enclosed area below where all the belts and motors for the workers' machines were placed, as well as heating and wiring, while ducts sucked all metal shavings, dust, and fumes down into containers in this sublevel, which could be hauled away directly through access gates in the exterior walls.

Bel Geddes admired Albert Kahn's Ford Laboratory at Dearborn, as an example

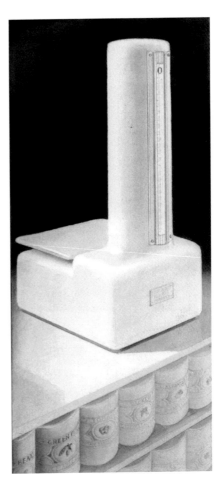

The Toledo counter scale: the standard 1928 model (*above*); the streamlined design by Bel Geddes, 1929 (*right*). Estate of Edith Lutyens Bel Geddes, Norman Bel Geddes Collection, Courtesy of the Harry Ransom Humanities Research Center.

of machinery inspiring efficient—and therefore, following his principles, aesthetically pleasing—architecture. Although not nearly as large as the Ford plant, the Toledo Scale project was a completely different order of factory environment. The large open spaces created by Bel Geddes' ingenious use of cantilevering, as well as his emphasis on light and cleanliness, were designed to create a worker-friendly environment. The structures were also designed to be flexible and expandable, with modular sections so that the internal configuration could easily be changed or extra space added.

Although some elements of Toledo Scale were never built because of the Depression, in *Horizons* Bel Geddes called his work on it "one of the most satisfying experiences of my life."[3] It was also influential. The effect of the broad horizontal bands formed by the windows of the administration building and laboratory, together with the concentric circles of the machine shop, is strikingly similar to Frank Lloyd Wright's

Bel Geddes' sketch for the layout of Toledo Scale Factory site (*above*), showing, from left to right, the laboratory, the administration tower and the circular machine shop, and the main factory, with shipping and receiving top, 1929–31. Estate of Edith Lutyens Bel Geddes, Norman Bel Geddes Collection, Courtesy of the Harry Ransom Humanities Research Center. Frank Lloyd Wright, Johnson Wax Administration Building (*opposite*), Racine, Wisconsin, 1937–39. Courtesy of Andrew Wood.

much-illustrated headquarters for Johnson Wax, designed seven years later. Wright also used the same construction technique as Bel Geddes for his laboratory tower, added to the Johnson Wax site at Racine, Wisconsin, in 1950. Only the unique interior columns in Wright's design, flaring out from a narrow base to broad interlocking circles that form the ceilings, are notably different. The similarities between Bel Geddes' architectural designs and Wright's buildings continue even decades later. So for instance, an "all-purpose" showcase/exhibition building, which Bel Geddes designed in 1942–43 (originally intended for General Motors, and proposed for Fifth Avenue in New York) in many ways—with its open circular interior and curving concrete façade—startlingly anticipates the iconic Guggenheim Museum, which Wright started work on in 1944–45 (when he presented a model to Solomon Guggenheim, even though construction difficulties and cost meant that it was still unfinished at Wright's death in 1959).

Not only did these buildings represent the modern era in their futuristic architectural form; they were also cheaper than traditional construction. Urban kept his eight-

story New School for Social Research within the modest $500,000 budget that the institution could afford, so unusual a step that the architectural journals remarked on it. Bel Geddes proudly publicized the fact that the contractor's estimate for the Toledo Scale Factory was $42.88 per square foot, twelve cents lower than the average construction costs for industrial buildings at the time (a saving on the factory building alone of $20,000—about $860,000 in today's money—and more than three times as much for the administration building). It was a strong selling point for the new style.

If the skyscraper is one of the dominating aspects of today's cities, another is the serried ranks of almost identical homes on the outskirts. Suburbia, in its modern manifestation as seemingly endless rows of separated houses, each surrounded by its own small yard, might also be seen as America's gift to twentieth-century living. This contribution may have seemed ambiguous, and in novels and films the suburbs have been portrayed as dysfunctional or demoralizing. In the decade following World War II, however, Americans embraced Levittown as a slice of heaven. At that time even critics could find nothing worse to call this new phenomenon than "Populux," as a comfortable fantasy turned out on the assembly line. Since then, at least partly because of Bel Geddes' efforts and influence, suburban design has matured into architecturally admired examples such as new developments like Celebration, Florida.

Although at the opposite end of the architectural scale from the skyscraper, the

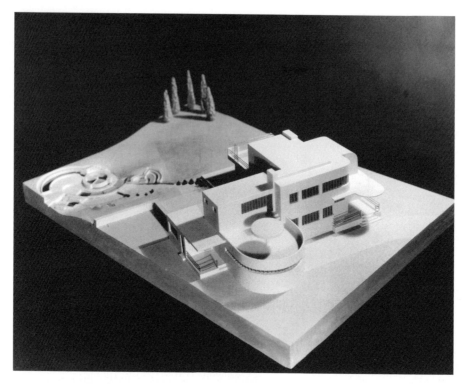

Two homes for ordinary families: (*above*) a scale model for House 3,
the "House of Tomorrow," based on plans and specifications drawn up by
Bel Geddes in 1930. Estate of Edith Lutyens Bel Geddes, Norman Bel Geddes Collection,
Courtesy of the Harry Ransom Humanities Research Center;
(*opposite*) Urban's house for Max Lerner, Lincoln, New York, designed in 1929.
Joseph Urban Papers, Rare Book and Manuscript Library, Columbia University.

standardized suburban house promotes an almost equally powerful American ideal:
the nuclear family, independence, and democratic equality. Even the darker side of
this ideal—conformity, materialism—was welcomed at the time as an antidote to the
insecurities of the long economic depression and war. Just as the shining glass towers
we associate with the modern style of skyscraper were introduced in the 1950s, so too
in the late 1940s and through the 1950s the first large tracts of suburban homes for
the masses were built. Suburbia and the skyscraper were the two sides of modernity
on the American plan.

Bel Geddes' socialist leanings, which came out clearly in his theater productions
such as *Dead End,* led him to design not only industrial workplaces, but also housing
for ordinary families. With the exception of his rejected plans for the United Nations,
he showed little interest in important public or commercial buildings and, unlike Jo-

seph Urban, never created houses for the super-rich. In contrast, Bel Geddes worked directly for the broad base of society, rather than counting on a trickle-down effect from the small elite at the top, although with the onset of the Great Depression, Urban also turned to the problem of creating modest housing for ordinary people. Yet there are marked similarities in the style of building both created, which clearly show the degree to which they were developing a shared and specifically modern idiom.

At the beginning of the 1930s Bel Geddes was developing a style of middle-class home, constructed around a lightweight steel frame that allowed a flexible arrangement of rooms. Channels in the frame, which carried wiring and plumbing, also served as heating or air-conditioning ducts, depending on season, creating a completely controlled environment within the house. As in the Toledo Scale factory, or indeed in Urban's New School building, windows (hermetically sealed) ran the whole

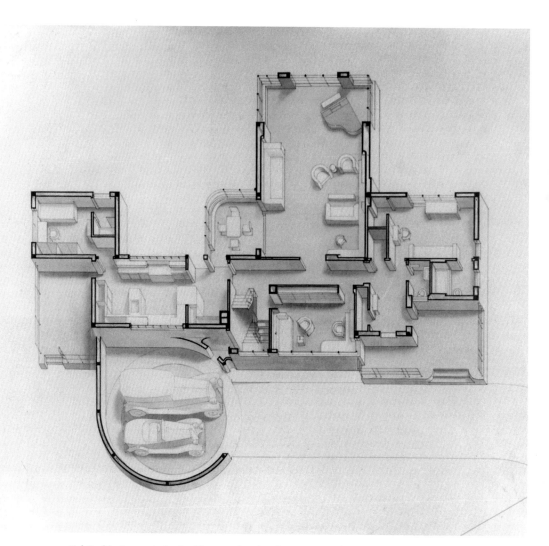

Bel Geddes' ground plan for House 3, showing the garage revolve, full-width windows, and wall ducts. Estate of Edith Lutyens Bel Geddes, Norman Bel Geddes Collection, Courtesy of the Harry Ransom Humanities Research Center.

length of the exterior walls in each room to provide even lighting; and at night the electric light—indirect, reflected on the ceiling from fixtures behind the tops of the walls—could be varied by dimmer switches. Cupboards and even furniture such as a desk, bookshelves, and kitchen and bathroom counters were built in. The garage had a revolving floor, so that cars could be driven straight in and be turned around to drive straight out again.

Although none of this technology was new, the way Bel Geddes applied it was strikingly original. For instance the variable-intensity electric lighting was taken directly from the theater, as was the revolving floor in the garage, but Bel Geddes was the first to propose the use of either for ordinary housing. He was also the first to hook interior house lights up to a photo-electric cell (in the offices he designed for the J. Walter Thompson advertising company in 1928) so that the intensity of the lighting changed automatically, dimming in response to the sun coming out from behind a cloud or brightening as dusk fell. His type of housing was literally a machine for living; and its curving corners, flat roofs, and absolutely plain walls exemplified his style of streamlined modernism.

Published in a series of articles for the *Ladies' Home Journal*, as well as in *Reader's Digest* and then in *Horizons*, pictures of his "House of Tomorrow" inspired quite a fashion during the 1930s. Bel Geddes demanded that his readers "start from the bottom, with our minds clear of the traditional styles and conventions of the past" and frames his architectural principles and approach in the characteristically modernist way he had done so much to define: "from a purely utilitarian basis, to create a type of architectural beauty which reflects the spirit of the age and will not soon be outdated." On the one hand, his aim was "to eliminate everything that is not necessary," and on the other he used cutting-edge materials and methods from industrial building ("reinforced concrete . . . steel cantilever—neither of which has ever been used in the dwelling house") to open up new perspectives. With such construction techniques "in pursuit of light and air . . . we can make our windows stretch the whole length of our rooms."[4]

Like Urban, beginning in the 1930s Bel Geddes received commissions to build several houses along these lines—one, which can still be seen in Philadelphia, as late as 1957. All across the country "streamlined" houses sprang up—larger, and built for the rich by various architects, but with the same semicircular projections, curving corners, flat roofs, and bands of windows running the length of the walls. Two of these, which are sometimes pointed to as examples of Bel Geddes' influence, are the Richard Mansell House at Mount Kisco, New York, designed by Edward Durrell Stone in 1934, and the Butler House in Des Moines, Iowa, built by George Kraetsch two years later. By the time the first of these appeared, however, Bel Geddes had already moved on, developing this concept into plans for standardized, low-cost homes, which were later picked up by the Housing Corporation of America.

Here flexibility, function, and economy were even more evident. The design could vary from one house to another, but every element of all the houses would be standard so that they could be prefabricated. His basic idea of creating houses from interchangeable modules also graphically illustrates the way Bel Geddes' theater experience intersected with his industrial design. Few plays take place in a single setting, and the traditional techniques for scene changes offered possibilities for housing that would be cheap—because all the basic scenery parts were standardized in shape and size—yet varied in style and appearance, even customized. At the same time, Bel Geddes was never content with the limitations of standard theatrical methods. He had taken inventive steps to mechanize the stage, and these also fed into his scheme for mass-produced family homes.

Conventional stage scenery was constructed out of canvas-covered "flats"—some with window or door cutouts—lashed together to form the shape of a room or a street scene. Backdrops, gauzes for various lighting effects, or "cut cloths" for foliage could also be dropped in from the "flies" above. But changing a setting was generally a slow business, and the more realistic the scene, the longer it took, requiring frequent intervals that broke the flow of the action. In 1928, faced with the problems of staging *The Patriot,* a fast-moving action that was also a historical epic requiring elaborate settings, Bel Geddes had taken these standard techniques into a completely new dimension.

Dramatizing the assassination of Tsar Paul I, the action shifted backward and forward among five settings. One scene (needed three times during the play) was the library of the patriotic conspirator, others included the boudoir of a baroness and various rooms and state chambers in the tsar's palace. In several scenes, characters exited from one place carrying on a dialogue that was resumed almost uninterrupted in the next. The standard solution would have been to set up the separate scenes on a revolving stage (as had been done for European productions of the play),[5] but revolves had a significant drawback. Even mounting two scenes on the circular floor cut the acting area of the stage in half, and each added scene made it smaller and more cramped. Yet palatial spaces were clearly needed to give a sense of the large issues and historical grandeur depicted in the play. So Bel Geddes developed a novel mechanism that made almost instantaneous changes possible, while allowing the actors to use the entire stage in each scene.

His solution was to construct two platforms, each holding one half of a scene, which pivoted out of the wings at each side on silent casters to meet in the center of the stage. When out of sight in the wings, one double set of scenery could be changed for another. In addition, different settings for the other scenes were lowered on steel wires from the flies—already completely constructed and solid (with the hinged walls of the tsar's audience chamber, for instance, weighing several tons)—and the previous ones whisked up, out of sight of the audience, while a ceiling, attached behind the top of the proscenium with hinges, came down to hide all the other pieces of scenery waiting overhead. It took less than a minute for these switches to be made. The curtain had barely been lowered before it was whisked up again to reveal a new

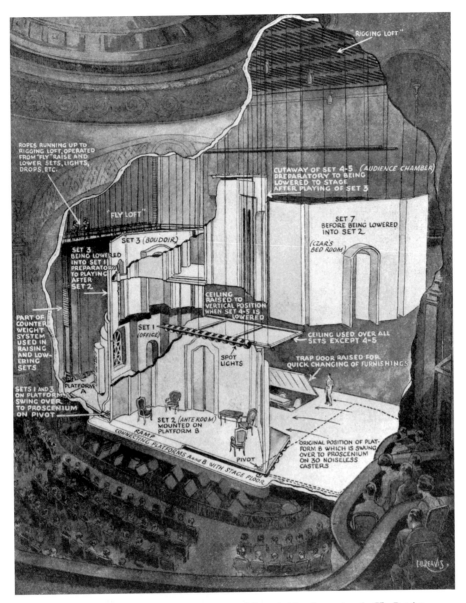

A diagram of the mechanism Bel Geddes used for switching the settings in *The Patriot* (also published in *Scientific American*, March 1928). Estate of Edith Lutyens Bel Geddes, Norman Bel Geddes Collection, Courtesy of the Harry Ransom Humanities Research Center.

Bel Geddes displaying a scale model of his prefabricated housing, from a 1941 advertising brochure (*above*). Scale models of the complete selection of prefabricated modular units necessary to erect one of Bel Geddes' low-cost houses (*opposite*). Estate of Edith Lutyens Bel Geddes, Norman Bel Geddes Collection, Courtesy of the Harry Ransom Humanities Research Center.

three-dimensional scene, in a bravura display of theatrical magic. The effect was so startling and realistic that reviewers enthused over the "enthralling" mobility of Bel Geddes' décor. The set attracted far more coverage than even the "gallant romanticism" of John Gielgud's Grand Duke Alexander.[6]

The mechanics Bel Geddes developed for staging *The Patriot* were so ingenious that *Scientific American* devoted an entire article to them.[7] Of course the heavy historical style of these settings was quite different from the modernistic simplicity of his mass-market housing. The completely prefabricated rooms of Bel Geddes' houses followed the same concept, however, and a later development of the designs even introduced comparable mechanisms to increase their flexibility.

Working with Raymond Hood in 1932–33, Urban had also created a "little house" that was standardized and could be built in different configurations. Their suburban design, although advanced for its time, seems very traditional in comparison with Bel Geddes' homes, with all houses sharing the same ground plan and only the function of the different spaces changing along with the external décor (numbers of windows, round or square, and so on).[8] In contrast, what Bel Geddes proposed was revolutionary. All elements of the homes he designed—both the individual rooms and the building materials—were modules, which could be fitted together in different ways

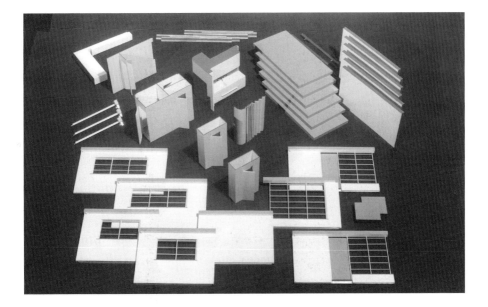

for a variety of living arrangements. The exterior walls and flat roof sections were manufactured in a "sandwich construction" of thin concrete sheets with an expanded steel core (to be filled with pipes, wiring, and insulation), while internal support was provided by the built-in cupboards that came as freestanding units. Bel Geddes' staff also developed specifications for complete prefabricated bathroom and kitchens with sinks, stoves, and cabinets as component parts of a single standardized unit.

The engineering firm of O'Brien-Fortin, which costed out Bel Geddes' designs in 1942, estimated a total of $3,220 per house—including stove, refrigerator, and bathtub—as compared to an average construction cost of $6,000–$8,000 for similar buildings at the time. Through Howard Hughes, whom he had interested in the project, Bel Geddes found a manufacturer: the Revere Company, for whom he wrote up specifications that it published in an illustrated booklet with the title *Better Living,* and his plans for prefabricated and flexible family housing were given extensive publicity, including front-page coverage in the *New York Times.*[9] By 1945 more than 800,000 copies had been distributed or requested from the company. The same unit housing designs also formed the basis of a national advertising campaign for Revere's brass and copper products. Several developers picked up on the idea, and orders were received for Milford, Connecticut (100 houses, from the New York builder Norman Winston), and the Washington, D.C., suburbs (3,500 houses, from McGovern construction—though it is unclear how many of these were actually erected).

In *Better Living* Bel Geddes emphasized that the high American standard of living was due to incorporating the latest scientific advances into the machinery of everyday life, and asked people to "Imagine a house with only 27 basic parts, which can be delivered at your building site in the morning and assembled into a finished home ready for you to move into by dinner time!"[10] In reality, during that first suburban boom prefabricated housing never reached the large-scale distribution needed to make it economically feasible. The general concept, however, as well as the look of these houses became widely adopted in suburban developments that expanded across the countryside after World War II, and Bel Geddes' designs for both houses and suburban layout certainly helped to set the standards for the homes of Middle America in the 1950s.

Bel Geddes continued to work on mass-produced home designs, exploring variously configured living arrangements and the possibilities for introducing machine-age elements. Between 1950 and 1953, he carried out time-and-motion studies of family occupations and developed a concept that he marketed under the trade name of "Expand-a-House." Echoing his interchangeable stage settings of more than twenty years before, though far simpler in operation as well as style, this unit had mechanically operated sliding walls and beds that folded up into cupboards, so that the bedroom walls could vanish into sockets in the walls of kitchen and bathroom, which were placed centrally and together formed the structural core of the house. Apart from these two relatively small rooms, the floor area could then be used for family activities, with the bedrooms and beds reappearing at the touch of a switch when needed. The designs were patented and a prospectus issued, but nothing came of this, perhaps because Bel Geddes tried to sell it as a franchise scheme instead of working with a manufacturing firm like Revere.[11]

Bel Geddes also proposed expanding the rudimentary trailers of the 1930s into "homes on wheels." The venture is interesting because of the light it throws on his hyperactive imagination, although he never took any steps to realize this particular vision. Among other things, a list of "Prophecies" he compiled for the J. Walter Thompson advertising agency in 1937 forecast double-wide trailers that would make it possible for a trailer to have "comfort equivalent to present-day housing." And, suggesting that up to 5 percent of the population might be living in such "moving homes," he anticipated there would be permanent sites around the country set up with facilities for them.[12] Mobile suburbs would match the mobility of American society, but the first trailer parks were still more than thirty years in the future. Similarly, even though Bel Geddes' concept of prefabricated housing was ahead of his time, with contemporary industrial techniques it has now become a practical option.

• • •

Bel Geddes was equally concerned with the positioning of houses on their lots to achieve private spaces within a limited area and to avoid monotony. Following up on *Better Living,* in the 1940s his design firm produced a book for the Rockefeller Institute on the layout of small towns and subdivisions.[13] This was hardly a new concern of city planners. Joseph Urban, working in collaboration with leading New York architects Wallace Harrison and Raymond Hood, had produced isometric drawings of neighborhood layouts in 1932. Its most famous manifestation was Frank Lloyd Wright's 1934 utopian proposal for Broadacre City, an expandable and endless suburbia dominated by the motorcar that he continued to develop until 1958. But the question of how suburbs should be organized gained extra urgency from the postwar housing shortage, which the Federal Housing Agency projected as being in the order of two and a half million units. As in Levittown, many of the postwar housing estates were laid out on the rigid grid plan that both Urban and Bel Geddes had attacked as soulless. Bel Geddes, however, demonstrated that curving roads linking residential crescents around cul-de-sacs, with houses angled and at staggered distances from the streets, allowed exactly the same number of units into a given area while maintaining a sense of privacy and variety. This kind of recommended lot layout, followed by some developers at the time, has become increasingly common.

Frank Lloyd Wright's continentwide vision was perhaps intended to be only inspirational. By contrast, Bel Geddes' book for the Rockefeller Institute was focused on immediate needs, and it led to a long-term relationship with Schine Theatrical Enterprises. The firm was still presided over by its founder, a colorful Russian immigrant who made his wealth from founding a chain of fifty-four movie houses and who had recently moved into the hotel business. In 1948–49 J. Myer Schine commissioned Bel Geddes to redesign a Los Angeles hotel, the Ambassador, and a commercial vacation development in Boca Raton, Florida.

Redesigning the main rooms of the Ambassador Hotel, Bel Geddes worked for a simplified and streamlined décor, with layered, subtly curving forms on the ceiling covering light fixtures. But he also added a new style of rental rooms: a row of double-level twin apartments that stretched in a sinuous line from the main hotel building to a new movie theater at the other end of the lot. In many ways the design for these apartments echoed his plans for suburban houses, even though they were built in a conventional way, instead of using modular construction. The hotel manager had protested (as frequently happened in the early stages of Bel Geddes' projects) that "some of the things he proposes are too drastic, expensive and visionary."[14] It was certainly not cheap. The renovation and expansion cost $2.5 million, a significant sum for those

Houses designed by Bel Geddes for Boca Raton (c. 1952) showing the
various combinations of styles and layouts achieved by his standardized approach.
House 3 exterior (*above*); House 3 ground plan (*opposite, top*);
House 11 ground plan (*opposite, bottom*). Estate of Edith Lutyens Bel Geddes,
Norman Bel Geddes Collection, Courtesy of the Harry Ransom Humanities Research Center.

days, though it does seem to have revived the Ambassador's profile and business, as
well as gaining significant media coverage and being hailed in the Los Angeles press.
The Boca Raton plan, based around Schine's flagship resort hotel—which had been a
money-losing private millionaires' club, founded by an eccentric and domineering ty-
coon who originally owned the whole township—was significantly more ambitious.

Joseph Urban had set the tone for Palm Beach, house by house, in the 1920s,
by his design for the Bath and Tennis Club on which the community centered, and
by the Sunrise shopping mall. Twenty years later, Bel Geddes' plans for Boca Raton
were broader in scope than Urban's, though directed further down the social scale
at middle-class consumers. At the same time he too was concerned with developing
a modern Florida architectural style, though he rejected Urban's Spanish colonial as
"excessively costly in today's terms" and called for wide expanses of windows and
the use of new building materials, to develop a new style based on "practicability
and economy." In a typically bold move, Bel Geddes produced a master plan for
the entire area. This (as he assertively wrote in his notes for the project) would

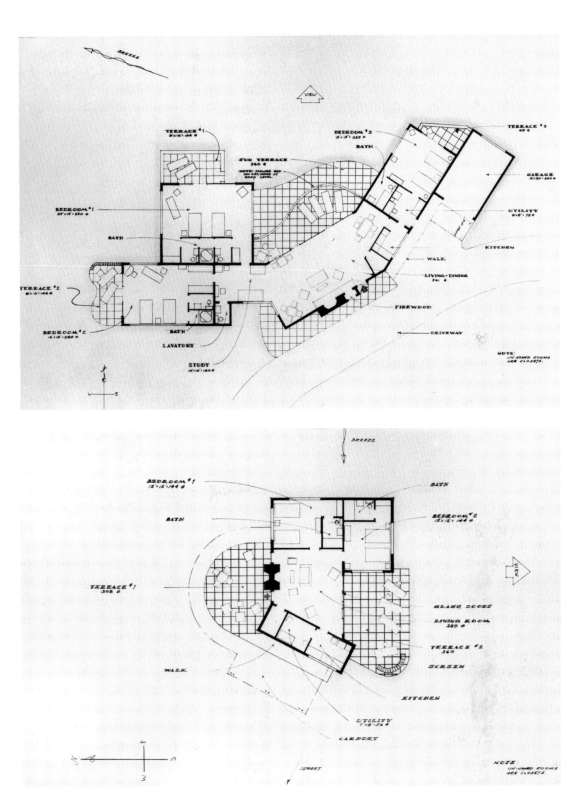

"provide the leadership in thought and planning so that their development will keep pace with ours."[15]

The new "Resort Colony" not only had cottages based on a slightly more elaborate version of his Housing Corporation of America model (Bel Geddes designed sixteen variations of size and ground plan), but also a shopping colonnade, a new sports area, and a roadside restaurant. A second, lower-cost hotel was also proposed, along with a yacht club. Modular in design, though not in construction, these cottages were high modern: flat roofs, with deep and at points curving overhangs shading walls of glass, simple columns, and a mix of concrete and contemporary sidings. Just as Urban had done earlier, these houses set a style of design that prevailed through the 1950s and 1960s, and is still common today.

For Bel Geddes, as a 1949 telephone conversation about publicity testifies, just as it was essential to "dramatize or dress up our little cookie" in order to get designs into *Life* or *Architectural Record,* so he objected to his design being called "just a house," specifically emphasizing that these Boca Raton dwellings had to be presented as "stage scenery" for a lifestyle.[16] The yacht club, whose sheer walls of glass overhung the water, with cantilevered flat roofs projecting above extensive decks in simple angular shapes, was even more clearly a modernist statement and very much the equivalent of a theater lobby advertising for contemporary America.

As for the existing town of Boca Raton, Bel Geddes designed a new town hall (incorporating the fire department, police station, and post office), hospital and professional office buildings, bus terminal adjoining the existing rail station, community auditorium, and recreational sports area. A new street layout was included, plus landscaping for the township. When these sweeping plans met resistance, he arranged for members of the town council to visit his recently opened Copa City entertainment complex, which conveniently was less than thirty miles away. The Boca Raton engineer responded, "I had no idea what could be done with basic materials as was done there—in fact that building is a revelation to a lot of people," and the council was won over.[17] Although by no means all of Bel Geddes' master plan was followed, enough elements were completed between 1949 and 1951 to change the face of the town. In addition to the cottages and restaurant, a new and relocated yacht club was built and the existing hotel was completely redesigned. Bel Geddes added a new wing, containing the colonnade of shops and an underground garage, terraces, and fountains.

Boca Raton attracted considerable interest, and as a direct result an international consortium commissioned Bel Geddes to design an even more elaborate resort in Spain. Yet however influential his town planning, however significant its long-term effect on the overall context in which the average American lived, however widespread his styling of their houses (still followed in general principle, despite changes in fashion), the work he and Urban did on the interiors of homes had still greater impact. Although I have followed their progress from redesigning society as a whole through the big things that determined the modern American society—cars and the highways built for them, the cityscape and public buildings—down to apartments and single-family homes, this by no means represents a chronological sequence.

Following their multifaceted imaginations and restlessly inquiring minds, they would focus on several of the different aspects of their modernist vision simultaneously, then—responding to the practical impetus of commercial commissions—switch to another selection, without completely abandoning any of their projects. It is true that Joseph Urban, in first establishing himself as an industrial designer, started small with fashions in clothing and décor for a tiny elite before expanding into increasingly larger architectural work. Yet from the beginning he was also making proposals for city planning. Bel Geddes, following in Urban's footsteps, was involved with both large- and small-scale work even in his earliest transfers from the stage to society. He created designs for whole cities side by side with women's jewelry, office buildings together with cars and refrigerators. And now the story—moving inward to individual experience—takes us to the level of private life. It is here, paradoxically, that Bel Geddes has had the most widespread, indeed worldwide, impact.

13

Lifestyle Begins in the Kitchen

CITIES MAY FRAME MODERN society, and high-rise apartments and suburban houses form the environment in which people live. But the kind of décor and furniture, the comforts and objects they surround themselves with in their homes, are what shape a particular lifestyle. Joseph Urban and Norman Bel Geddes were not alone in designing the beds and tables the American public chose to buy, any more than they had been with the clothes people wore. Even more than with fashion, furnishings come from many sources. Still, each of them helped to define the modern image inside the American home through designing a range of key products that served as catalysts for the new modern style.

Their inspiration, even in this most practical field, came, as with all their work, from the theater. Writing an introduction for the annual Architectural League exhibition in 1933, Urban commented on the way stage scenery reflects current architecture, and theatrical "properties" (like furniture) express the aesthetic values of the time. Singling out the movie settings on display as well as the costume drawings and models of stage interiors being exhibited, he further asserted that "theater very often takes the lead and points the way to artistic development in interior decoration and other allied arts."[1] And there is a close connection between his and Bel Geddes' Broadway and Hollywood settings, and their commercial work for furniture and fabric manufacturers. These designs for very ordinary household objects were possibly more influential than their large landmark architectural or urban-planning projects.

Urban's fame for interiors went back decades. Already with *The Rainbow Girl* in April 1918 theater reviewers noted that in presenting an "actual home" on the stage in place of his highly decorative but operatic palaces, Urban had taken on the role of "interior decorator." A wit in the *New York Morning Telegraph* even thought his scenery worthy of poetry:

> The Urban sets with beauty bloom,
> If art collectors chance to see
> That backdrop of a breakfast room,
> They'll start a raid on K & E.[2]

The comic notion that audiences might besiege the office of Broadway producers Klaw & Erlanger, like housewives at a department store sale, was not entirely far-fetched. Just three years later, in July 1921, *Architectural Review* discussed Urban's scenery for the *Ziegfeld Follies* as the source of a new style in interior design, singling out his use of color as affecting the way people decorated their homes.

On stage and off, Urban used a vibrant palette to establish a clear emotional tone in each room, corresponding to its function. Even in the black-and-white movies that he designed and directed for William Randolph Hearst, and later Fox, Urban tried to promote his sense of color by redesigning the system of lighting, confident that "the mind of the spectator can be made to think in colors even when they are not shown."[3] For a revue or a film set in modern times, his interior scenes were specifically intended as examples of a new style.

This was particularly clear in the movies he made, as with the radically simplified Art Nouveau home pictured in *The Young Diana* starring Marion Davies, which anticipates the characteristic look of the 1930s (though produced by Urban in 1922). The interiors in this film contained chairs and tables designed (like every detail of the sets) by Urban himself. These exact items were shortly to be manufactured by the Mallin Furniture Company, so that, having been to the movie, the audience could actually go out and buy the identical seat they had seen Marion Davies reclining on, or the bed she had been lying in. The same was true of the scenes Urban designed for Broadway. Home life was clearly intended to copy art.

Just as styles of dress encouraged specific activities so the way people outfitted their living quarters determined how they lived, conditioning personal attitudes as well as general social expectations. Urban's view (frequently expressed in newspaper interviews) was that the pace and outdoor emphasis of modern life required a new simplicity in décor, just as it did in residential architecture. Out with "the endless hangings and the depressing somberness" of the past, and with old-style furniture or anything imitated from elsewhere, he cried to the *Sunday Journal* in 1920. Such relics were as out of place in a modern American home as wearing a top hat with a sports jacket. As he often repeated: "We must create something of our own, something which belongs to us."[4]

Urban had already done several interiors for apartments in Vienna, including his own, before he left Austria for Boston in 1911. Strongly decorative in the Jugendstil manner, these were usually commissioned by patrons who had visited Urban's home for one of his parties (which were already famous), or seen his work in the art exhibitions of the Hagenbund.[5] By contrast, in America his style of home décor was quite different, and instead of being limited to personal example, it was the wider spread of images through theater or cinema that primarily attracted his clients. In more than one case, when people commissioned Urban to decorate rooms in their houses, they wanted a replica of what they had seen on Broadway.

His brilliant and fantastic sets for *The Garden of Paradise* in 1914 brought him his first interior design jobs. Similarly, toward the end of his career, the *Brooklyn Eagle* article on Urban in 1930 was illustrated with a montage of four photographs, all clearly interlinked: two of his recent stage sets, one of a reception room in William

The setting for a scene in *The Young Diana* (1922) showcasing Urban's chairs.
Joseph Urban Papers, Rare Book and Manuscript Library, Columbia University.

Examples from the Urban line of furniture
manufactured by the Mallin Company,
1924–25. Joseph Urban Papers, Rare Book
and Manuscript Library, Columbia University.

Randolph Hearst's house that Urban had designed, and the other showing one of the full-scale model rooms he had created for the Metropolitan Museum of Art's 1929 exhibition on "The Architect and the Industrial Arts."[6] The relationship between these photographs graphically demonstrates the influence of theatrical scenery on interior design. In Urban's hands they become interchangeable.

In exactly the same way, Bel Geddes also had been creating images of modern homes for the Broadway stage. These ranged from his scenery for smart comedies of contemporary life like the Shubert production of *He and She* in 1924 to his own plays about modern America, *The Rugged Individualist* in 1935 and *The Red Dress* in 1937. Like Urban, in many instances he not only designed the sets (wallpaper, curtains, color schemes) but also stage props: the beds, tables, and chairs. Several of these plays had been about forward-looking or fashionable characters, and it was a short step from that to designing modernistic furniture for the real houses that the audience lived in.

But where Urban's lushly colored scenery generally represented an idealized high society, and attracted mostly an elite clientele, Bel Geddes' plays were more likely to show the lives of ordinary people. This difference in social focus was reflected in the kind of home décor and furnishings each produced for the commercial market.

For example, a reviewer for *Theatre Magazine* recounted that a woman in the seat next to his at Urban's first *Ziegfeld Follies* production remarked, "That's an awfully nice kind of drapery." He concluded, somewhat patronizingly, that the *Follies* might not be such trivial entertainment after all, since "This woman's education was being advanced by the new colors and forms shown to her."[7] Four years later Urban was designing a whole line of modernistic textile patterns for Frank Silk Mills. Marketed as "Franco Prints," these echoed some of his *Ziegfeld Follies* designs and were widely used for drapes (as well as women's dresses, handbags, and shoes). Not only were they an expensive material—silk—they were rich in color, simply breathing luxury. He also created chintzes for upholstery and new styles of lace curtains for other manufacturers, while professional journals reported in 1931 that he was selecting window-shade designs for the entire trade.[8]

By contrast, when a decade later Bel Geddes turned to tablecloths and curtains, his designs were intended quite specifically to symbolize modernist concepts and contemporaneity, as well as popular appeal. In proposing a 1940 wallpaper patterned with penguins, he stressed that these "typify cleanliness, are comic little animals, and will be in the news shortly since Admiral Byrd has just arrived in the South Polar regions."[9] Still more modernistic in its material, this was vinyl wallpaper which, along with his tablecloths and curtains, was manufactured from a "revolutionary" Col-O-Tex plasticized material—by Columbus Coated Fabrics. In 1940 plastics were absolutely

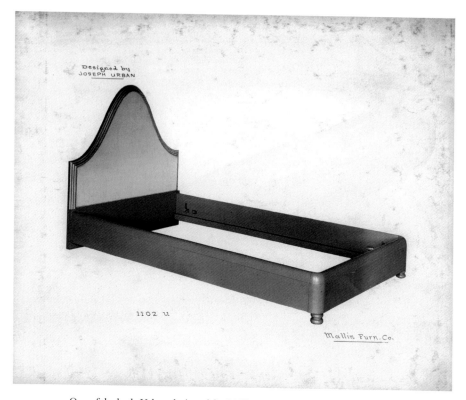

One of the beds Urban designed for Mallin, 1924–25. Joseph Urban Papers,
Rare Book and Manuscript Library, Columbia University.

the latest thing. When Du Pont introduced nylon, the world's first totally synthetic
fiber, in 1938, the announcement that it was made solely of coal, water, and air had
dazzled consumers. Tupperware, first invented in 1939 and made of polyethylene, was
to swamp suburbia with its ubiquitous parties of the 1950s. Rather than having the
associations with down-market cheapness they later came to acquire, these materials
were looked on as cutting-edge, "miracle" fibers. And Bel Geddes' preference for the
machine-age, mass-market qualities of plastic-coated cloths for dining tables or window coverings is typical of his vision. It also marks the development of the modernist
style over the twenty years since Urban had introduced it to America.

No piece of furniture could be more basic than a bed, and an even clearer example of the way Art Deco modernism evolved is the type of bed Urban and Bel
Geddes each designed. Urban's models for Mallin Furniture in the 1920s had radically simplified lines, while remaining sensuous. Made entirely of wood, the beds
featured headboards that either formed a single exaggerated curve or had veneers

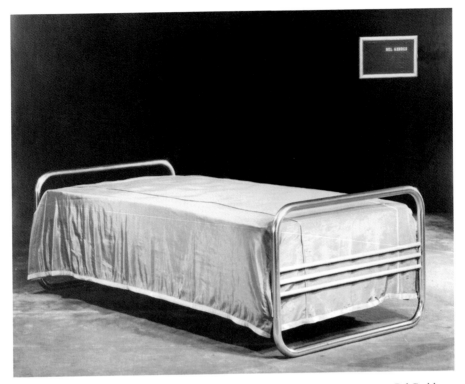

One of the beds Bel Geddes designed for Simmons, 1928–29. Estate of Edith Lutyens Bel Geddes, Norman Bel Geddes Collection, Courtesy of the Harry Ransom Humanities Research Center.

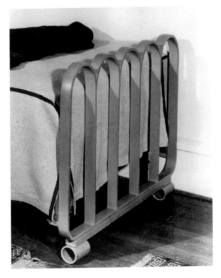

The footboard on one of Bel Geddes' beds for the Rome Bed Company, 1933–34. Estate of Edith Lutyens Bel Geddes, Norman Bel Geddes Collection, Courtesy of the Harry Ransom Humanities Research Center.

with sharply angular geometric patterns. Bel Geddes started out with still simpler types of beds in the late 1920s, manufactured by Simmons, at that time the largest bed-making company in the country. Deliberately undisguised steel or plastic, these bed frames represented extreme minimalism, while the range of models he designed for the Rome Bed Company (which reached stores in 1934) were expressions of the machine age. Bel Geddes quite consciously conceived of his design work as a single whole, with beds and cars following exactly the same aesthetic.[10] The curves of the bedstead were industrial, and the legs were made of small sections of steel pipe. The whole effect was a declaration of a stripped-down, efficient lifestyle. It was also highly popular: as the *Herald Tribune* commented in 1929, Bel Geddes' metal furniture was "known throughout the country."[11]

Both these wood and steel styles are in their own ways elegant, and both have a theatrical flourish that communicates a very specific and modern message. Although their cost was not all that different, Urban's beds have an aura of luxury, while Bel Geddes' make a statement of pure functionalism.

Urban was convinced that conditions of life in America during the 1920s were quite new—at least in cities like New York, which were at the forefront of social change—but that the way people lived had not yet caught up. As he put it in a 1930 interview: "We eat differently and more hastily; we have less leisure, and when we sit down we expect to jump up frequently to answer the telephone, to tend to some business or to do something else. Our tables, our dishes, our chairs and all our furniture should conform to this change in tempo."[12] He designed a complete range of household as well as office furniture with this in mind: semicircular armchairs, banded in black, with curving backs; desks with extremely plain clean lines, either finished in shiny black or covered with wood veneer in the same fractured geometry as some of his bed headboards; even carpets for the floors with a jagged mosaic of colors. Manufactured by the Baker Furniture Company as well as Mallin, these were distributed in stores across America.

This new type of furniture required an appropriate backdrop. Urban also designed the décor of complete apartments for people in Chicago and New York, as well as interiors for several houses, including Hearst's New York mansion, each of which was given extensive coverage in fashion and lifestyle magazines. As he had done previously in Vienna, when he first moved to New York he designed both the décor and all the custom-made furniture for his new family home at Yonkers—which was then featured in *Vogue* and *House and Garden,* among other journals.

At the time he was making over his cramped Victorian cottage, Urban was going through a messy divorce (tactfully never mentioned by the many articles about Urban's renovation), and his aim was to create a modern setting for his new American wife. Ripping out all the gingerbread moldings, he used thin painted strips outlining fake panels on the walls to give an impression of geometric austerity (which the reporters found severe, but highly original): black on white in the living room, white on black in the dining room, gold on gold in the music room. Above the shoulder-high paneling, walls and ceiling were painted shades of delicate gray. Elsewhere the tone was bright and light, with clear pastel colors, and in 1919 the impression was unusual. Every striking detail was reported. The window blinds (maroon); the sofa (with shelves built in along the back and arms on its rear to form a low bookcase on its outside, a piece that Urban was to repeat in designs for manufacturers and reuse elsewhere); the tight patterns of small flowers on the carpets he had specially made for the house.

Several articles also described his champagne lifestyle in these surroundings, consuming quantities of caviar and wine surrounded by four large, shaggy sheepdogs. Urban was careful to boast to the journalists, who all wrote about the color schemes and simplicity of the whole with enthusiasm and exclamation marks, that the entire renovation had cost him just five hundred dollars. Stressing "economical principles" and "novel artistic effects" (a combination highlighted by *Photo Journal* in a heavily illustrated report of December 1919) was a pretty plain way of saying that "Urban design" was open for business.[13]

Two particular apartments Urban designed, in 1929 and just before his death in 1933, show the way his American-modern style of décor evolved. One apartment, in Chicago, was commissioned by a lawyer (who had been involved with Urban's rede-sign of the Central Park Casino) for his sixteen-year-old daughter. Remembering in later life, she said that Urban had conceived her room as a fanciful setting for youthful happiness: "a girl is asleep on a hill looking down upon a flowered meadow."[14] It was a concept that might have come directly from the *Follies*. One of Urban's curving-backed beds was set on a raised semicircular dais with steps down to the floor, all carpeted with a tight floral pattern. Urban designed all the furnishings, complete with carpets, drapes, lamps, and built-in shelving. The light from the windows out onto the twenty-seventh-floor terrace—covered by thin blue, green, and yellow drapes, dotted in a schematic representation of trailing leaves—reflected off black lacquered bookcases, dressing table, or (in the study) writing desk. These elements were all built into shining black vitrolite walls.

The other apartment was designed for the sophisticated life of a New York so-cialite, the writer Katherine Brush. Two stories high, the living room presented an image of stark simplicity. Apart from one wall where there were two tall windows, which was painted dark blue to emphasize the shadow-effect of the light from out-side, all the surfaces and upholstery were sharp white. The carpet, square sides of

Urban's modern home décor: sketch shown at the American Design Exhibition, 1928 (*opposite, top*);
a Chicago apartment, with Mary Roberts in her bedroom (*above*), and her study (*opposite, bottom*),
1929. Estate of Edith Lutyens Bel Geddes, Norman Bel Geddes Collection,
Courtesy of the Harry Ransom Humanities Research Center.

the couches (again backed by low bookcases), and tables were all black. This was offset by touches of geranium red on one couch against a wall and the insides of the built-in bookshelves flanking it, in the window-drapes, and in big red squares woven into the carpet. Two large circular mirrors reflected each other on either side of the room. It was a domesticated equivalent of the Park Avenue Restaurant Urban had designed two years earlier, which used the same circular mirrors. Here, however, this stark modernism was deliberately contrasted with the two rooms that led off from the living area: a lemon-yellow and orange sunroom, and a striking circular study paneled at the bottom with green leather quilted in geometric squares, with polished redwood stretching above to a silver ceiling.

The décor of these apartments each garnered considerable publicity, with *House and Garden* headlining its illustrated piece "Katherine Brush Goes Completely Modern" (January 1933) and *Life* giving it a big spread.[15] Even three years later articles on this apartment were still appearing in journals like *Arts and Decoration* (August 1936), while Urban's design for the Chicago apartment was almost immediately hailed as a classic (its bedroom is now in the Cincinnati Art Museum).

The various rooms graphically illustrate the range within Urban's modernism, from delicate femininity to utilitarian elegance, and the clarity with which each room expresses its different function and the lifestyle of its inhabitants in an idealized form is intrinsically theatrical. Recognizing this, one commentator enthusiastically compared Katherine Brush's study, with its semicircular writing desk, to the kind of chief executive's office that might appear in a 1930s Hollywood extravaganza.[16]

There was another, far more directly influential occasion, where Urban's interior designs were specifically presented as stage settings, though not in the theater. This was at the "Architect and the Industrial Arts" exhibition held by the Metropolitan Museum of Art in 1929, where the main displays were a number of complete, full-sized "rooms." Two of these were by Urban, illustrating other intriguing variations on his simplified Art Deco modernism: a man's study with bold geometrical patterns and a glass-walled conservatory for a penthouse roof (see page 281).

Urban's influence on the way Americans furnished their homes spread widely during the 1920s and well into the 1930s. Through designs exhibited at the Metropolitan Museum of Art and in his own New York gallery-store, and popularized through magazines like *House and Garden,* he created a fashion for décor derived from the theater. Trade journals had always taken particular note of Urban's work. A 1920 issue of *Upholsterer and Interior Decorator* drew the connection between his stage props and furniture, while a 1921 issue of *Architectural Review* pointed out that the large number of stage designs in that year's Architectural League exhibition at the Metropolitan

The study in Katherine Brush's apartment, designed by Urban in 1933.
Joseph Urban Papers, Rare Book and Manuscript Library, Columbia University.

was "a striking recognition" of "the relation of stage settings to architecture." It also remarked on the need for interior designers to follow the way Urban's settings used "colors and forms to convey a message and create an atmosphere." Much the same commentary recurs in the *Magazine of Light* (illustrating his shades and blinds) or *Metal Arts* (featuring his interiors) in 1929–30. As the *New Yorker* said in 1931, "Until a few years ago the designers employed by manufacturers merely corrected the ugly lines created by machinery or stuck on meaningless decoration. The first break" into a unified design ethic where designers were brought into the process at the beginning, creating the "concept" for the object or machine to be manufactured "came ... under the aegis of Joseph Urban."[17] The same article stressed the importance of the theatrical connection, going on to point out that the popularity of Urban's work had made it common practice for manufacturers to employ leading young scene designers, and citing not only Bel Geddes' furnishings and kitchen equipment, but also a piano by Lee Simonson and silks by Robert Edmond Jones. It was a revolution, out of which came the modern lifestyle of America.

While Urban's dramatic use of color and sweeping shapes obviously owed much to Broadway, Bel Geddes' minimalism and strict functionalism were equally derived from his stage productions. Although mainly remembered for the hyperrealism of *The Miracle* or *Dead End,* in fact (as with his *Hamlet,* and even more modernistic in style, his setting for O'Neill's expressionistic *Lazarus Laughed*) the majority of his Broadway work was abstract or highly simplified. Perhaps the most successful of these shows was his 1930 version of *Lysistrata,* which ran for more than three hundred performances, setting an all-time record for a Greek classic on Broadway. The scenery consisted of a great sweep of stairs, rising to a row of four plain pillars, between rugged-sided platforms. These were colored nonrepresentationally, with reds shading into grays, blues, and yellows. Yet the New York reviewers unhesitatingly identified these minimalist shapes with "a high pitched acropolis" or "the ancient Greek amphitheatre," as well as immediately classifying the effect specifically "modernistic." Hailed as "a triumph of simplicity," Bel Geddes' *Lysistrata* won particular praise from Raymond Hood (the architect who had collaborated with Urban on plans for a new Metropolitan Opera building) as "the *best* stage pictures I have *ever* seen" because they were so "architecturally impressive."[18] As Bel Geddes had written of contemporary industrial design in general in 1928: "The new school [of theatrical designers, in which he counted himself as the leader] worked in terms of light and form and colors. They built settings that had duplicates nowhere except in their own minds. In many important respects modernistic furniture, as it is known today, is a utilitarian expression of their stage designs."[19]

Like Urban, Bel Geddes continued to design furniture for the American home

Bel Geddes' modernist stage setting for *Lysistrata*, Broadway, 1930.
Estate of Edith Lutyens Bel Geddes, Norman Bel Geddes Collection,
Courtesy of the Harry Ransom Humanities Research Center.

throughout his career. *Ladies' Home Journal* and *Reader's Digest* both carried long illustrated articles in 1931 on the style of interior décor and furnishings that would be suited to the "House of Tomorrow" he had designed. This was all as modernist as its flat roof and curving walls. Bel Geddes was already designing machine-age steel-tube chairs for Simmons, and the same kind of simplified shapes, with any styling directly related to function, reappear in the chesterfields and armchairs he did for Valley Upholstery in 1947.

Between them, Bel Geddes and Urban carried their modernist ethic into the smallest details of people's lives. Urban had designed colorful candy boxes, and even modern typefaces for printing. In 1929, Hartman Trunks employed him to create the fabrics and decorative finishes for a line of suitcases and bags, and Bel Geddes followed suit in 1945, designing the first luggage made out of plastics. Bel Geddes also created plastic bar trays and soap dispensers that appeared on people's kitchen counters and in their bathrooms, as well as a whole line of knick-knacks and decorative

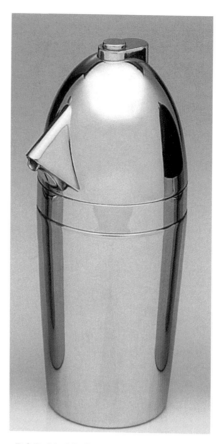

Bel Geddes' Soda King siphon bottle, 1938.
Estate of Edith Lutyens Bel Geddes,
Norman Bel Geddes Collection,
Courtesy of the Harry Ransom
Humanities Research Center.

objects—modernistic copper and brass trays, electric lamps, candlesticks, cigarette boxes and ashtrays, streamlined soda siphons, the Manhattan tray, Skyscraper cocktail shaker, and metal goblets (all now museum pieces: see page 11)—that adorned the coffee tables and mantelpieces of the nation. He even carried modernist design through leisure activities. Surrounded by all these in their homes, people could have been playing a board game based on horseracing that Bel Geddes patented in 1932.

But Bel Geddes' major impact came through the home appliances he designed. Writing on the 1939 World's Fair for the *New York Times,* H. G. Wells observed, "half the gadgets in a modern home are made of stuffs unheard of in 1900. At present only the gadgets. But the rest of our dwelling places will follow."[20] One of the exhibits he had in mind was the Frigidaire showroom that was part of Bel Geddes' Futurama display.

New materials like plastics and aluminum not only made radical new structures possible, but also demanded new styling that expressed their innovative qualities, and nowhere did this have more impact on everyday life than in the kitchen. By the early 1930s Bel Geddes was already involved in designing stoves and refrigerators, applying the same principles as with his houses and furniture: "simplicity, freedom from intricate decoration, reliance upon the beauty of form" and "in tune with our ever progressing civilization," as he had expressed it to *Ladies' Home Journal* in January 1931. His stoves for the Standard Gas Equipment Company were truly revolutionary. Designed in 1932 and patented in 1933, they remained the standard into the 1970s, and (with very minor modifications) the same shape and structure still survives in the average stove today.

The market leader at the time was the Magic Chef, a square box on tapering legs, introduced by the American Stove Company in 1929–30. But the front surface and lid of this was marbleized in imitation of a living-room cabinet, with elaborate drawer pulls. The stoves Bel Geddes produced just two years later for SGE—in a sharp contrast that he pointed out in his book *Horizons*—were entirely of flat white enamel with rounded corners and straight chrome handles on a solid base.

Up till then stoves (and fridges) had been heavy sheet or cast iron because the surfaces were structural. Glossy enamel could not be welded or even screwed in place (the fragile surface would crack) and so could not bear weight. To gain the new, clean lines he envisaged, Bel Geddes came up with a completely new type of construction, which he compared to a skyscraper in miniature: an independent steel frame, onto which the thin enamel skin was attached with hooked clips (invented by Bel Geddes himself), which were formed of bends in the edges of the metal sheets that fit into one another via slots. Bel Geddes went on to do very similar stoves for Philco in 1933. Other manufacturers immediately adopted all the elements of this design, and it remains the way stoves and refrigerators are made.

In addition, Bel Geddes streamlined the production process. SGE had been manufacturing about one hundred models in various sizes and configurations, each with different sized broilers and ovens. Bel Geddes simplified this by devising standard modules, all of which were interchangeable: three sizes of broiler, five sizes of utility drawer, a single oven, and so on. The result was "a cooking machine," and one that undersold the competition.

In 1932 Bel Geddes designed his first refrigerator, for General Electric, which employed the same manufacturing principles. Until then the Monitor type was standard, with its cooling coils exposed on the top. Bel Geddes began with a simplified

The Magic Chef gas stove, designed by the New York School of Fine and Applied Art, 1929 (*above*);
Bel Geddes' SGE stove, 1932 (*opposite*). Estate of Edith Lutyens Bel Geddes,
Norman Bel Geddes Collection, Courtesy of the Harry Ransom Humanities Research Center.

model of the Monitor, but in the same year produced a prototype for GE that (as he
proudly claimed) was the first to have hidden coils. Two years later, in 1934, Raymond
Loewy followed with the Sears Coldspot, a very similar design which he too claimed
to be the first refrigerator to have its mechanism concealed. With Sears, Roebuck
marketing it into every corner of the United States, this model immediately became
the industry standard. But to claim, as Loewy later did in his book *Industrial Design*,
that his was the earliest, or that this "classic case history of industrial design applied

to mass production marks the beginning of the profession in America" is misleading, to say the least.[21] Bel Geddes' stoves had already set the streamlined design and
construction technique, while both he and Urban had been employed as industrial
designers for more than a decade previously.

   Loewy and Bel Geddes continued to dominate the design of refrigerators—the
largest and most obvious appliance in any modern kitchen—with Bel Geddes producing models for Frigidaire and Electrolux during the 1930s. These were the appliances

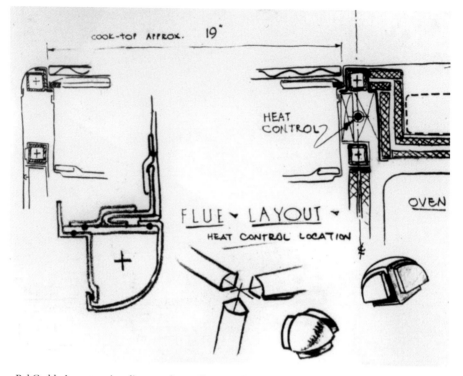

Bel Geddes' construction diagrams for appliances. The new technique for joining aluminum sheets (*above*); interchangeable modules for SGE stoves (*opposite*). Estate of Edith Lutyens Bel Geddes, Norman Bel Geddes Collection, Courtesy of the Harry Ransom Humanities Research Center.

on display in the GE exhibit that the "time-travelers" saw at the end of the Futurama ride at the 1939 World's Fair (see page 138). His role as an innovator is clear in his patents for the construction of the casing and mechanism of the hidden door hinges and the handle, the layout of interior shelving, plus the design of the back-mounted cooling coils. In the 1940s he created still more streamlined shapes for the Nash-Kelvinator refrigerator, one even placing the freezer next to the cooler compartment, rather than above, with double doors of unequal size as in today's top-of-the-line models.

White, as Bel Geddes noted in *Horizons,* is universally accepted as the most sanitary color; and his concern for unity in design led from the glossy white enamel of stoves and refrigerators to kitchens as a whole. Bel Geddes insisted that the kitchen cupboards should be white, too, and in modules echoing the proportions of the appliances. The result was the "white kitchen," a clean, state-of-the-art center, which, as *Fortune* noted (reacting with some ambivalence to his "House of Tomorrow") would be as antiseptic as a hospital in its "porcelain and surgical white."[22] And already in the Frigidaire display at the New York World's Fair, Bel Geddes designed a model

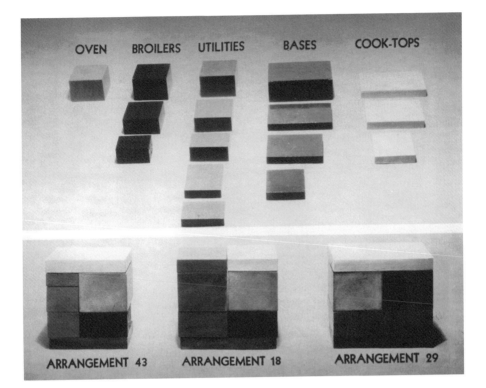

kitchen that flowed into a sitting area, anticipating the family room of today. Apart from the traditional farmhouse, where the kitchen table was where people ate, kitchens had been separated from the living areas in the home. As in Urban's Yonkers house, the kitchen was frequently located in the basement. Now it could become a focus for family life.

This is a case where the design of a machine had a truly revolutionary impact. It relocated the center of activity from the (male-dominated and formal) reception rooms at the front of a house to the far more family-oriented housewife's area at the back. If it is hard to credit such a far-reaching effect simply to styling, consider that Bel Geddes based his designs on extensive public surveys. Whatever the project, he started with customer sampling (the first industrial designer to use this now standard technique). For instance, in coming up with the concept for the stove, which the SGE trade journal publicized in 1932 as "typical of the three-dimensional quality of the new industrial design," he and his staff interviewed 1,200 "representative women users." The same article also, significantly, paid tribute to the way his stage experience made the simplicity of design so expressively modern, calling Bel Geddes "unique in the thoroughness of his approach, in his *theatrical* gestures."[23] In a 1933 issue, which hailed the new gas

Bel Geddes' modern refrigerator for Electrolux, c. 1935. Estate of Edith Lutyens Bel Geddes,
Norman Bel Geddes Collection, Courtesy of the Harry Ransom Humanities Research Center.

The completely white kitchen in the Frigidaire exhibit for the 1939 New York World's Fair at the GM Building. The refrigerator (also by Bel Geddes) is basically the same as the one he designed for Servel in 1934, and his stove is a variation on his 1932 design for SGE. The tubular steel chairs and table were also designed by Bel Geddes. Estate of Edith Lutyens Bel Geddes, Norman Bel Geddes Collection, Courtesy of the Harry Ransom Humanities Research Center.

ranges as having "the smooth, sweeping lines of a skyscraper, divested of all gadgets, sharp corners," SGE pointed out that Bel Geddes' design was the "starting point for the future evolution of all kitchen equipment."[24] Indeed the public interest was so widespread that, as the advertising manager of SGE commented, no other stoves "manufactured in the last twenty years can have received as much free advertising combined as this Geddes model."[25] He cites articles in *House and Garden, American Home, Arts and Decorations, Stylist, American Builder, Fortune, Better Homes and Gardens,* even *Field and Stream.* Five years later, in 1937, these stoves were still being

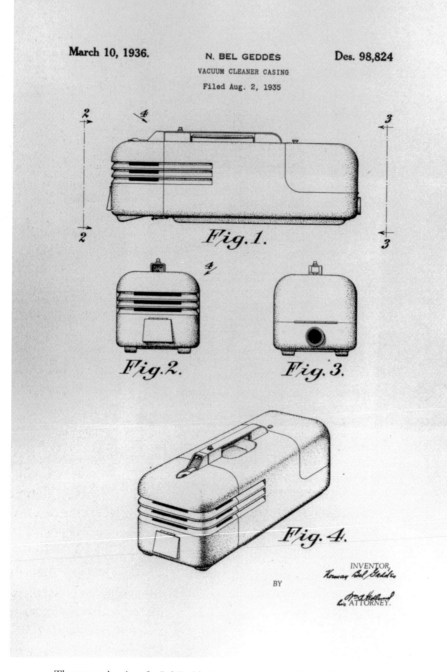

The patent drawings for Bel Geddes' vacuum-cleaner casing for Electrolux, 1936.
Estate of Edith Lutyens Bel Geddes, Norman Bel Geddes Collection,
Courtesy of the Harry Ransom Humanities Research Center.

singled out as the prime example of the changed relation between form and function introduced by the newly recognized profession of industrial designer.[26]

Stoves, fridges, and kitchens, while certainly the most central, were by no means the only things in the woman's household domain through which Bel Geddes influenced home life. He redesigned vacuum cleaners for Electrolux (which he patented in 1936) and RCA (1944), for which he also designed a washing machine, as well as electric radiators. As his 1934 report for Electrolux shows, although the external design of such appliances was primarily to create an "impelling visual appeal" through "an *impression* of . . . modern simplified efficiency," Bel Geddes was equally concerned with their internal operation (for example, "improving efficiency of air passage through the suction system" of the vacuum cleaner).[27]

These models are closely related to the home appliances manufactured worldwide today. Following in his footsteps, Loewy added designs for the Frigidaire chest-freezer and various other appliances, including a room air-conditioner and a cream separator, while Henry Dreyfuss contributed the Ingraham alarm clock and the upright Hoover vacuum cleaner. Between them, with Loewy picking up where Bel Geddes left off and projecting his designs into the 1970s, Urban and Bel Geddes designed the home life of the average American family during the period when modern American culture was at its prime, and on to the present.

However significant the streamlined styling and modular variations in appliances and living spaces, the low-slung cars and multilane highways, creating the objects and physical environment was not in itself enough to shift the way people conceived their lives. Urban and Bel Geddes had to turn their theatrical flair to publicizing their new vision if it was to reach the "tipping point."[28] Futurama had been immensely compelling, yet communicating what it meant to be modern was a continuing challenge for both designers. They had to sell the lifestyle they were envisaging, to spread its image as widely as possible, if America was to adopt it.

14

Selling Modernity

HOWEVER STANDARD THEY may seem to our eyes today, the modernistic beds, undecorated stoves, and streamlined household objects that Joseph Urban and Norman Bel Geddes created must have looked radically novel, even out of place, when they first appeared. Both designers quickly realized the need to provide a modern context for their wares. Because the store window was still the main venue for advertising merchandise in the 1920s, marketing displays in stores were among the earliest commercial projects each took up.

In 1922 Urban was restyling counter and window displays for various store chains. He transformed these into stage settings for the merchandise, and this theatrical ambience is by no means merely metaphorical, as Urban included scenic pieces (even a stage curtain from his *Ziegfeld Follies* of the previous year in one Lyon and Healey storefront) and used stage lighting. Placing a mannequin in modern clothing by a few selected pieces of furniture, backed by an eighteen-foot-high curving screen (doubling for a stage cyclorama) and flanked with an oversize reproduction of an icon art object—a Klimt painting or a Paul Manship sculpture or a Clarence White photograph—he created symbolic evocations of an idealized lifestyle. Framed by an arch placed diagonally across the corner, which acted as a proscenium, such "scenes" presented his fabrics and furnishings as the epitome of modern living.

In the standard store window of the early 1920s, merchants crammed as much as they could, with little attempt to arrange it artistically. Furniture was arranged separately in one window, clothes (on dressmakers' headless dummies) or rows of shoes (on small stands) by themselves in another. Urban's vivid pictures were striking in comparison to what they replaced, and his concept was widely copied in store windows all along the Main Streets of America.

In other hands, however, the backgrounds tended to overwhelm the merchandise, and turned into clichéd theme scenes (a typical example being "the Gift Spirit of Christmas" in one Fifth Avenue window display, where mannequins draped with pearls appeared in a classical Greek interior). For Bel Geddes, already inspired by streamlining, this was merely anachronistic clutter of another sort. A new statement of the modern lifestyle was needed. So when in 1927 George Simon, who had been impressed by the sweeping but simple scenes for his Broadway show *Arabesque* just over a year earlier, invited Bel Geddes to redo the displays for the Franklin Simon store on Fifth Avenue, the designer set out to create images of striking minimalism.

In an early version of his flexible modular construction for gas stoves, he created interchangeable panels and units with a variety of textures (metal, glass, fabric) and colors (yellow, blue, and red, each in twelve shades) constructed in four standard sizes. These could be put together as pyramids, a flat wall, or a curving screen, while texture and color was selected to contrast or harmonize with the hats, shoes, or perfume bottles on display. The window displays followed the combinations Bel Geddes had worked out on a large-scale model of the storefront in his design offices, which were card-indexed so that the store personnel could change the setup easily and at minimal cost. Bel Geddes also produced a completely new style of mannequin. Eliminating the realistic wax figures usual at that time, he had glass mannequins made to display clothing (which could be illuminated from within to reveal the delicacy of lingerie) and semiabstract heads of gleaming metal for hats and scarves.

The unity of treatment and background, and the simplification or transparency of the human effigy, together with a system of spotlights that Bel Geddes borrowed from his stage shows, particularly impressed *Display World,* which gave a special review of Franklin Simon's new window treatments in January 1928. Theatricality infused the whole design: as Bel Geddes put it in his "Job History" for the project, "the store window is really a stage on which the merchandise are the actors."[1] As with theatrical stars who shine brightest with a small cast surrounding them, he severely limited the number of objects on display. One large window, for instance, contained only a glass platform, carrying a single handbag, together with a single brightly colored and sharply lit hat and scarf on an aluminum bust. The sight literally stopped traffic. As Bel Geddes noted with considerable glee, pedestrians flocked across Fifth Avenue and the crowds around the window grew so dense that (according to Bel Geddes' account) the police had to call out reserves to prevent them from blocking the street.

Believing this event might have been a fluke, after a few weeks Bel Geddes repeated it—and found the result much the same. Crowds gathered; drivers stopped their cars to gawk. His designs were so successful that he was rehired by Franklin Simon to extend them in 1928, and again in 1929. And (as Bel Geddes wryly noted) within barely three months of unveiling his first displays, all the store windows on Fifth Avenue had changed to follow his lead. His Franklin Simon displays were the start of the modern simplified trend in store advertising.

The transition is neatly illustrated by a *Women's Wear Daily* article on the new display methods in leading New York stores in 1928. Windows that year showed a radical change: everywhere they were filled with "livable" or symbolic scenes.[2] Lord and Taylor and Wanamaker were specializing in nooks of rooms that "the well bred woman will recognize as a hint of a room she knows," in the style set by Joseph Urban. Arnold Constable and McCreary offered more fanciful scenes like "Lindbergh's Flight" (with silhouettes of the plane and mannequins costumed like the aviator) or "the City of Tomorrow" (reflecting Bel Geddes' Shell Oil film in terms of the futuristic science-fiction fad of the period) as illustrations of the way Urban's trendsetting ideas on merchandise display were being interpreted by his followers. At the same time, other stores (such as Saks) were singled out for their minimalist abstraction:

A typical Franklin Simon window in 1927, before Bel Geddes' designs were introduced (*above*); one of Bel Geddes' window treatments for Franklin Simon using the panels and special units, which stopped traffic on Fifth Avenue (*opposite*). Estate of Edith Lutyens Bel Geddes, Norman Bel Geddes Collection, Courtesy of the Harry Ransom Humanities Research Center.

an asymmetrical "disregard of the traditional balance in window displays" (to the reporter's evident surprise) with shining aluminum heads on the mannequins and features reduced to just one or two curves—clear signs of Bel Geddes' influence.

Installing new styles of window display, of course, was cheap. But it also led to changing the entire appearance of the shop, giving a new feel to the shopping experience. Shortly after his Lyon and Healey success, Urban was commissioned to do a complete makeover of the huge Kaufmann department store in Pittsburgh, for which he provided high American Modern designs, with an entryway like a brightly lit theater marquee. Then in 1928 he was commissioned to remodel Bedell's, a women's clothing store on 34th Street in New York.

Reshaping everything from the street façade to the elevators, Urban turned the whole building into an extended window display. Using the same gleaming black vitrolite on the outside that he had proposed for the Reinhardt Theatre, and replacing all the street-level walls (apart from the doorway in the center) with showcase windows through which the whole ground floor could be seen, he created so distinctive an image that no trademark was needed. Bedell's became the only store in New York without its name on the outside. Instead, high up on a lacelike black glass and silver metal grill curving out above the main entrance, and integrated into its frilly pattern, were women's silhouettes forming a frieze of changing fashions through the nineteenth century. It dominated the block, forming an unmistakable trademark. As Urban observed in an article for *American Architect,* because advertising and architecture were the two quintessentially American art forms, any modernist building should be "the sandwich board of its owner."[3]

The front façade of the Bedell store on 34th Street, designed by Joseph Urban, 1929.
Joseph Urban Papers, Rare Book and Manuscript Library, Columbia University.

Walking in through the two-story circular lobby formed by this silver grill, customers found themselves in a vestibule occupying over one-third of the ground floor,
enclosed by arcades of plate-glass showcases—just like the window displays facing
out into the street. The cases had glass backs, so that both they and the store windows
could also be viewed from inside the store. Lights shining down through translucent
top panels brightly illuminated each glass case—and the clothes, some of which would
have been inspired by Urban himself, or cut from cloth he had designed. The only
decoration came in silver fanlike fluted tops to the black vitrolite columns supporting
the ceiling and in the elevators, which were given mesmerizing geometric surrounds
and had jewellike flower paintings on shining black lacquer covering their interiors.
Together with the filigree grill above the main entry, these supplied accents of frivolous luxury. The whole building became a glossy and elegant image of high fashion
in which consumers, seeing each other through the glass cases along with the mannequins inside, were very much part of the display.

Bedell's also influenced the whole concept of retail marketing, and the way people went about one of the most popular American pastimes, shopping. Described and illustrated by every major architectural journal, Urban's design for the Bedell Company was hailed as distinctively "modern," a specifically "American" model for other stores, and its showcase lobby also clearly inspired other architects.[4] One was Morris Lapidus, who gained the reputation of having revolutionized retailing through the stores he designed for retail chains during the 1930s and into the 1940s—Postman's, Bond clothing, Kay Jewelers, Barton candy—exploiting what he liked to call the moth complex. Their entryways led the pavement deep inside the stores, lined with eye-level illuminated display cases that ran continuously across the street front and on each side along the walls to the doors. Lapidus (who was studying architecture at Columbia when the Bedell store opened) had wanted to become a stage designer, and he used bold colors and sweeping curves in his shops, just like Urban.

Bel Geddes, too, produced store plans and window displays for all Beck Shoe stores across the United States in 1942, which were similar to those Lapidus was designing. But far more striking were the venues Bel Geddes created in 1946, combining shopping and entertainment. The one that received the most publicity because of its novel construction techniques was Copa City in Florida, where the only dividing partitions in the huge space were sinuously curving plate-glass screens that formed boutique display cases. Outfitted with Bel Geddes–designed furniture and fittings, these separated the main dinner-dance and performance area from the entryway and from the clublike studio (see pages 95–97). As in Urban's foyer at the Bedell store, the display cases were specifically designed so that the Copa customers could see straight through, so that the clothing and accessories of the new lifestyle on sale framed the public activities on either side.

On a still larger scale, Bel Geddes redesigned the Commonwealth Edison Building in Chicago to create a street-level showroom (where the first display installed was an exhibition of his own industrial designs). A continuous wall of glass was flanked on the outside by a line of slim columns forming an exterior arcade all round the building (which occupied an entire city block). The open-plan interior contained both showrooms and a TV studio visible to passersby, turning the whole ground floor into a giant advertising venue. It also effectively symbolized Bel Geddes' concept of modernity in its brightness and transparency, as well as in its apparent repeal of the laws of gravity through the impression that there was nothing holding up the whole massive weight of the upper floors of the building.

Here Bel Geddes was following Urban's guiding principle that the function of any building should be expressed in its architecture. The Bedell store was a triumphant demonstration. In addition to a building's purpose, however, Urban also took its

Joseph Urban's double-sided showcase foyer in the Bedell store, 1929 (*above*).
Joseph Urban Papers, Rare Book and Manuscript Library, Columbia University.
Bel Geddes' foyer in Copa City, with its curving glass walls separating the entry, studio,
and dining/dance space, 1946 (*opposite*). Estate of Edith Lutyens Bel Geddes,
Norman Bel Geddes Collection, Courtesy of the Harry Ransom Humanities Research Center.

location into account. What suited sophisticated Manhattan would be out of place in Florida. So another store Urban built in Palm Beach was given a quasi-Spanish style, with tiled roofs and an open, arched entryway, like the Bath and Tennis Club and the various mansions he was building there around the same time.

But rather than a single building, this Florida store of Urban's, the Sunrise Building, occupied a complete block on the outskirts of Palm Beach and contained more than twenty stores, anchored by a movie theater. Designed in 1925, it was a prototype for a whole new lifestyle, and eventually for the modern shopping mall. The innovation that makes the Sunrise Building such a key development on the American architectural scene is Urban's combination of shopping and entertainment, with audiences for the screen becoming customers for the stores, and shoppers being given a reason beyond immediate purchases to spend time at the mall. This was almost immediately picked up and became standard by the time of Bel Geddes' Copa City just over twenty years later.

Approaching the Paramount movie theater in the Sunrise complex, spectators had to pass through the arcade and patio of stores, the whole ambience being designed (as Urban noted in his book *Theatres*) "to invite loitering" and window-shopping. Although the Bedell store—and the similar entrance grill that Urban's firm later provided for Bonwit Teller on Fifth Avenue—are no longer there (the Bonwit Teller

The prototype shopping mall: one of Urban's elevations for the Sunrise Building,
looking down into the curving interior patio, 1925. Joseph Urban Papers,
Rare Book and Manuscript Library, Columbia University.

building was demolished to make way for Trump Tower), the Sunrise Building was restored in the late 1980s. The movie theater is now a department store, its cool green and silver murals of fantastic fish and waving fronds of seaweed stripped away.[5] Yet, even if small in comparison with contemporary suburban shopping malls, Urban's overall design is still very much a modern one.

Stores and shopping malls were, of course, not the only retail outlets. Outside the cities the Sears catalogue ruled, and Bel Geddes was involved in this kind of shopping too, not only through his menial work as a young draftsman, though that experience would have made him acutely aware of the problems of this type of direct marketing. Now in the mid-1930s he set out to bring the look and feel of print advertising into his vision of the modern world. First redesigning the format and typography for Montgomery Ward's mail-order catalogues, he turned his attention to the kind of marketing that appeared in journals and magazines. In 1939 he undertook a major restyling of advertisements in Cromwell-Collier publications, among them the leading lifestyle glossies *Women's Home Companion, Collier's,* and *The American Magazine.* Their circulation reached 2.25 million households, and Bel Geddes came up with eye-catching new ways of presenting visual ads that shouted modernity—and produced a gain in circulation of more than 70,000 over the previous year.

In place of advertising images printed on pages separate from the text, his layouts integrated words and picture, using the double spread of the opened magazine as his basic unit. At its simplest, a single drawing or photograph would appear across the bottom half of two facing pages, automatically drawing the attention of anyone reading the text in the top halves. Other more imaginative layouts recognized that the eye subliminally completes an interrupted line or fills in the gap between two areas of color. These included a "zigzag spread" with text printed over the picture in a square block on the bottom outside left of one page and another on the top outside right of the next, leaving a band of uninterrupted picture all the way up on both sides of the central fold, or a "strip spread" where the upper third of a picture covered the top section of two facing pages and the lower third appeared at the foot of both pages, with a band of text across the middle. Bel Geddes labeled these "heroic" ads, because even though broken up by blocks of "story," in each case the image was double the size of the standard full-page picture. Then there was the "bookmark" double-page foldout, and even an "animated spread," where a continuous series of pictures ran across the top of a left-hand page, on over the whole of the next two pages, and across the bottom of the fourth (right-hand) page.

Such novel layouts were quite striking at the time. Bel Geddes created an entire advertising campaign for Cromwell-Collier, addressed to advertisers, which linked *The American Magazine* with this "revolutionary contribution to advertising." He went on to redesign the layout and typography for various trade publications like *Think* and even *Business Machines.* Significantly, he associated the innovation and its popularity with "that discontent with status quo which has made this the most progressive nation on earth."[6] Offering flexibility as well as versatility, and attracting interest by changes in visual pace, these formats rapidly became standard for the magazine industry.

Being directly involved in advertising, and indeed in the advertising of advertising, was nothing new for Bel Geddes. Ten years earlier one of his first architectural ventures had been designing offices for an advertising agency, J. Walter Thompson. Using a color scheme of greens and gray, with vertical strips of brass and black vitrolite to accentuate the height of the rooms (particularly in a two-story conference hall), he created an image of sharp but elegant modernity. (Black vitrolite, Urban's favorite material, had become closely identified with American Art Deco.) Every detail from chairs and tables to ashtrays, all designed by Bel Geddes, contributed to a unified effect that seemed so much like a stage setting it was reviewed by *Theatre Arts*

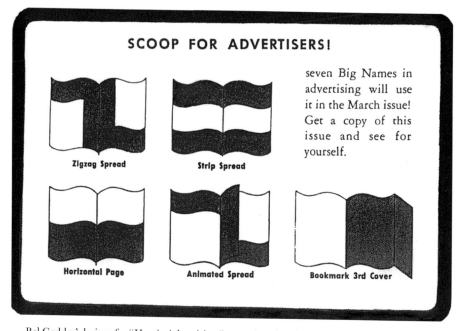

SCOOP FOR ADVERTISERS!

Zigzag Spread

Strip Spread

seven Big Names in advertising will use it in the March issue! Get a copy of this issue and see for yourself.

Horizontal Page

Animated Spread

Bookmark 3rd Cover

Bel Geddes' designs for "Heroic Advertising," 1939. An advertisement for the new ad layouts in a brochure put out by Cromwell-Collier illustrating the various "heroic" formats (*above*); mock-up of a "ZigZig spread" flowing over two pages of text (*opposite*). Estate of Edith Lutyens Bel Geddes, Norman Bel Geddes Collection, Courtesy of the Harry Ransom Humanities Research Center.

Monthly in 1929 as a quintessential expression of "the power and drama of the large modern advertising agency," and led to an article in the *New York Times* captioned "The Decorator as a Minister of Trade."[7] It was also remarkably similar in some of its lines to the New School for Social Research, which Urban was designing at the same time.

Far more significantly, Bel Geddes also took a hand in developing the sort of brand images, now so central in marketing, which encapsulated modernity in their simplified shapes or streamlined lettering. After working with Firestone on the first puncture-proof tire in 1935, Bel Geddes persuaded company executives that the firm needed a distinctive logo and lettering for its name—which he then provided. When Hire's Root Beer was founded, Bel Geddes designed not only their trademark but also a distinctive shape of bottle and the entire advertising campaign to launch their product.

Together and in competition with Raymond Loewy, he went on to design a range of logos and packaging in the 1940s. In 1940 Loewy created a new look for Lucky Strike cigarette packaging; in 1941 Bel Geddes was designing cigarette vend-

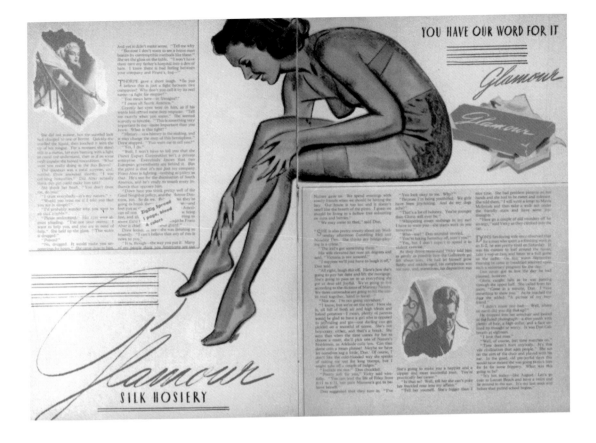

ing machines for the U-Need-a-Pack Company as well as the Rowe Manufacturing Corporation. Bel Geddes designed the logo, packaging, and ads for Sunshine Biscuits. Loewy did the same for the Nabisco conglomerate. Bel Geddes provided the corporate image for IBM, giving a coherent look to their front offices, products, and delivery. And so on.

It was the start of the trademark revolution in consumer culture. Brand logos, together with vibrant packaging and a unified image, became more than ways of marketing specific foods or manufactured products. Today advertising obviously sells a fantasy image, an attitude, an illusion of glamour focused on the brand. The average American may be exposed to more than one thousand advertisements daily, and their power is often attacked as dangerously addictive and as corrupting the way we see ourselves or others. In the early days of the 1920s, however, advertising was widely accepted as a liberating force that fueled social progress by turning the products of American culture into a vision of the culture itself.

Bruce Barton, the founder of one of the first and most successful advertising agencies

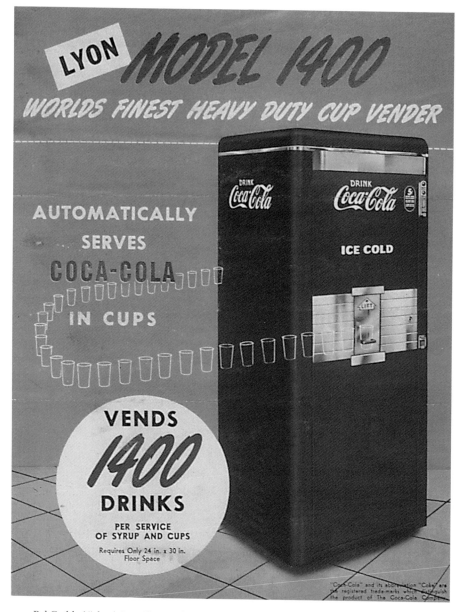

Bel Geddes' "classic" vending machine for Coca-Cola (the color is bright red in the original advertisement by the manufacturer, Mills Industries, 1944). Estate of Edith Lutyens Bel Geddes, Norman Bel Geddes Collection, Courtesy of the Harry Ransom Humanities Research Center.

who became a congressman and was even considered a potential presidential candidate, built his career on this perception. As he proclaimed in a 1927 speech, which he published as "The Creed of an Advertising Man," advertising was "the creative force that has generated jobs, new ideas . . . the spark plug on the cylinder of mass-production, and essential to the continuance of the democratic process."[8] Advertising sustained, even created, the American way of life—and brands served as its icons.

One example that sociologists like to cite is laundry detergents, which represent not only clean clothes but also how mothers should care for their children. Coca-Cola is an even more obvious symbol for an entire American lifestyle. Bel Geddes was specifically commissioned to create "an exclusive Coca-Cola personality" with a "hard-boiled" look, expressed in "a machine that shouts 'Here is a Coca-Cola source!'"[9] The vending machines he designed became one of the most common objects on the American scene. They were everywhere. Only 10 percent were estimated to be in stores, over half stood in factories and offices, and others were placed in gas stations and parking lots, public buildings, railroad stations, schools, hospitals, and recreation centers.

Even today, Coca-Cola stands as shorthand for "America" all over the world. Its "hard-boiled" bright red dispensers (still influenced by Bel Geddes) and "classic" bottles (with their instantly identifiable, slender curving shape contributed by Loewy) are still highly evocative, and helped spread the concept of branding through Europe. Particularly in Britain, where the new consumer culture arrived late, held back by the drabness of wartime rationing that was lifted only in the early 1950s, the new American style of marketing arrived with an overwhelming bang: commercial television, self-service stores, brightly packaged convenience goods that leapt off the shelves. Pepsodent toothpaste, Heinz soups, Britvic juices, Nabisco breakfast cereals (all with packaging by Loewy's London firm) dazzled the British housewife with the promise of a clean and colorful life. Above all, they promoted the modernist ideal of change, the preference for the new over traditional values, which Urban and Bel Geddes had done so much to develop and which by the 1960s had become characteristic of America.

Even if occasionally their names were used in ads for products they designed (as Bel Geddes' was by Chrysler in mounting their 1934 sales campaign for the Airflow car), generally the models were marketed simply under the manufacturer's logo. None of the public realized, when they visited the Bedell store, purchased Simmons furniture, or chose Franco Prints curtains for their homes that these had been designed by Joseph Urban. Similarly, Bel Geddes' hand was invisible in Fifth Avenue window displays, the eye-catching layout in Cromwell-Collier magazines, to say nothing of the Standard Gas stove or Coca-Cola. Although all these stood as tangible advertisements for their vision, if the distinctively modern culture they envisaged was to be fully accepted in America, they needed to show the broader themes unifying the disparate objects and environments they created. Their visions had to be written down—and illustrated.

Despite all their other commercial and theatrical commitments, Bel Geddes and Urban each took the time to write major books. Hampered perhaps by his slightly imperfect grasp of English, Urban wrote just one book, which was limited to designs for proposed theaters, although these designs contained the seeds of the modernist architecture that, translated into the nontheatrical terms of the New School building, helped to form the International Style. Far more crucially, Bel Geddes' 1932 *Horizons* was the first comprehensive definition of modern design principles, comparing them to historical examples and applying them to almost every aspect of living. He wrote about not only theater design, but all kinds of household products, equipment, and furniture; housing, restaurants, factories, and city planning; and particularly transport, from trains (anticipating Raymond Loewy and Henry Dreyfuss) and airplane design to airports, cars, and buses (again clearly foreshadowing Loewy).[10] One example of the way *Horizons* promoted Bel Geddes' ideas is his plans for a streamlined ocean liner.

Illustrated extensively in the book, this projected ship had a rounded, completely enclosed shell tapering towards the stern, and with the smokestacks encased in the upper curves. Sections in the shell opened and slid back for air and sunlight, or to launch lifeboats housed inside the skin. This was still the age of competition between the great steamships for the fastest Atlantic run, and such complete streamlining would, so Bel Geddes estimated, cut transatlantic crossings by an entire day. Although the liner was never built, as illustrated in the book the concept was certainly influential.

Almost immediately after the publication of *Horizons*—and despite Bel Geddes having taken out a patent on his ship design—miniaturized copies began to appear in ferryboats like the *Princess Anne*, designed by Loewy for the Virginia Ferry Company in 1933, which went into service across the Chesapeake in 1936, or the *MV Kalakala* (1935), which ran from Seattle to Bremerton. Both had the same rounded shells, and the way the smokestack and upper-works were enclosed on the *Princess Anne* was strikingly similar to the illustrations for the ocean liner in *Horizons*.

As self-promotion in this particular field, his book hardly had quite the success Bel Geddes hoped for. Although commissioned to design a streamlined motor-yacht for the Axel Wenner-Gren boatyard, which went into production in 1934, Bel Geddes himself was never given a chance at any larger kind of ship, which would have put his name unmistakably on the marine map. However, it was *Horizons*, as much as the

Bel Geddes with his scale model for an ocean liner, c. 1932.
Estate of Edith Lutyens Bel Geddes, Norman Bel Geddes Collection,
Courtesy of the Harry Ransom Humanities Research Center.

Raymond Loewy on the upper deck of the *Princess Anne*, 1936.
Courtesy of Laurence Loewy.

Airflow car, which led *Fortune* to call Bel Geddes "the father of streamlining."[11] More recently his ocean liner design has been singled out as "indisputably classic."[12]

In each area he dealt with, Bel Geddes showed how functional, streamlined design might change ordinary people's way of living and shape a new society. The ideas promoted in *Horizons* found their way into popular culture (as in films like *Things to Come*), and the book had many imitators. Walter Dorwin Teague's *Design This Day*, written almost a decade later in 1940, and Henry Dreyfuss's 1955 *Designing for People* both follow almost the same format. So does Raymond Loewy's 1979 book documenting his own career, *Industrial Design*, though it is more purely pictorial and descriptive. Bel Geddes also published detailed descriptions of his ideas for highway design and construction together with the implications for urban planning in *Magic Motorways*, as well as an autobiography—though when he died he had written about his career only up to 1925, before he branched out into commercial design. As a consequence, his autobiography, *Miracle in the Evening*, unfortunately contributed to the highly misleading view that up to now has dismissed Bel Geddes as being almost exclusively concerned with theater.

More directly, Bel Geddes followed up on *Horizons* by founding his own School of Design in 1939. Operating in conjunction with Norman Bel Geddes and Company (his industrial/architectural design firm) and located on the same floor of the Rockefeller Plaza as its offices, the school offered courses on every commercial application of design: industry, architecture, and interior decoration, as well as topography and model making. These were all based in the aesthetic of modern design, functionalism, and principles of streamlining, stressing hands-on experience and practical training. They were an extension of his earlier highly successful classes in theater design, started in 1921 at the Master School of United Artists, which had been attended by Henry Dreyfuss and Mordecai Gorelik, among others, and where by all accounts Bel Geddes had been a spellbinding (as well as pugnaciously opinionated) lecturer. Bel Geddes' School of Design was specifically intended to spread his own concepts, in addition to developing talent for his own enterprises.[13]

Quite apart from being a utilitarian workshop for housing associates, draftsmen, and secretaries, as well as a space in which classes were conducted, Bel Geddes' offices themselves were advertisements for his designs. The same element of advertising was even clearer in Urban's offices, because they predated Bel Geddes' establishment by more than a decade. Both men were significant entrepreneurs, each employing (at the height of their businesses) more than fifty people. The difference between Urban's "scenery-shop" in Swampscott, while designing for the Boston Opera, and his Fifth Avenue offices is striking. Swampscott was simply utilitarian, a large wooden shed; New York presented an ambiance of vibrant modernity. The décor and the

The image of modernity: a circular drafting room, with silver ceiling and featuring chairs
Urban designed for the Mallin Furniture Company, as well as sculpture by Austrian artists
(also exhibited in his Fifth Avenue store), in the offices of Urban's firm on Fifth Avenue, New York,
c. 1930. Joseph Urban Papers, Rare Book and Manuscript Library, Columbia University.

architecture, with the individual offices fanning out from a circular central space, were
intended to condition the way his employees worked, as well as offering an attractive
example of the modern lifestyle for the customers.

In addition, beyond the direct influence of his teaching, or the projects commissioned by the customers who came to his office, or even the inspirational impact of
his books, particularly *Horizons*, Bel Geddes' concept of modernity was spread by
all his major competitors in the United States. The official Raymond Loewy website cites an assertion in the *New York Times Book Review*, "Mr. Loewy has indeed
changed the shape of the modern world,"[14] which certainly has a great deal of truth:
Loewy remained active for thirty years after Bel Geddes had vanished from the scene,
dying in 1986 at the age of ninety-two. Yet as the example of the streamlined boat

demonstrates—or the design of streamlined cars and trains, and the design of refrigerators discussed earlier—for all the competitiveness between them, the vision Loewy so effectively promoted throughout his life was that of Bel Geddes, and behind Bel Geddes there was Joseph Urban. No single designer, not even with the energy of Urban or Bel Geddes and with the large staffs they employed, could hope to single-handedly change the shape of the world. It took the disparate efforts of a whole group of gifted designers, who carried the influence of Urban and Bel Geddes forward to the following generation. This included not only Raymond Loewy but also architects like Raymond Hood, and more strictly industrial designers like Dreyfuss and Teague.

Equally significant—and certifying the importance of their work more officially—is the fact that examples of the furniture designed by both Urban and Bel Geddes, as well as Bel Geddes' radio cabinets for Philco in 1931, were acquired early on for the permanent collection of the Museum of Modern Art. As Bel Geddes noted in his self-congratulating way, these were "the first ever radio cabinets ever considered to be furniture of artistic merit."[15] Their chairs and cocktail shakers and commercial designs of all kinds were also collected and exhibited in many other places throughout the 1920s and 1930s, and are now prized possessions of the Metropolitan Museum of Art and the Brooklyn Museum, as well as MoMA. Urban opened his own Fifth Avenue gallery in 1922; Bel Geddes' car designs were put on display in Detroit under the auspices of Henry Ford himself in 1933; and during their lifetimes their work appeared at museums of art or museums of science and industry in New York, Chicago, San Francisco, and Toledo. The Association of Art Museums organized a national tour, and their designs went abroad, from the Italian National Exposition in Milan to the Grand Palace in Cairo. All helped to spread their vision.

The Metropolitan Museum of Art and the Museum of Modern Art were far more central. In contrast to other museums, MoMA prided itself (as it still does) on being a trendsetter. It focused on collecting the best examples representing contemporary design that would not only educate the public, but also serve as inspiration for students and professionals. As for the Met, it was one of the most significant institutions of its kind in America and indeed the world; and its special exhibitions had an extremely high public profile—as they still do.

One of the Met's crucial exhibitions was "The Architect and the Industrial Arts" in 1929. Joseph Urban was on the committee that coordinated the overall display, along with his close associates Raymond Hood and Ely Kahn. Echoing his view—repeatedly expressed throughout the 1920s—that it was up to America to define the form and concept of modern life, the aim of the exhibition was, as the *American Architect* reported, "to encourage confidence on the part of the general public in the development of a

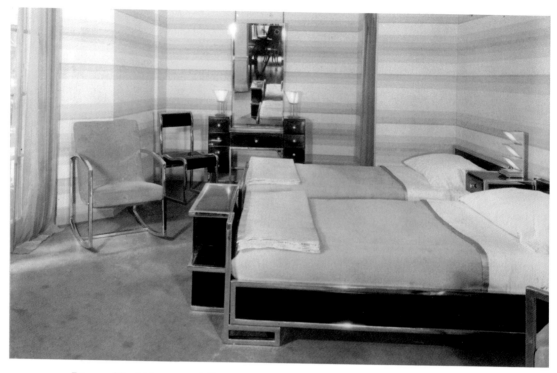

Décor and furnishings as art. A Simmons bed suite exhibited at the Chicago Museum of Science and Industry, 1933 (*above*). Every detail, including the horizontally striped wallpaper and drapes, furnishings, and light fixtures, was designed by Bel Geddes. Estate of Edith Lutyens Bel Geddes, Norman Bel Geddes Collection, Courtesy of the Harry Ransom Humanities Research Center. The rooftop conservatory designed by Urban, in the path-breaking 1929 exhibition at the Metropolitan Museum of Art (*opposite*). Joseph Urban Papers, Rare Book and Manuscript Library, Columbia University.

distinctive American style of interior architecture."[16] Notoriously, when the United States had been invited to exhibit at the 1925 Exposition Internationale des Arts Décoratifs et Industriels Modernes in Paris, the American panel set up to coordinate the national entry had turned down the invitation, because in their view there was no such thing as modern design in America. This 1929 exhibition was specifically a declaration of just how much had changed, largely because of Urban himself, in barely four years.

It was also the first exhibition at the Met to show complete rooms: layout, décor, furniture, even lamps and teacups, each one created specially by an individual architect for this exhibition. Literally stage sets, displaying the context of modern living, two of these were by Urban himself: a man's den/study, and a glass-walled conservatory for a penthouse roof. Both defined by triangles and zigzag patterns, these two

room displays presented a radically simplified form of Art Deco that was unmistakably contemporary. They also demonstrated Urban's dominance in the new stylistic movement. Although the other exhibitors were among the leading architects of their day, each of them contributed only a single room. It was also Urban's displays that were selected as cover pictures by several magazines, including the October issue of *Woman's Journal*.

The various "rooms" on exhibit offered models for every area in an apartment, as well as business offices, and while Urban's décor was more simplified than the others, all were remarkably similar in style. Together they made a unified statement about how a specifically American culture might express itself in the modern world. As self-promotion, this exhibition could hardly have been surpassed. Usually the Met mounted these spring shows for a single month, but the response was so overwhelming that the museum kept the exhibition open for the whole summer and into the fall of 1929.

MoMA also promoted this new aesthetic, with its "Machine Art" exhibition of 1934—a ship's propeller hanging outside the museum and a ball bearing wheel on the cover of the show catalogue. "Machine Art" deified pure function, whereas for

Urban, as for Bel Geddes and his followers, the crucial element was always the form of an object. Certainly Bel Geddes' Airflow cars, or trains like the *Twentieth Century Limited* by Henry Dreyfuss, may have been more efficient than the earlier designs they replaced, but the key to their shape was psychological. The Airflow styling evoked speed, the sleek torpedo-like shells placed over the standard boiler, wheels, and pistons of the railway engines symbolized modernity and the power of the machine. All these designs expressed the idea of functionalism in an imaginatively convincing way, and their principles remain the credo for MoMA's collection, which continues to influence future design by encapsulating the best of the present. Salvaged in the 1950s and still in the office of the Philip Johnson Chief Curator of the Department of Architecture and Design, even after the rebuilding of the museum, is a poster from the "Machine Art" exhibition:

GOOD DESIGN
Fulfils its function
Respects its materials
Is suited to method of production
Combines these in Imaginative Expression

Contemporary design is still the mandate of MoMA—though their exhibitions are now frequently retrospective. Recently there has been renewed interest in the crucial era between America's victorious emergence from World War I and the fifties, throughout the New York art world. In 2000, the Met exhibited "American Modern, 1925–1940: Design for a New Age," while Bel Geddes' Manhattan tray and Skyscraper cocktail shaker made an iconic appearance in the 1999 "American Century" show mounted at the Whitney Museum of American Art. The names of Urban and Bel Geddes may largely have been forgotten. But the movement they started, and did so much to shape, continues.

Beyond their books and the exhibitions that transmitted their vision, both Urban and Bel Geddes were always sensitive to the possibilities of new media. They were expert communicators. Quite as much as their designs, it was this that made them so effective in shaping the modern American lifestyle. Both had transferred their success in using the mass appeal of theater to the expanded reach offered by the movies, and just as Urban played a key role in the early years of the film industry, so the younger Bel Geddes picked up the potential offered by technologies that opened even wider horizons. He was interested in radio, and sought to exploit the potential in the rapidly emerging television industry. He even became involved in the very start of the computer revolution, proving particularly prescient about the key forces driving the development of the contemporary world. In 1943, in response to the question of what would be the "greatest product inventions or improvements" in the postwar era, he singled out electronics, forecasting that they would "come closer to mechanically reproducing many of the limited and simple functions of the human brain."[17] Notably, as well as having apparently complete confidence in an American victory, even so soon after Pearl Harbor, he is imagining developments consistent with computers and artificial intelligence.

Four years after this, in 1947, Bel Geddes was designing not only the corporate image for IBM, but also the exterior shell for the IBM calculator at Harvard. The entire design of the shell, which was constructed of chromed steel and Lucite, with Plexiglas covers, gave an unmistakably modernist style to the cumbersome calculating machine—the earliest prototype of the computer. When IBM decided to launch it with an exhibition, Bel Geddes proposed displaying an office of the future. To create this he redesigned both IBM's accounting machines and its new electric typewriter, together with a secretary's desk and workstation (following ergonometric principles and complete with a sliding shelf for the typewriter plus desktop plug-ins). The exhibit was set up in the front office of the Harvard building, and initially, to attract public attention, outside the doors was parked a delivery truck with a highly streamlined body derived from the designs Bel Geddes had published in *Horizons*. The display eventually became permanent, the electric typewriter became the secretarial standard for the next three decades, and the workstations were subsequently used in the corporate offices of IBM as well as several New York firms.

Of course the other major electronic influences on contemporary life are television and personal communications. Most of the firms Bel Geddes worked for in designing his kitchen appliances and household equipment were in the electrical business, meaning they were also involved with the development of the modern media world. In fact, given his interest in communications, it is hardly surprising that by 1930 Bel Geddes had won an exclusive contract with Philco to design all their "radio, phonograph, talking moving-picture and television cabinets." Quite apart from being considered so advanced that MoMA collected several of these pieces as "classics" of contemporary design along with some of his other furniture, they were also highly popular. Philco sold more than 4 million of Bel Geddes' radio sets by the end of 1932, capturing 50 percent of the North American market.

Bel Geddes continued with this through the 1940s, creating simplified modernistic casings for RCA, Majestic Radio, and Federal Telephone and Radio, even a wartime "Patriot Table Radio" that mimicked the American flag in its red, white, and blue plastic. In a series of 1942 concept designs for RCA, he anticipated remote control

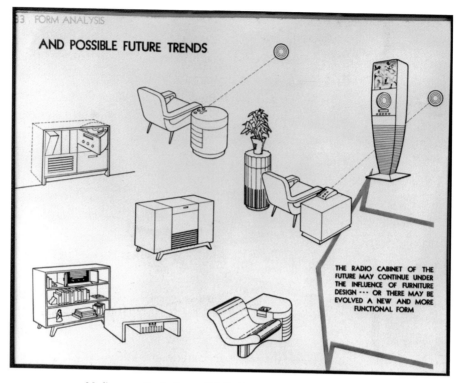

AND POSSIBLE FUTURE TRENDS

THE RADIO CABINET OF THE
FUTURE MAY CONTINUE UNDER
THE INFLUENCE OF FURNITURE
DESIGN ··· OR THERE MAY BE
EVOLVED A NEW AND MORE
FUNCTIONAL FORM

Media rooms for the home: Bel Geddes' concept designs for RCA.
Estate of Edith Lutyens Bel Geddes, Norman Bel Geddes Collection,
Courtesy of the Harry Ransom Humanities Research Center.

sound and channel controls, media towers for living rooms, and built-in wall screens and speakers. He also came up with a miniaturized slim-line radio with recessed controls for RCA in 1946, which was intended to be carried by a strap hung from the shoulder. Although using subminiature Raytheon tubes, rather than the transistors that appeared only in the 1950s, with its pocket size and earpiece this must count as an early prototype of the highly popular and now almost ubiquitous Walkman.

However important this sort of personal mini-radio may have turned out to be for the youth lifestyle of the last decade, Bel Geddes' widest influence in the field came from his work as a behind-the-scenes pioneer in the booming postwar field of television. In 1950, ABC hired him to design its Sixth Avenue New York studio, including the production facilities as well as the exterior appearance of the building, the public entrance, and the lobby. He produced a quasi-modernist industrial look, matching his concept of television.

A year later he was contracted by NBC as a "consultant and designer in such immediate phases of television as staging [of drama shows], lighting, studio planning,

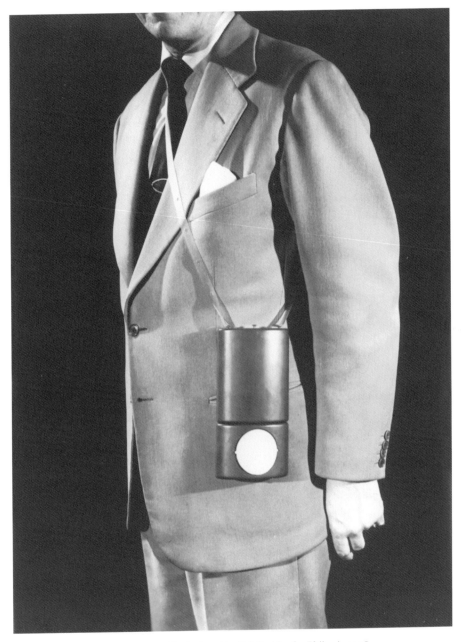

The shoulder radio designed by Bel Geddes for Philco in 1946.
Estate of Edith Lutyens Bel Geddes, Norman Bel Geddes Collection,
Courtesy of the Harry Ransom Humanities Research Center.

architectural design, presentation ideas, future developments in TV production."[18] The studios he designed were "revolutionary," as one NBC executive remarked. This was Pat Weaver, NBC's chief programmer from 1949 to 1953, who himself had won fame as an innovator by introducing "magazine advertising" (where instead of one firm "owning" an entire series, each show was divided between several firms, allowing the network to control programming) and "event" programming with one-show spectaculars. At the time many programs were still recorded live in front of a studio audience, and Bel Geddes laid out a completely flexible building for "assembly line television production" (as it was referred to in NBC interdepartmental memos) to replace their Manhattan facilities. Studios had movable walls that could be opened to include banks of seats for spectators, or configured for variable performance spaces, with a grid covering the whole area above, along which motorized cameras, lights, and microphones could move in all directions during the filming. NBC estimated that this would increase the output of their New York studios from 50 to around 120 half-hour shows a week, although to some extent this depended on the use of remote-controlled "slave cameras."

As might be expected, the unions objected to such "industrial methods of mechanization." So only the more conventional parts of this structure were built, even though these plans forecast many of the elements in today's high-tech television studios. However, the importance of Bel Geddes' contribution as a consultant is indicated by his arrangements with NBC. His annual contract was renewed continually until his death in 1958, paying him $50,000 a year plus expenses (a significant sum for the time). Still more to the point, Pat Weaver left NBC in 1953, along with two other executives, to join Bel Geddes in setting up an independent television production company that developed "dramatized feature journalism." These programs would make up for the as-yet unknown ubiquity of shoulder-held or helicopter-mounted cameras, as well as today's ability to transmit visual material from almost anywhere into the studio, by filming acted presentations of current happenings. As a news story developed, it might be developed into a full-length docudrama. But the setup was also intended to be capable of producing almost immediate up-to-the-minute footage. In some ways it counts as an early version of that equally artificial and orchestrated contemporary form, "reality television."[19]

Retrospectively, this late episode in Bel Geddes' career, which links him so firmly to our contemporary world, crystallizes the interweaving of theater and everyday reality in almost every aspect of his and Joseph Urban's work. In this case, when film was poor quality or (as all too common) unavailable, dramatized reproductions substituted for and might sometimes even be taken as news reports. Broadly speaking, this same principle was what made their designs so influential. As with the Florida

Spanish mansions of Palm Beach, or the Futurama display at the New York World's Fair, stage scenes were turned into the settings for people's lives and delineated the world they would want to inhabit. Styled to capture the essential qualities of modernity, the Chrysler Airflow or the New School for Social Research transmitted images of American life, becoming self-fulfilling realities. It was a highly productive merging of the street and theater.

AFTERWORD

Then and Now

LOOKING BACK, THE IMPACT and influence of Joseph Urban and Norman Bel Geddes on practically every aspect of American life is simply astounding. But I had no idea of this when I came across the documents they had left behind. Aware that each had done some work outside the theater, I had initially been looking for material about their scene designs for the stage.[1] I was not at all expecting what I found, and the task of reading their papers, usually a dry and dusty occupation, became a real eye-opener. Letter after letter, in idiosyncratic handwriting or old-fashioned typewriter carbons, set out their vision or described their dealings with William Randolph Hearst, Robert Moses, and Frank Lloyd Wright, executives from Coca-Cola, Cadillac, and Chrysler, Standard Gas, Texaco, GE, and NBC—people and firms so well-known that they had become national icons. Architectural plans and engineering blueprints, design sketches, and scale models showed things that were utterly familiar. It had never occurred to me that the shape and look of a car or a refrigerator might have been created by an individual—but here they were in the files of Urban and Bel Geddes.

Elevations and design drawings and endless photos of their work presented snapshots of the world around me. I'd walked past a few of those buildings on the street, though many others had been demolished. Some of the appliances and furnishings were no longer being manufactured, but their style or outline could be clearly seen in the products on display in stores or homes or offices. I had been looking for material on theater, and discovered the outlines of a whole universe: the world we all live in.

Theater was there, too. And as I explored their stage work, from the Metropolitan Opera to Broadway and the *Ziegfeld Follies,* I gradually realized there was a great deal in common between the scenery and costume designs that Urban and Bel Geddes had done for their shows, and all their architectural and industrial work outside the theater. Trademark details like parrots or the vibrant colors, which made the settings of Urban's shows so immediately identifiable, were reproduced in buildings such as Mar-a-Lago and the New School for Social Research. Bel Geddes' modular stage settings and the manufacturing modules he developed for his gas stoves were much the same. Looking from one to the other, it wasn't just that there were similarities between the theatrical and industrial designs each had created. The techniques they used in the commercial world came directly from the stage. There was practically no difference in their approach. Everything—the lush décor Urban created for people's apartments, or Bel Geddes' stripped-down suburban houses—was intrinsically theatrical. What made Bel Geddes' streamlined cars and the whiteness of his kitchens so effective? A quintessentially dramatic, symbolic, and expressive quality in that sweeping shape and that clean color. The aura of Broadway had been brought to Main Street. This gave their image of modernity such imaginative appeal—and immediately suggested why the American model had become so widely adopted as a modern lifestyle.

Another realization that slowly emerged was that Urban and Bel Geddes were very aware of their importance on the American cultural scene. As entrepreneurs, running their own businesses, they had generated extensive records that were invaluable in showing how they worked. The way they had organized these records also gave a faint, yet unmistakable impression of their personalities. There was something obsessive about the way Bel Geddes documented every aspect of each project, writing up summaries after the event and filing all the details in separate folders. Similarly, Urban's large leather-bound albums, into which he pasted every single newspaper clipping that even mentioned his name, betrayed a certain vanity. In addition, the sheer volume of everything they preserved suggests how sure they must have felt of a claim on the attention of future generations.

Thinking about that, I was struck by how unique Urban and Bel Geddes had turned out to be. Part of this was their promotion of a clear concept of modernity through their own designs, which were all the more convincing and attractive because of their intrinsic theatrical flair. Equally singular was how their vision was broadcast and amplified through their influence on others. Designers like Raymond Loewy, Henry Dreyfuss, and Walter Dorwin Teague had copied the style they had set and continued it into the 1970s—and, in the long-lived Loewy's case, up to the 1990s. Morris Lapidus (who gave Miami its distinctive look) had popularized, or some might say parodied, their concept of modernism in the Florida resort hotels he created during the 1950s and 1960s. The Sans Souci, Fontainebleau, Americana, Delano, and Eden Roc combined Urban's columns (attenuated to "beanpoles") with the biomorphic curves of Bel Geddes' Copa City, although in an over-the-top, blatantly kitschy form that was encapsulated in the title of Lapidus's 1966 autobiography, *Too Much Is Never Enough*. Although contemporary life seems to move ever faster, there seems to have been no real advance in the definition of modernism since Urban and Bel Geddes.

Their vision of what it means to be modern, incorporated in commercial logos and the styling of consumer goods, has gained a truly global spread, maintaining its imaginative power, and continuing to be a part of home life as well as encapsulating the golden age of postwar America. One particularly vivid example of this is a housewife's apron from Spain. A popular purchase in Madrid today, the front of the apron features a black-and-white picture of a refrigerator being opened by a languidly elegant woman in a sweeping floor-length gown, with a Spanish slogan that translates as, "I'm going to be a star, too."

The image is an advertisement for Philco from the 1950s, and there is of course an element of ironic retro use, even perhaps tongue-in-cheek kitsch, in reproducing it on an ostensibly utilitarian garment. But the styling of the refrigerator—rounded corners

Continuing influence: a popular kitchen apron from Spain, 1999.
Courtesy of John Dawson.

at the top and decorative grill of horizontal ridges down one side of the front—comes straight from an earlier model by Bel Geddes, and there is a strong sense of nostalgia as well as the suggestion that this apron epitomizes the elegance of today's high-tech kitchen. It forms a tangible, if equivocal, acknowledgment of the global spread of the American culture Bel Geddes helped to create.

But where are the Urbans and Bel Geddes of today? Who now is promoting a different vision of modernity sufficiently unified and broad-reaching to define a new lifestyle? There is no longer any significant input from the Broadway theater, which gave their concept such dramatic impact. A number of contemporary designers who have made a significant impact, as for instance Milton Glaser, whose career has stretched from newspaper and magazine redesign (including the *Washington Post* and *Time*) to the Grand Union supermarket chain and the "I♥NY" logo. This logo has been copied everywhere, yet Glaser has hardly defined anything like a complete lifestyle, as Urban and Bel Geddes managed to do. Perhaps because nobody—not even Milton Glaser—now seems to have the same breadth as Urban or Bel Geddes, or work in such a variety of fields. The nearest equivalent is probably Michael Graves, an architect whose firm covers interior décor as well as designing rugs for Glen Eden Wool Carpet, and a variety of household products. Yet these are still following the modernist template designed by Bel Geddes.

New ideas of modernity may be appearing—as with Frank Gehry's wildly curving metal-clad museums and symphony halls, which are so highly praised for their contemporary image, although they seem a baroque extension of Bel Geddes' Futurama Building at the New York World's Fair and, in an exaggerated form, pick up on some of the elements in Urban's architectural projects. But today's futuristic buildings have not reached Main Street. Over the past decades architectural and industrial designs have at best been eclectic. The bland and indistinguishable glass box of the 1960s has given way to bizarre stylistic eclecticism (like Philip Johnson's postmodern AT&T building, topped by a neoclassical broken pediment) or the complex shapes now made possible by computer software. But with each building asserting its stylistic uniqueness or the unique identity of its architect, there is no common style.

There is at least one contemporary stage-designer and director who crosses into other areas, Robert Wilson—widely seen as America's leading avant-garde theater artist through the 1980s and into the 1990s—yet the furniture, landscapes, and architectural objects Wilson has created are all purely abstract. His chairs have been collected by MoMA and by many other museums, as Urban's and Bel Geddes' furniture was. However, missing one leg (like his Kafka Chair) or elongated into thin verticals (like the Einstein Chair, which does not have a seat), they are impossible to sit on.

Impressive as artistic images, these represent the ideal of chairs as abstract postmodern aesthetic, not designs for manufacture and popular use.

The modern style, which Urban and Bel Geddes began developing in the 1920s, reached its peak in the 1940s and 1950s. It would be logical to expect a new idiom of modernity to have emerged by now; but nothing strikes the eye. Despite many attempts, no advance has become generally accepted across American society. And perhaps—despite the speed of technological advance, the disruptiveness of intervening history in the Vietnam war or the race riots of the 1960s and 1970s and the emergence of new social groupings, the recovery of the sense of being (in Madeleine Albright's phrase) "the essential nation"—the way Americans live remains basically unchanged.

Perhaps a single decade is still too soon for a new style to have spread, and maybe the tragic destruction of the World Trade Center will signal the end of the modern concept that has held sway for so much of the past century, with whatever replaces it representing a new era. Yet the definition of modernity these two designers introduced was so coherent and convincing that it has retained its popular appeal. In any case, the work of Joseph Urban and Norman Bel Geddes still conditions our lifestyle today. The world defined by their designs is very much the one we live in. Their achievement is both an object lesson and inspiration.

Notes

A NOTE ON SOURCES

Documentation on the design work of both Joseph Urban and Norman Bel Geddes is relatively complete, since they ran commercial businesses with staffs to organize files, and in each case the complete collection is housed in a single institution. The Geddes papers are held by the Harry Ransom Humanities Research Center at the University of Texas, Austin, while Urban's papers were acquired through his daughter Gretl by the Butler Library at Columbia University in New York. The catalogues of both these collections are available online and give the exact location of all items referred to. The complexity of Bel Geddes' filing system has sometimes also required listing the box and folder number in a note.

In one important instance the standards of documentation have changed in the years since the material in these collections was first gathered. The clipping services or secretaries, whose job it was to garner all the news reports about the many activities of Urban or Bel Geddes, frequently omitted the place of publication, and sometimes the date or even the title of a newspaper clipping, while in other cases the tag bearing this information has disappeared or become illegible. The problem is compounded in the case of Joseph Urban, whose clippings were glued into a series of leather-bound albums, which were in such poor condition that some time ago the pages were microfilmed and discarded. Even so, the actual year of a newspaper report can generally be ascertained from the sequential nature of the Urban scrapbooks, which is retained in the microfilm copy, or in the case of Bel Geddes from the date of the particular job file, making it possible to cite from this material. And in estimating the wider social influence of their designs, newspapers and journals offer the best record, particularly in the middle decades of the twentieth century. As these collections so clearly demonstrate, journalistic life was far more varied and vibrant at this time than it is today, with every town having one or more independent newspapers, and hundreds of trades publishing their own journals.

1
STYLING FOR THE MODERN AGE

1. For a particularly acute discussion of the introduction of the phrases "the American Way of Life" and "the American Dream," see Warren I. Susman, *Culture as History* (New York: Pantheon Books, 1984), p. 154.

2. Notably in the most recent and extensive exhibition of Art Deco covering the whole period from 1910 to 1939–40, mounted by the Victoria and Albert Museum in 2003, America is represented primarily by a boat-tailed Auburn roadster and a film clip of the dancer Josephine Baker in a Paris performance—and the 464-page catalogue devotes a total of eight pages to America: less than Shanghai or even Australia (although the Chrysler Building does make an appearance in the opening "Style and the Age" section). While the designs of Urban and Bel Geddes were in some ways associated with the Art Deco movement—and indeed Bel Geddes' work is represented in one or two photos and objects—the relative absence of American design signals its distinctness: indeed the one section specifically on America (pp. 361–69) is titled "From Art Deco to Streamlining."

3. *Arts and Decoration,* May 1928, p. 56. Austrian Paul Frankel came to the United States in 1915, after World War I had broken out in Europe; *New Yorker,* 29 August 1931, p. 155.

4. *Miami Beach Sun,* 28 December 1948.

5. See Henry Dreyfuss, *Designing for People,* 1967 ed., pp. 24–25 (first published New York: Simon and Schuster, 1955).

6. *Report of a Commission Appointed by the Secretary of Commerce to Visit and Report upon the International Exposition of Modern Decorative and Industrial Art in Paris,* Washington, D.C., 1926, p. 16, and *Decorative Furnisher,* May 1925, pp. 81–82. See also *New York Times,* 16 February 1925.

7. A good example of this desperate gaiety is given in the final nightclub scene of Noël Coward's 1931 play *Cavalcade.*

8. Another example would be the interior décor and furnishings by Donald Deskey—but again his Art Deco work was limited to the years 1929–30.

9. This becomes clearer in a book titled *American Art Deco,* by Alistair Duncan, published by Thames and Hudson in 1986. However, the visible change in style is not recognized in Duncan's text. The book was reissued in 1999, and this bias became reflected in the 2000–2001 Metropolitan Museum of Art exhibition on "American Modern: 1925–1940—Design for a New Age."

10. Duncan gives more attention to Urban than to any other person, except perhaps Deskey, while ranking Bel Geddes with Frank Lloyd Wright and just below Ely Jacques Kahn.

11. Although only a vague sense of the color patterns can be gained from the black-and-white photograph shown here, Urban's original watercolor design is printed in the catalogue for a 2000 exhibition of Urban's work at Columbia University: *Architect of Dreams,* ed. Arnold Aronson, p. 28.

12. Built in 1930–31, and sadly torn down in the 1960s, the main structure of this entryway is preserved in the Victoria and Albert Museum.

13. See *New Yorker,* 29 August 1931, p. 155.

14. One of the proponents of this was the French sociologist André Siegfried, who notably declared, "Today, as a result of the revolutionary changes brought about by modern methods of production the American people are now creating on a vast scale an entirely original social structure which bears only a superficial resemblance to the European. It may even be a new age" (*America Comes of Age* [New York: Harcourt, Brace, 1927], p. 347).

2
EGOS AT WORK

1. Although some sociologists—like Daniel Roche, *A History of Everyday Things: The Birth of Consumption in France, 1600–1800* (New York: Cambridge University Press, 2000)—have argued that consumerism is a long-standing phenomenon, to observers in America at the time it was clear that the 1920s marked a significant change in the nexus of advertising, industrial production, and commercial competition that produced a new type of consumer society, giving rise to a marked change in the role of design: see Stuart Chase, *The Economy of Abundance* (New York: Macmillan, 1934). In fact the first book to mention consumers only appeared at the very beginning of the decade: Percy Redfern, *Self and Society: Social and Economic Problems from the Hitherto Neglected Point of View of the Consumer* (London: E. Benn, 1930).

2. For an extended discussion of this period in his career, see Randolph Carter and Robert Cole, *Joseph Urban* (New York: Abbeville Press, 1992), pp. 9–45.

3. Bel Geddes' claims of penury, as for instance in his autobiography, *Miracle in the Evening: An*

Autobiography, ed. William Kelley (New York: Doubleday, 1960), pp. 17ff.—or an interview in the *New York American,* 2 March 1924, where he claimed, "I never went to school—I had to pick my education up where I could find it—I never even went to art school" (a claim contradicted by his autobiography), are hardly borne out by the family photographs, which show Norman and his brother at various ages up to their early twenties, together with their family home. This was a large three-story clapboard mansion with elaborate gingerbread trim and even a turret, and as young men the brothers are fashionably dressed, as well as elegantly posed.

4. Bel Geddes, *Miracle in the Evening,* pp. 122–24. Almost all the detail about Bel Geddes' early life and pre-theatrical career comes from this autobiography. The only corroborating sources are an occasional photo of him with colleagues at the Peninsular Engraving Company.

5. Bel Geddes' youthful political views are shown by the 1916 correspondence around *INWHICH* (Bel Geddes Collection, Harry Ransom Collection [hereafter HRC], Personal Files).

6. Cited by Otto Teegen in "Joseph Urban's Philosophy of Color," *Architecture,* May 1934, p. 257.

7. While anti-traditionalist, the Vienna Secession movement, founded in 1897 by a group of painters that included Gustav Klimt and Oskar Kokoschka (as well as Urban), remained in the aesthetic realm of high art.

8. Summer issue, ed. Charles Holme: the photos are reproduced by Carter and Cole, *Joseph Urban,* p. 37.

9. Carter and Cole assume that it was this professional jealousy, accompanied by accusations of dishonest conduct and an unsuccessful libel suit by Urban, which motivated his departure to the States (see *Joseph Urban,* p. 42). Given his character, however, more likely the draw was the chance to have sole artistic control of an opera company (which was simply not possible within the hierarchical theater system of Vienna) as well possibly as an awareness of wider opportunities in America.

10. An impression of the club's meetings, and of Urban's dominant role, is given by Walter H. Kilham, *Raymond Hood, Architect* (New York: Architectural Book Publishers, 1974), pp. 79–80. Sadly, there is no record of the recipe for Urban's uniquely named cocktail.

11. *INWHICH,* 3 August 1915 (n.p.).

12. The costs for Bel Geddes' reconfiguration of the Century Theatre for Reinhardt's 1924 *Miracle* production were not much less; and even today, a complete theater may be built for performing a single show—as with the Princess Theater in Toronto, constructed specifically to house *Miss Saigon* (and completely paid for by the run of that production).

13. Percy MacKaye, brochure, William Chauncy Langdon archive, Brown University.

14. Cited in *Survey,* 4 July 1914, p. 372.

15. That Lindbergh may also have found it politic to name his plane after St. Louis in recognition of funding by businessmen from that city is an alternative explanation. However the pioneering spirit celebrated by the pageant, together with the symbolism of that final airplane, was certainly the initial inspiration.

16. Program, June 1916: housed in the manuscript collection of Brown University Library.

17. Exhibited in London, Brussels, and New York between 1922 and 1928, Bel Geddes' designs for *The Divine Comedy* were published extraordinarily widely. They appeared in several books, including Sheldon Cheney's *A Primer of Modern Art* (New York: Liveright, 1924) and George Sheringham's *Design in the Theatre* (New York: B. Blom, 1927), and were printed and reprinted in numerous journals—a brief listing includes: *Theatre Arts* (October 1921); *Century* (April 1922); *New Republic* (3 January 1923, 2 January 1924, 20 February 1929); *The Architectural Record* and *American Architect* (both July 1924); *Commonweal,* 17 March 1926, 28 July 1926); *The Dial*

(May 1926); *Theatre Arts Monthly* (June 1926); *Illustrated London News* (21 January 1928)—as well as Bel Geddes' own book of photos illustrating all the scenes on the model stage that he constructed: *A Project for a Theatrical Presentation of the Divine Comedy of Dante Alighieri* (New York: Theatre Arts, 1924).

18. See Reinhardt, foreword to Bel Geddes' book, *A Project for a Theatrical Presentation of the Divine Comedy of Dante Alighieri.*

19. In addition to being a poet and artist, William Morris founded one of the most important firms of interior decorators in nineteenth-century Britain, as well as running a whole cottage industry that did everything from weaving and making furniture to manufacturing rolls of wallpaper, and printing books. The extent to which he almost single-handedly created the physical context for English society at the time is what makes the late Victorian lifestyle so easily identifiable. Morris applied his art to architecture and to every aspect of house interiors—chairs and all sorts of other furniture, tapestries, stained-glass windows, wallpaper, tiles, and carpets—and formulated a whole concept of culture that he publicized through lectures and his writings. He directly inspired the numerous Arts and Crafts societies that sprang up across England in the 1890s, whose principles were copied by the new wave of architects like C. F. A. Voysey and Baillie Scott, as well as influencing the German Werkbund, the Vienna Secessionists (one of whose leading artists was Gustav Klimt), and their rivals the Hagenbund founded by Urban. His ideas reached America through Oscar Wilde's 1882 lecture tour, where Wilde the aesthete spoke on "Art and the Handicraftsman" and "House Decoration."

20. *New Yorker,* 29 August 1931, p. 155.

21. Cover story of the October 1934 issue "Both Fish and Fowl," 9, no. 2, responding to Bel Geddes' publication of *Horizons* (Boston: Little, Brown, 1932).

22. Somewhat gratuitous in context (in his autobiographical promotion of the new profession of industrial design, *Designing for People* [New York: Simon and Schuster, 1955], p. 75), Dreyfuss's comment reveals the jealous competitiveness between these designers.

23. Typescript, Raymond Loewy Clippings file, Cooper-Hewitt Museum, New York.

24. *Life,* 2 May 1949, p. 70.

25. Dreyfuss, *Designing for People,* p. 75.

3

THEATRICAL FASHIONS

1. For a fuller picture of Russell's career, Urban's recruitment, and the productions he mounted, see Quaintance Eaton, *The Boston Opera Company* (New York: Appleton-Century, 1965).

2. Editorial, *Boston Evening Transcript,* 11 January 1912.

3. Typescript (Columbia): "Modern Decorative Stagecraft," published in *Opera,* 1913 (clipping with partial date).

4. Color is primary for all Urban's work, both on stage and in manufacturing and fashion. However, it was not possible to reproduce any of the illustrations for this book in color. In the case of Bel Geddes this hardly matters, since almost all the documentation of his work is in black-and-white, or (for instance with his *Divine Comedy* renderings) shades of umber, and what concerned him was primarily structural qualities. By contrast, Urban was a colorist; and so it is difficult to understand the true impact of his work without color prints. However, many images of Urban's New York career, in particular his colorful theater designs for the Met and for Broadway, have been mounted on the Columbia website, and can be viewed at: http://www.columbia.edu/cu/web/eresources/archives/rbml/urban.

5. *Boston Evening Transcript,* 25 September 1912.

6. Urban's sole book, *Theatres* (New York: Theatre Arts Press, 1929), is unpaginated.

7. Mizzi Lefler, Unpublished diary, Urban Collection, Columbia University.

8. Interview by Oliver Saylor, cited in an unpublished typescript "Shadowland," dated 1923 (n.p., Urban Collection, Columbia University).

9. The same range of adjectives appears in practically all the New York papers in response to each edition of the *Follies,* from 22 June 1915 (Urban's first "edition") through at least 1919, when the annual show featured Irving Berlin's hit "A Pretty Girl Is Like a Melody."

10. More detail on *Around the Map,* and on the Klaw and Erlangen operation, can be found in Mary Henderson's excellent study *The New Amsterdam: The Biography of a Broadway Theatre* (New York: Hyperion, 1997).

11. Lady (Lucy) Duff Gordon gives a titillating account of her career in her autobiographical memoirs, *Discretions and Indiscretions* (New York: Frederick A. Stokes, 1932)—although in typical self-aggrandizement she refuses to allow Urban any credit for the *Follies.* For a modern feminist reading of the crossover between her lingerie modeling shows and the London stage, see Sheila Stowell and Joel H. Kaplan, *Theatre and Fashion: Oscar Wilde to the Suffragettes* (New York: Cambridge University Press, 1994), pp. 39–40.

12. *New York Globe and Advertiser,* 2 November 1915.

13. For more details on the life and art of Gordon Conway, see the lavishly illustrated *Gordon Conway: Fashioning a New Woman* (Austin: University of Texas Press, 1997).

14. When she did finally return in 1936, ill and having split up with her unreliable husband, Gordon Conway was almost unable to find work, her only contract being to design wallpaper for Anderson Textiles in 1937.

15. *Hotel Review,* July 1915.

16. *New York Sun,* 2 November 1915.

17. *New York Sun,* 26 June 1917; *Arts and Decoration,* October 1919.

18. The shocked response is from the *New York Tribune,* but was duplicated in several papers.

19. The clipping from the *Cincinnati Commercial Tribune* comes from Urban's scrapbook, and was undated though the year is clear from other clippings on the same page. The same sentiments were expressed by the *Journal,* 18 September 1917, and *Commercial Tribune,* 2 May 1920.

20. *Buffalo News,* 16 March 1926, and *Minneapolis Journal,* 28 March 1926.

21. *New York Sun,* 22 June 1915.

22. *Sunday World,* 18 January 1920.

23. Scene listings in *Ziegfeld Follies* program, 1926 and 1927.

24. *American Architect,* August 1928.

25. *New York Evening Post,* 5 and 12 March 1927; *New York American,* 26 March 1927.

26. *New York Herald Tribune,* 23 June 1927.

4

STAGE AND SCREEN

1. *Theatres* (n.p.).

2. Typescript notes by Gretl Urban (possibly intended as material for a biography of her father) in the Urban Collection, Columbia; Ely Jacques Kahn, *Architectural Record,* May 1927, p. 396. The response of theatrical reviewers can be summed up in Brooks Atkinson's comment: "The most extravagant and bizarre cycloramas of imaginative designing this side of fairyland. . . . It sets a standard. Mr. Ziegfeld must take care lest his productions on stage prove inferior

to the sweep of carnival beauty on the walls of his theatre" (*New York Times*, 4 February 1927).

3. The influence of the Ziegfeld Theatre was still being promoted even after Urban's death, as by an illustrated article in *Architecture*, May 1934.

4. Urban's plans for the Reinhardt Theatre were broadly publicized and attracted admiration, as in "Wedding Theatre Beauty to Ballyhoo," *New York Times Magazine*, 19 August 1928, p. 10.

5. *Theatres* (n.p.).

6. The *New York Tribune* reviewer noted, "Even before 'The Miracle' began, sacred music met your ears, and a lady in a nun's wimple showed you to your pew. Slim saints in painted windows were at every hand, the lights dim and religious, and you could hear, occasionally, the soft beating of church bells" (16 January 1924). "The air is heavy with incense," the critic for the *Pittsburgh Gazette* observed, and once the bells began to toll, "the populace is streaming through the four doors and advancing [down the aisles through the audiences] on the altar, singing, intoning, praying, suffering" (21 January 1924). The *New York Times* (20 January 1924) concurred: "The theatre never attained so closely as in this presentation to the ideal of a unified mass atmosphere."

7. Written after first viewing Bel Geddes' designs and dated Salzburg, 25 August 1923, Bel Geddes Collection, JF 85, HRC.

8. *Theatre Arts Monthly*, March 1924, pp. 273–74.

9. *Scientific American*, March 1924; *Architectural Record*, April 1924.

10. "We Nominate for the Hall of Fame: N.B.G.," *Vanity Fair*, May 1924. Details about the Foote-MacDougal lawsuit are in Bel Geddes Collection, HRC, JF 85. h18).

11. As well as completely remodeling the Century Theatre (twice) and the Belasco Theatre—though on a one-off basis for specific shows, the spectacle of *The Miracle* in 1924, the ultrarealistic *Dead End* in 1935, a musical skating-extravaganza *It Happened on Ice* in 1940—Bel Geddes also redesigned the Century Roof Theatre, and created the Denishawn Dance Theatre (for Ruth St. Denis) in Los Angeles, the Palm Beach Theatre (working with Joseph Urban), and the Roxy Theatre in New York.

12. This was printed as a booklet by the Norman Bel Geddes Corporation, and circulated to potential investors, including Charlie Chaplin, Danny Kaye, Elia Kazan, and Laurence Olivier. A typescript of the introduction, giving these figures, has been preserved (HRC 627. p-1). Slightly different figures were given by the *New York Herald Tribune* for 3 September 1949, where the number of theaters in New York was estimated to have diminished from a high of 75 to 38.

13. Statistics published in the *New York Times,* 3 December 1950. Bel Geddes' plans for hotel theaters had been published, with complete architectural details, three years earlier in the *New York Times Magazine,* 30 November 1947, pp. 24–25, 56–57.

14. Bel Geddes, Film Scenario, "New York Story"/"Manhattan," 1926 (based on a story by Forrest Halsey), HRC.

15. For instance, *Evening Globe,* 3 July 1920.

16. Cited by Lee Simonson, *The Stage Is Set* (New York: Theatre Arts Books, 1964), p. 22. A letter from Mary Urban to Alfred Keller, 6 April 1921, describes how Urban quite deliberately went against the movie practice (standard even then) of filming on location, because by constructing and lighting a set he gained the control "to make his pictures a series of studied compositions, not just good photographs" (Urban Collection, Columbia).

17. For a detailed discussion of the relationship between Urban's films and his furniture, see Chapter 14.

18. Reported in the *Evening Journal* (Los Angeles), 22 April 1925, and *New Yorker,* 25 June 1927.

19. The layouts can be directly compared in the Bel Geddes Collection, HRC, between sketches

for *Feet of Clay* (JF 92. MP.1 e.1), the Resort Hotel (JF 689.5), and the Island Dance Restaurant for the Chicago World's Fair (published in *Horizons,* illus. 154).
20. Urban's Sunrise shopping center is discussed below (chapter 14).
21. New York *Herald,* 16 August 1924.
22. *Light* (San Antonio), 10 August 1924.

5
SOCIETY SCENERY

1. Some idea of this can be gained from the color reproduction of Urban's original design, reprinted by Carter and Cole, *Joseph Urban,* p. 196.
2. 20 December 1922. Similar comments recur in several other enthusiastic newspaper reviews.
3. *New York Times,* 4 June 1929. The title of the article tellingly recognized the theatricality of the Casino: "Opening Rehearsal at the Park Casino."
4. Urban, *New York Times,* 4 June 1929, and *Architectural Record,* July 1929.
5. These details and more are reported in Robert A. Caro's biography of Robert Moses, *The Power Broker* (New York: Alfred A. Knopf, 1974), pp. 338–39.
6. *Architectural Record,* August 1929.
7. *New York Evening Graphic,* 4 November 1931.
8. Materials from the maritime Museum, San Francisco, cited in Donald J. Bush, *The Streamlined Decade* (New York: George Braziller, 1975), p. 149.
9. 28 December 1948.
10. *Engineering News Record,* 12 May 1949, script reprinted in *Copa City Magazine,* 1951, pp. 5–7, *Miami Beach Florida Sun,* 24 December 1948, and typescript of radio interview, 22 December 1948 (HRC: Norman Bel Geddes 584 i-1). Despite all the publicity, the owner of Copa City, Murray Weiniger, was unable to recoup the $35,000 he claimed to be spending per week on the cabaret and floor show, and filed for bankruptcy just over six months after the opening, leaving Bel Geddes unpaid, which caused him significant financial difficulties.
11. Unidentified newspaper clipping pasted in the album kept by Urban (Columbia).
12. *Brooklyn Eagle,* 30 March 1930.
13. Bel Geddes in the *New Republic,* 20 January 1941; *New York Journal and American,* 8 April 1941. These sentiments were also echoed by the enthusiastic headlines of the *New York Times* and the *New York Post* for the same day, both of which specifically praised both the use of plastic and the theatrical structuring of the procession as novelties.

6
A CENTURY OF PROGRESS

1. The "White City" inspired a book by a popular preacher of the time: Josiah Strong's *The Twentieth Century City* (1898), which proclaimed "the city redeemed is a vision of the revelation, the symbol itself of Heaven, Heaven on earth" (p. 181). For illustration of this theme in American architecture, see Ruth Eaton, *Ideal Cities: Utopianism and the (Un)built Environment* (London: Thames and Hudson, 2002).
2. The contemporary sense of the future being ushered in by the new technologies at the Columbian Exposition—and a sense of the power represented by electrical dynamos—is well illustrated by a memoir that became extremely influential; see *The Education of Henry Adams: An Autobiography* (Massachusetts Historical Society, 1918), p. 341.

3. Despite the names of the Coney Island resorts, evoking undersea adventure, space travel, and the archetypes of the subconscious, these were all amusement parks filled with rides, roller coasters and Ferris wheels, boardwalks, and booths—in contrast to the later theme parks designed by Disney or Urban (see Chapter 8), in which everything contributes to a specific fantasy: either a children's fairy tale, such as "Hansel and Gretel" (Urban) or "Sleeping Beauty" (Disney).

4. Urban's personal copy is in the Urban Collection, Columbia.

5. "Chicago Fair," typescript (production box 47: Urban Collection, Columbia).

6. 7 May 1933, Letter in the Urban Collection, Columbia.

7. Percy MacKaye, letter, 29 September 1929, in Bel Geddes' job file under "World Finder."

8. Steele MacKaye died just three weeks after the completion of his Scenitorium, and little of his proposed dramatic program seems to have been presented.

9. The letter was dated 23 October 1929. The more than thirty recipients included a who's who of experimental theater: Granville Barker, Jean Cocteau, Paul Green, Gordon Craig, Leopold Jessner, Louis Jouvet, Pablo Picasso, Luigi Pirandello, Oscar Schlemmer (of the Bauhaus), Igor Stravinski, Alexander Tairoff, as well as Max Reinhardt (with whom Bel Geddes had a long-standing theatrical relationship), and architects such as Frank Lloyd Wright. Bel Geddes Collection, HRC.

10. Terence Gray, 17 September 1929; Fuerst, 22 September 1929, MacKaye, 29 September 1929 (all in the Bel Geddes Collection, HRC).

11. For example: *New York Times,* 16 November 1930; *Fortune,* October 1930, p. 96.

12. This sketch is held in Box 182, n-1, HRC.

13. 23 October 1929.

14. For instance, in 1867 the Paris International Exposition covered 41 acres and attracted 6,805,969 visitors: the Centennial Exposition in Philadelphia the same year covered 48 acres and drew 9,892,625 visitors. For other comparisons, see introductory essay by Robert W. Rydell, *The Books of the Fairs: Materials About World's Fairs, 1834–1916, in the Smithsonian Institution Libraries* (Chicago: American Library Association, 1992).

15. *Architecture,* May 1934.

16. Among others who have noted this connection is Bush, *Streamlined Decade,* p. 153.

17. Egmont Arens and Roy Sheldon, *Consumer Engineering: A New Technique for Prosperity* (New York: Arno Press, 1932).

18. *Horizons,* p. 4. In this book Bel Geddes was also responsible for coining the term "machine art," declaring "Art will be achieved by the machine," p. 292. The term has come to be the label for the design of this period.

19. Harold Clurman, *The Fervent Years: The Story of the Group Theatre and the Thirties* (New York: Knopf, 1945), p. 48; *Horizons,* pp. 3, 289–90.

20. These figures come from a history of the magazines: Lee Server's *Danger Is My Business* (San Francisco: Chronicle Books, 1993).

21. Quotations come directly from the movie (London Films, 1936, directed by Alex Korda), and from *Things to Come: A Film Story Based on the Material Contained in His History of the Future, The Shape of Things to Come* by H. G. Wells (London: Cresset Press, 1935), p. 56.

22. Norman V. Carlisle and Frank B. Latham, *Miracles Ahead! Better Living in the Postwar World* (New York: Macmillan, 1944).

23. Unidentified newspaper clipping in the Loewy papers, Cooper-Hewitt Museum, New York.

24. *Business Week,* 10 June 1933.

25. *Designing for People* (1967 ed.), p. 111.

1. Videorecording of the film *The World of Tomorrow*, directed by Lance Bird and Tom Johnson, written by John Crowley (1940; New York: Media Study, 1986).
2. Color supplement, *New York Times*, 5 March 1939.
3. Also quoted in Susman, *Culture as History*, p. 214.
4. *Nation*, 8 May 1939.
5. *GM Horizons and Highways Press Guide*, 1940, p. 28.
6. See Chapter 11.
7. The Gallup survey was reported in the *New York Times*, 17 May 1939: the second most popular, behind Bel Geddes' Futurama, was judged to be the City of Tomorrow in the Perisphere. Clips of Futurama from *The World of Tomorrow* can be viewed at http://xroads.virginia.edu/~1930s/DISPLAY/39wf/frame.htm.
8. *Sunday News*, 25 June 1939. For examples of professional journals: *Road Builder's News*, or *Automotive Industries*, both 1 May 1939, which gave Futurama a three- and five-page report respectively, and *Popular Mechanics*, August 1940. In the *Cincinnati Post*, 6 July 1939, Futurama was reviewed by its science editor.
9. Brooks Atkinson, *New York Times*, 29 October 1935 (his exclamation point).
10. As Eleanor Roosevelt recounts, *New York World Telegram*, 17 February 1937. Other articles on the social importance of the play appeared in *Commonweal*, 8 November 1935; *America*, 30 November 1935; *Catholic World*, 2 December 1935.
11. Case history of the GM intersection, citing GM memos: typescript dictated by Bel Geddes 8 August 1941 and 29 September 1941 (emphasis added).
12. According to the photographic record, these futuristic vehicles appeared on the life-size section of the Futurama display for only the second year of the World's Fair (1940), since at least initially the cars and trucks on the full-scale city intersection at the end of the ride were GM's current 1939 models.
13. Bel Geddes, "Description of the General Motors Building and Exhibit for the New York World's Fair," typescript, 8 September 1939, p. 15.
14. Excerpts from the words spoken by the "whispering voice" were widely reported, as in the *New York Times*, 19 April 1939.
15. Memo from Bel Geddes, 30 June 1941.
16. Bel Geddes, "Description," typescript, 8 September 1939, p. 31.
17. *Sunday News*, 18 June 1939, and *New York Post*, 11 May 1939.
18. Bel Geddes, "Description," typescript, 8 September 1939, p. 14.
19. "Futurama Facts," the equivalent of a commemorative theater program, offered a twenty-page overview of photos, descriptions, and quotations from the sound track (undated and unpaginated).
20. 11 June 1939.
21. President and vice president of General Motors, W. Knudsen and R. Grant, cited in GM press release, 14 April 1939. Also cited in "Case History of the GM Intersection," typescript, n.p. (dictated by Bel Geddes 29 September 1941. HRC 381.56–57).
22. It received extensive press attention over the next several years; for instance, *Cosmopolitan*, in January 1940, gave it a seven-page spread entitled "Pattern for a Brave New World" (pp. 38–39, 82–87).
23. *American City*, July 1939; *New York Post*, 11 May 1939. The 1940 figures were given in *PM* (New York), 28 August 1940.

24. As a University of Virginia website devoted to the New York 1939–40 World's Fair comments: it is no "coincidence that the mileage of paved roads in America rose from 387,000 miles in 1920 to roughly 2,946,000 miles by 1970. General Motors staked its claim to the future by providing a comprehensive worldview in which it was to be the chief proponent of a better quality of life, and it did so at a crucial point in the redevelopment of the nation. Its message not only changed the face and the scale of advertising and marketing forever; it changed the ways in which Americans live, move, and build. GM's vision of 1960 was not too far off the mark, minus the floating dirigible hangars and auto-gyros" (http://xroads.virginia.edu/~1930s/DISPLAY/39wf/frame .htm). However, floating airfields were specifically Bel Geddes' vision, as were the motorways; and with the exception of the science-fiction "auto-gyros" (which he dismissed), his name could be accurately substituted for every reference to GM in this document.

8
THE WORLD OF TOMORROW

1. *Sales Service News Letter* (Chicago), 8 May 1939.
2. *New York Herald Tribune*, 28 April 1939.
3. *Magic Motorways* (New York: Random House, 1940) had a significant and long-lasting effect from being associated with the striking Shell Oil "City of Tomorrow" advertising campaign of 1937–38, as well as being in effect an extended scientific and engineering commentary on Futurama.
4. Press release, 1 August 1942, for the Graham-Paige Company, Bel Geddes Collection, HRC, JF 161.14; Norman V. Carlisle and Frank B. Latham, *Miracles Ahead! Better Living in the Postwar World* (New York: Macmillan, 1944), pp. 18, 4, 43.
5. Proposal to client: typescript, April 1938, p. 1, Bel Geddes Collection, HRC, JF 381.3. Bel Geddes continually published "predictions": these were also repeated in *Ladies' Home Journal*, January 1931 (on p. 10 of the HRC copy Bel Geddes has noted these were written in 1930), and *Life*, 5 June 1939.
6. For the complete 1964–65 *New York World's Fair Guidebook* to the General Motors Pavilion, see: http://peace.expoarchive.com/6465/transportation/trpav07.shtml.
7. *New York Times*, "Guide to the World's Fair," 5 May 1940. Also cited in Allen Abel, Review Section, *National Post* (Canada), 1 January 2000.
8. Fairyland website: http://www.fairyland.org/facts.html.
9. Wheatsworth was sold to the National Biscuit Company, now Nabisco, and in the 1950s Urban's Gingerbread Castle was closed. It fell into disrepair, but is now being restored. See www .dupontcastle.com/castles/gingerbread.html. (The correspondence on this website also asserts the influence of Urban's theme park on Disney, as well as offering evidence for its long-standing popularity.)
10. Cited by Roy Disney, *New York Times*, 3 February 1967, and http://www.wdwinfo.com/wdwinfo/ guides/epcot/ep-futureworld.htm. Additional information about EPCOT can be found in Beth Dunlop's *Building a Dream: The Art of Disney Architecture* (New York: Abrams, 1996).
11. *A Pictorial Souvenir of Walt Disney World:* www.intercot.com/edc/Horizons/index.html.
12. Typescript of conversation between Bel Geddes and R. Warner (U.S. Coordinator for the Brussels World's Fair), 5 March 1957 (Bel Geddes Collection, HRC).
13. Memo to Henry Cabot Lodge (U.S. State Department), March 1947, pp. 7–8 (Bel Geddes Collection, HRC).
14. Ibid.

9
CAR CULTURE

1. Cited in Susman, *Culture as History,* p. 108.
2. Hailed as such by (among others) André Siegfried, *America Comes of Age,* "Fordism"—as it came to be known—was based on Frederick Taylor's time-and-motion studies, and enthusiastically adopted in Soviet Russia.
3. Prefatory note in Bel Geddes' personal copy, Bel Geddes Collection, HRC.
4. Interview with Munro Innes: typescript, n.d., Bel Geddes Collection, HRC, JF 161.
5. Details of the design, and the difficulties experienced in making accurate measurements, are given in memos and minutes of meetings with Chrysler executives, as well as in a typescript summary by Bel Geddes: Bel Geddes Collection, HRC, JF 268 and 271.
6. *Saturday Evening Post,* 16 December 1933.
7. Typescript minutes, Bel Geddes Collection, HRC, JF 271.1 (emphasis added).
8. *Chrysler Pictorial News,* 1, no. 1 (1934); also reprinted in the *New York American,* 4 January 1934.
9. *New York Times,* 16 May 1999, WK 3.
10. Clipping (n.d.), Bel Geddes Collection, HRC, JF 415.
11. *Newsweek,* 22 August 1955.
12. Maurice Evans first appeared in America in 1935 as Romeo with Katharine Cornell, and made a wartime reputation by touring a GI version of *Hamlet* to troops across the Pacific. He appeared prominently in the "Hallmark Hall of Fame" TV productions of the 1950s. In line with the trend of the time, he established Maurice Evans Industrials as an "Industrial Show Production Unit" with his silhouette as Hamlet, traditional skull in hand, for its logo (a somewhat misleading guarantee of "high culture" for commerce).
13. *Advertising Age,* 20 October 1958. After New York, the 1958 Motorama transferred to the Commonwealth Armory in Boston for a further fifty-seven performances.
14. The script, contract, briefing notes, and clippings (from which all the quotations in this and the preceding paragraphs come) are held in the Maurice Evans Industrials Collection at the New York Public Library for the Performing Arts Lincoln Center.
15. *New York Mirror Magazine,* 24 November 1957.
16. A telling photo of this 1949 "Fish-tail" Cadillac (never manufactured) is published in Donald Bush, *The Streamlined Decade,* p. 114.
17. When Czechoslovakian designers created the Tatra car in 1934, it was rear-engined and streamlined, with a small vertical fin running up the back, just like Bel Geddes' designs published in *Horizons* two years earlier. The connection between the design of the 1936/37 Volkswagen and the 1934 Tatra (manufactured in Czechoslovakia until the German annexation in 1938, when production was stopped because it was in direct competition with the Volkswagen) has been noted in *Automobile Quarterly* 7, no. 3 (1969), p. 311. The earliest Beetle prototype appeared in 1935.

10
STREET SCENES

1. Josiah Strong, *The Twentieth Century City* (New York: Baker and Taylor, 1898), p. 18.
2. For a discussion of this utopian trend in urban design by many American architects, see Donald James, *Imagining the Modern City* (Minneapolis: University of Minnesota Press, 1999).

3. For example: Simon Guy, Simon Marvin, and Timothy Moss, *Infrastructures in Transition: Urban Networks, Buildings, Plans* (Sterling, Va.: Earthscan Publication, 2001).

4. The degree to which the Shell Oil model anticipated Futurama can be seen in the original plans, which called for a sequence of twelve different advertisements—only six of which were to be in urban settings, the remainder covering arterial highways running through mountainous country, across a river, skirting a metropolitan centre and "night driving."

5. Typescript, n.p., and minutes of meeting, 10 November 1936, Bel Geddes Collection, HRC, JF 356 f.1 and 2.

6. *New York Times,* 1 August 1937; *Architectural Forum,* July 1937.

7. Typescript, n.p., Bel Geddes Collection, HRC, JF 356 f.4.

8. Miller McClintock, script for presentation, National Planning Conference, Detroit, 1 June 1937, pp. 4–5. The Harvard Group, founded in 1920, had proposed and developed the first traffic light.

9. At a meeting on 16 November 1936, Shell executives insisted—over Bel Geddes' protest—that the city model put pedestrians underground, with the major roads above: in the World's Fair model for Futurama Bel Geddes reversed this, reverting to his original concept in putting the pedestrians on elevated walkways.

10. McClintock, script for presentation, National Planning Conference, pp. 4, 8.

11. Typescript, "List of situations" (minutes of meeting with Shell Oil representative, 10 November 1936); typescript notes of meeting between Bel Geddes and Dr. Miller McClintock, 1 December 1936. Bel Geddes Collection, HRC, JF 356.2.

12. McClintock, reported in the *Terre Haute Tribune Star,* 26 September 1937.

13. *Philadelphia Record,* 1 August 1937; *Life,* 15 September 1937.

14. *New York Sun,* 26 July 1937; *Life,* 30 August 1937, 1 November 1937. All the other newspapers cited—and many more—published pieces between the beginning of August and December 1937 (see the clippings folder, JF 356, in the Bel Geddes Collection, HRC). *Cleveland Plain Dealer,* 2 October 1937; *Journal of Commerce and Commercial,* 15 June 1937; *Architectural Forum,* July 1937.

15. For many of the details in this summarized treatment of Robert Moses's career I am indebted to the excellent study by Robert Caro, *The Power Broker: Robert Moses and the Fall of New York* (New York: Knopf, 1974). Another view is offered by Joel Schwartz, *The New York Approach: Robert Moses, Urban Liberals and Redevelopment of the City* (Columbus: Ohio State University Press, 1993).

16. *New York Sun,* 2 June 1937.

17. *News* (New York), September 1937; correspondence, 8–17 July 1937, Bel Geddes Collection, HRC, JF 356 f.1.

18. For instance, *New York World Telegram,* 27 June 1945; *Rochester Democrat and Chronicle,* 30 July 1945.

19. Notes and memo dated 9 August 1946, Bel Geddes Collection, HRC, JF 562. Bel Geddes' claim may technically be true, at least in terms of the multiuse concept of this airport building, as well as its modular reproducibility. His air station and terminal may also have represented a first in America. However, a custom-designed airport terminal had already been built at Gatwick in the United Kingdom by the architectural firm of Hoar, Marlow & Lovett in 1936. Well in advance of its time, this shows influence of Bel Geddes' designs published in *Horizons* four years earlier. It was circular, with four retractable telescopic tunnels—one at each quadrant—to take passengers under cover to an aircraft door. It does not seem to have been replicated at other British airports.

20. *Toledo Blade,* undated clipping in Bel Geddes' job file.

21. A partial script (typescript, n.p.) is included in Bel Geddes Collection, HRC, JF 525.

22. *Architectural Forum,* August 1945, pp. 199–204; *Toledo Blade,* 12 October 1945; publicity release, Hamilton Wright Company, 1945, Bel Geddes Collection, HRC, JF 525.6.

23. For instance, *Chicago News,* 8 June 1945; *Building Service,* October 1946.

24. *Life,* 17 September 1945 (Overseas Edition for the U.S. Marine Corps). Also published in the Home edition, pp. 87–94.

25. For instance, see Eleanor Roosevelt in *New York World Telegram,* 25 May 1939.

26. *New York Sun* and *New York World Telegram,* both 27 June 1945; *New York World Telegram* and *Rochester Democrat and Chronicle,* both 30 July 1945.

27. See Geoffrey Moorhouse, *Imperial City: The Rise and Rise of New York* (London: Hodder and Stoughton, 1988).

11
REACHING FOR THE SKY

1. Donald Trump, cited in Jonathan Mandell, *Trump Tower* (New York: Lyle Stuart, 1984), p. 27.

2. Theodore Starrett (a builder involved with the Flatiron Building) in response to a contract for a hundred-story skyscraper—ironically never constructed: cited in Paul Goldberger, *The Skyscraper* (New York: Knopf, 1981), p. 8.

3. These architectural blueprints, forming the set design for *Iron Men,* are preserved in the Bel Geddes Collection, HRC, JF 353.

4. A description of this lunch club is given by Walter K. Kilham, *Raymond Hood, Architect* (New York: Architectural Book Publishers, 1981), pp. 79f. Sadly, no recipe for Urban's cocktail survives.

5. Theodore Muller, *Architectural Review,* June 1929, p. 945.

6. *New Yorker,* 28 March 1928, p. 75.

7. Urban, cited in Deems Taylor, *Musical America,* 8 October 1927, and memo by Urban (dated 17 October 1927), which also cites Murchison's reported comments, in the Urban Collection, Columbia. A slightly different interpretation is put forward in the far longer discussion of the Metropolitan Opera project by Carter and Cole, *Joseph Urban,* pp. 221ff.

8. For discussions of Urban's influence on Rockefeller Center, see Carol H. Krinsky, *Rockefeller Center* (New York: Oxford University Press, 1978), pp. 178–80, and Carter and Cole, *Joseph Urban,* p. 209.

9. Urban's disparaging but accurate comment about the imitative quality of American architecture in this period was reprinted in several newspapers: the one cited is in "Stage Sets or Beach Clubs Urban's Style Is Distinctive," *New York Evening Post,* 30 June 1930.

10. *Architectural Forum,* 1928, reprinted in Robert McCarter, *Frank Lloyd Wright* (London: Phaidon Press, 1997), p. 277.

11. Copies of the New School brochures, and of the public tender for the building, are held in the Urban Collection, Columbia.

12. New School, publicity broadsheet, 1929, Urban Collection, Columbia.

13. *Architectural Record,* February 1931, devoted almost the entire issue to the New School.

14. The title of an essay published in Edmund Wilson, *The American Jitters* (New York: Charles Scribner's Sons, 1931), p. 28.

15. New School, publicity brochure, 1930, Urban Collection, Columbia; Shepard Vogelgesang, *Architectural Record,* February 1931, p. 143.

16. Philip Johnson, "The Architecture of the New School," *Arts,* March 1931, p. 393.

17. *Christian Science Monitor,* 31 August 1931.

18. The official Russian specifications, plus supporting material used by Urban in preparing his bid for the project, including street maps and photographs of Moscow, are held in the Urban Collection, Columbia.

19. Typescript (n.p.), Urban Collection, Columbia, box 32.

20. Ibid.

21. "Flexible Theatre," *New York Times Magazine,* 30 November 1947. He revised and expanded this article for *Theatre Arts,* June–July 1948.

22. *Chicago Daily News,* 24 October 1930.

23. Articles (uniformly enthusiastic) on Bel Geddes' aerial restaurant appeared in a wide number of newspapers and journals, including: *Philadelphia Public Ledger,* 4 May 1930; *Popular Mechanics,* July 1930, p. 88; *Architecture,* July 1930, pp. 11–13; *Creative Art,* August 1930, pp. 146f.

12
SUBURBAN HEAVEN

1. *Horizons,* p. 23.

2. Ibid., p. 225.

3. Ibid., p. 206.

4. *Ladies' Home Journal,* April 1931. The series, started in the January issue, ran until July 1931. A compressed version was also published in *Reader's Digest,* May 1931.

5. *The Patriot,* by Alfred Neumann, was originally performed in Berlin, directed by Karl Heinz Martin, in 1927.

6. *Theatre Arts Monthly,* March 1928.

7. *Scientific American,* March 1928, pp. 249–50.

8. A sketch by Urban shows six configurations of a single house, but all have a balcony and chimney in identical placement. Although it is clear that a garage can be switched for living space, the differences between one house and the next are primarily cosmetic and limited to external appearance.

9. *New York Times,* 15 March 1942.

10. "Better Living," pamphlet published by Revere Corp., September 1941. Also published in *Saturday Evening Post,* 27 September 1941.

11. Details on this project are contained in the Bel Geddes Collection, HRC, JF 631.

12. Typescript, n.p., Bel Geddes Collection, HRC, JF 356.3.

13. "Presentation on Low Cost Housing to the President by the Housing Corp. of America," Rockefeller Institute, December 1939, typescript held in the Bel Geddes Collection, HRC, JF 400.1.

14. J. E. Benton, response to Bel Geddes' initial report, letter of 11 September 1948 to Myer Schine, Bel Geddes Collection, HRC, JF 592.1.

15. Bel Geddes, "Program for an Overall Development of Boca Raton," undated, Bel Geddes Collection, HRC, JF 591.1.

16. Typescript of record 210, side 2, 7 February 1949, Bel Geddes Collection, HRC, JF 591-2.

17. Tony Lamont, letter to Bel Geddes, 21 February 1949, Bel Geddes Collection, HRC, JF 591-1.

1. Urban, article on the exhibition of the Arts of the Theatre in the annual Architectural League show, written for the *New York Times*, April 1933. A typescript copy is preserved in the Urban Collection, Columbia.

2. *New York Post*, 22 April 1918; *New York Morning Telegraph*, 1 November 1915.

3. *Sunday Journal*, 3 October 1920.

4. Ibid.

5. For details on Urban's work before coming to America, see Carter and Cole, *Joseph Urban*, chapter 1.

6. *Brooklyn Eagle*, 30 March 1930.

7. Willis Steele, 1915 typescript draft of articles, Urban Collection, Columbia.

8. Several clippings note this in the scrapbook (Urban Collection, Columbia), but the date and, apart from *Metal Arts*, the names of the journals are either missing or illegible.

9. Minutes of meeting with Columbus executives, 27 February 1940, Bel Geddes Collection, HRC, JF 407.

10. In an interview for *Automobile Topics* in 1938, Bel Geddes compared the functionalism of his car designs for Graham Paige with his metal furniture and his stoves, all of which were openly presented as steel, "instead of as an imitation of wood." Munro Innes, typescript, Bel Geddes Collection, HRC, JF 161.4.

11. *New York Herald Tribune*, 16 October 1929.

12. *Brooklyn Eagle*, 30 March 1930.

13. *Photo Journal*, (?) December 1919, repeated in *Vogue* of the same month [clippings with partially obscured date], Urban Collection, Columbia.

14. Mary Fanton Roberts, *Arts and Decoration*, August 1936.

15. *House and Garden*, January 1933, pp. 33f.

16. *New York Sun*, 3 January 1933.

17. *Upholsterer and Interior Decorator*, September 1920; *Architectural Review*, July 1921; *New Yorker*, August 1931.

18. *Evening Courier*, 29 April 1930; *Town Crier*, 5 May 1930; *Theatre*, September 1930; *Record*, 29 April 1930. Hood's review was published in the *Sun*, 6 May 1930 (his emphasis).

19. Typescript, Bel Geddes Collection, HRC, JF 161, published in *Creative Art: A Magazine of Fine and Applied Art*, October 1928.

20. Special World's Fair supplement, March 1939.

21. Raymond Loewy, *Industrial Design* (Woodstock, N.Y.: Overlook Press, 1979), p. 98.

22. "Color in Industry," *Fortune*, 1 February 1930.

23. "Yes! Something Has Happened in Gas Ranges!" (my emphasis), SGE publicity pamphlet, 1932; a copy is held in the Bel Geddes Collection, HRC, JF 267.8.

24. *Philadelphia Gas Works News*, April 1933, pp. 4–5.

25. Copy of internal SGE memo, Bel Geddes Collection, HRC, JF 267.

26. T. S. Kennedy, cited in *American Enameller*, May 1934; *Kansas City Times*, 27 January 1937.

27. Typescript, n.p. (my emphasis), Bel Geddes Collection, HRC, JF 301.1.

28. Malcolm Gladwell's phrase describing the way in which a relatively small change in public consciousness can result in a societywide shift: see *The Tipping Point: How Little Things Can Make a Big Difference* (Boston: Little, Brown, 2000).

1. Typescript, undated, n.p., Bel Geddes Collection, HRC, JF 134.

2. *Women's Wear Daily*, 12 January 1928. Similar observations were made by *Display World*, December 1927.

3. *American Architect*, 20 September 1928.

4. *Architectural Forum*, June 1929, p. 945; *Architecture and Building*, July 1929, p. 200.

5. The fish designs on the walls were by Gretl Urban (an example wrongly attributed is printed in Carter and Cole, *Joseph Urban*, p. 176).

6. *Time*, 1 February 1941. Also published in Cromwell-Collier brochures, 1940 and 1941 (Bel Geddes Collection, HRC, JF 359). As background Bel Geddes did extensive public surveys of newsstand purchasing patterns and readers' preferences for color, layout, typefaces, and so on.

7. *Theatre Arts Monthly*, July 1929; *New York Times Magazine*, 23 June 1929.

8. Bruce Barton, *The Man Nobody Knows* (London: Constable, 1925), p. 81. Also quoted in Susman, *Culture as History*, p. 128.

9. Company memo of February 1944, typescript in Bel Geddes Collection, HRC, JF 419.

10. A review of *Art and the Machine* (a study of the "new profession" of industrial designers and, significantly, written by theater critics Sheldon and Martha Cheney), in the *Kansas City Times*, 27 January 1937, noted that the final shape in "evolution chart of motorcars by Raymond Loewy," published in the book and leading to a teardrop shape with a single rear fin, was almost exactly identical to Bel Geddes' Motor Car 8, designed in 1931 and published in *Horizons*, pp. 54, 55, 56, 57.

11. *Fortune*, February 1934.

12. Bush, *Streamlined Decade*, p. 182.

13. Unfortunately, unlike his classes at the Master School of United Artists, there seems to be no record in Bel Geddes' files of the names of students who attended his School of Design, although at least one person who subsequently worked for Bel Geddes' industrial design studio had trained there.

14. See www.raymondloewy.com.

15. *American Architect*, March 1929.

16. Bel Geddes, memorandum to Mills Industries, 16 November 1943, typescript, Bel Geddes Collection, HRC, JF 509. He was also far ahead of his time in other technological ways. For example, in 1940 Bel Geddes was developing an "aerial torpedo" controlled by radio and using TV for "terrain vision." Over two years before the V-1 and V-2 rockets had been developed by the Germans, Bel Geddes' plans were restricted to a propeller-driven craft, which was judged too impractical at the time. What he was envisaging was clearly a prototype of the cruise missile, though what he actually came up with was almost a clone to the unmanned drones used for reconnaissance by the U.S. Army today.

17. NBC contract, 18 April 1951. The extensive nature of Bel Geddes' involvement with the television industry is indicated by the number of files kept by his office. See Bel Geddes Collection, HRC, JF 654, 656, 683, 688, 693.

18. Copies of internal NBC memos and transcripts of meetings, Bel Geddes Collection, HRC, JF 688.j.7.

19. Notes, Bel Geddes Collection, HRC, JF 693. The other NBC executives were John Nesbitt and

Jim Sylvester. Bel Geddes' job files contain two folders that give some indication of possible programming: "John Nesbitt—Telephone Hour TV" and "You Are There." Unfortunately, the documentation on these projects is missing.

AFTERWORD

1. My original aim was to compile documentation for *Twentieth-Century British and American Theatre: A Critical Guide to Archives* (Aldershot, U.K.: Ashgate, 1999).

Index

Numbers in bold refer to illustrations.
Abdin Palace (Cairo), 19
Adam and Eva, 74
Advertising Age, 166
Aida, 38
Albany (New York), 179
Albright, Madeleine, 294
Alen, William Van, 47, 192
Amazing Stories, 111
Ambassador Hotel (Los Angeles), 227–228
American Architect, 54, 65, 263, 279
American Art Deco, 269
American Broadcasting Company (ABC), 284
American Builder, 255
American City, 143
American Home, 255
American Hotels Corporation, 71
American Institute of Public Opinion, 121
American Magazine, The, 269
American Radiator Building (New York), 203
American Stove Company, 249
Americana Hotel (Miami), 291
Amphibia, 71
Andersen, Hans Christian, 42
Anderson, Sherwood, 72, 193
Andrews, John, 209
Andrews, W. Earle, 183
Anti-Establishment League, 19
Apple Computers Inc. (iPod), 2
Aquacade (New York World's Fair, *1939*), 123
Aquatic Park Casino (San Francisco), 92
Arabesque, 260
Arc de Triomphe (Paris), 181
Architect and the Industrial Arts Exhibition, 244
Architectural Forum, 146, 175, 178, 182, 186
Architectural League Exhibition (*1929*), 69, 109;
    (*1933*), 234: (*1921*), 244
Architectural League of New York, 193
Architectural Record, **61**, 68, 91, 200, 201, 230
Architectural Review, 193, 195, 234, 244
Architecture, 110
Armstrong, Louis, 14
Army Air Force School of Applied Tactics, 147
Around the Map, 42–43, **43**, 47
Art Deco, 4, 13, 14, 43, 84, 105, 108; In America, 10–11;
    And the International Exhibition (Paris), 9–10, 11;
    Related to Urban, 42–43, 84, 238, 244, 281
Art Nouveau, 2, 8–10, 13, 108; Related to Urban, 20,
    22, 235
Arts, 201
Arts and Crafts Movement (England), 20
Arts and Decoration, 48, 78, 244, 255
Association of Art Museums, 279
Astaire, Fred, 85
Astor Hotel (New York), 203

AT&T Corp., 152, 293
Atlantic Beach Club (Long Island), 91, 92, **94**, 96
Atlantic Crossing, 71
Austria, 18, 19–22
Austrian Pavilion (St. Louis World's Fair), 20
Avant-Garde, 107, 293
Axel Wenner-Gren Co., 274

Baker Furniture Co., 240
Baker, George Pierce, 69
Baker, Josephine, 10
Baltimore American, 178
Barnum & Bailey Circus. *See* Ringling Brothers Barnum
    and Bailey Circus
Barnum, P. T., 103
Barrymore, Lionel, 76
Barton Candy Co., 265
Barton, Bruce, 271
Bauhaus (Germany), 4, 9, 14, 204
Baum, Frank L., 104
Beard, Charles, 201
Beaux Arts Style, 8, 102, 104, 106
Beck Shoe, 265
Bedell Store (New York), 8, 203, 262–267, **264**, **266**,
    273
Belasco Theater (New York), 125
Bell telephone, 7, 32, 148
Ben Hur, 30
Bennett, J. H., 150
Berkshire Hotel (New York), 85
Berlin (Germany), 25, 204
Berlin, Irving, 44
Bermuda, 71
Bernard, Oliver, 13
Better Homes and Gardens, 255
Better Living, 225–227, 308
Biddle, Anthony, 88
Big Parade, 72
Blackfoot Reservation, Montana, 19
Blackpool (UK), 104
Block, Paul, 182, 183
Boas, Franz, 201
Boca Raton, Florida, 227–230, **228**, **229**
Bogart, Humphrey, 128
Bohr, Neils, 146
Bolton Canyon, 30
Bolton, Guy, 193
Bond Clothing Stores Inc., 265
Bonstelle, Jessie, 25
Bonwit Teller Store (New York), 267
Book-Cadillac Hotel (Detroit), 95
Boston (Massachusetts), 38, 175, 177, 235; And Urban,
    28, 31, 39, 42
Boston Evening Transcript, 87
Boston Opera, 38, 39, 73, 156, 277

Bowman-Biltmore Hotel Group, 85
Brando, Marlon, 204
Breer, C. H., 161
Bremerton (Washington), 274
Britvic Co., 273
Broadacre City (Wright), 110, 227
Broadway Limited, 34
Bronx (New York), 189
Bronx Zoo (New York), 22
Bronx-Whitestone Bridge, 180
Brooklyn (New York), 84, 182, 187; Civic Center, 181;
    Hospital, 189; Museum, 279
Brooklyn Bridge, 189, 193, 199
Brooklyn Eagle, 235, 97
Brown, John Mason, 139
Brush, Katherine, 241, 244, **245**
Brussels, Belgium, 152
"Buck Rogers" (Philip Francis Nowlan, *Amazing
    Stories*), 111, 112
Buffalo (New York), 148
Buffalo Bill (William Frederick Cody), 103
Buffalo News, 49
Bunshaft, Gordon, 199
Burlington Northern Railroad, 115
Business Machines, 269
Butler House (Des Moines), 221
Byrd, Admiral Richard E., 237

Cadillac cars (General Motors), 6, 156, 168, 290;
    Cadillac LaSalle, 157; "Dagmar" Cadillac, 163, 168
Cairo, Egypt, 19, 279
Caliban of the Yellow Sands, 27–28, **29**, 107
Camp, Mrs. Alex, 74
Canadian National Tower (CN Tower, Toronto), 209,
    211, 214
Capra, Frank, 121
Carnegie Hall (New York), 49
Carroll, Earl, 44
Carson, Edward E., 209
Carson Pirie Scott Building (Chicago), 9
Casino of Science Stage Show (New York World's Fair,
    1939), 123
Cathedral of Christ the Redeemer (Moscow), 206
Catholic Theatre Movement, 128
Celebration (Florida), 217
Central Park (New York), 7, 88, 89
Central Park Casino (New York), 88–91, **89**, **90**, 97, 98,
    179, 241
Central Park Zoo (New York), 89
Central Theatre (New York), 76
"Century Girl, The" (*Follies*), 47
Century Theatre (New York), 42, 47, 66, **67**, 69, 85
Challenge to Liberty, 104
Chambless, Edgar, 172–173
Chaplin, Charles, 73
Charm School, The, 46
Chaulnes, Duchess de, 44
Chesapeake (Virginia), 274
Chevrolet Corvette, 163
Chicago Art Institute, 19
Chicago Daily News, 209
Chicago Opera, 19

Chicago River (Illinois), 103
Chicago Tribune, 203
Chicago Tribune Tower, 193
Chicago World's Fair/"A Century of Progress" (*1933*), 4,
    72, 75, **77**, 104, 120, 193, 209; Contribution of Urban
    and Bel Geddes, 102, 105–106; Influence, 110–112;
    Theatre program, 30, 107–110, 122, 203, 204
Christian Science Monitor, 178
Chrysler Building (New York), 10, 47, 48, 65, 192, 197
Chrysler cars (General Motors), 6, 8, 14; Airflow, 159,
    160–166, **160**, **162**, 273, 277, 287; De Soto, 128;
    Dodge, 41, 156; Dodge Durango, 163
Chrysler Corp. (General Motors), 128, 157, 159, 161, 163,
    164, 165, 273, 290
Chrysler Pictorial News, 161
Cincinnati (Ohio), **62**, 63, 84, 86, 183
Cincinnati Art Museum, 244
Cincinnati Commercial Tribune, 49
City Beautiful Movement, 172
City of Salinas, **114**
"City of Tomorrow." *See* Democracity
Cleveland Auto Show, 178
Cleveland Institute of Art, 19
Cleveland Plain Dealer, 178
Coca-Cola Co., 8, 94, **272**, 273, 290
Coconut Grove (Palm Beach), 51
Cohoes American, 178
Cold War, The, 14
Collier's, 19, 269
Col-O-Tex Company Ltd., 237
Columbia (Massachusetts), 180
Columbia University (New York), 265
Columbian Exposition (1893), 8, 60, 102–104, 107, 110,
    172
Columbus, Christopher, 106
Columbus Coated Fabrics, 237
Columbus Day, 103
Commonwealth Edison Building (Chicago), 265
Community League of Greater Boston, 28
Community Youth Center (New York), 127
Condé Nast Publications, 46
Coney Island (Brooklyn), 104, 149, 179
Congress Hotel (Chicago), 85
Conklin and Rossant, 172
Connecticut Yankee, A, 72
Consumer Engineering: A New Technique for Prosperity,
    111
Conway, Gordon, 33, **45**, 46, 47, 97
Cook County Morgue (Illinois), 19
Copa City (Florida), 85, 98, 230, 267, 291; Construction,
    95, **96**, **97**, 204, 265
Copland, Aaron, 201
"Coquette" lamp, **11**
Cosmopolitan Theatre (New York), 8, 76, **78**, 78–79
Craig, Gordon, 27
Criterion Theatre (New York), 75, 76
Cromwell-Collier Publications, 268–269, **270**, **271**, 273
Cross Bay Bridge, New York, 180
Cross-Bronx Expressway, New York, 180
"Crystal Lassies" (New York World's Fair *1939*), 122
Cunard Building (New York), 195

Dallas (Texas), 74
Dante Alighieri, 26, 30
Darcy, J. J., 181
Davies, Marion, 72, 74–75, 78, 235
De Soto cars. *See* Chrysler
Dead End, 71, 130, 139, 141, 142, 175, 218; Production, 125–127, **126, 127**; Effect, 128, 157, 246
Dearborn, Michigan, 94, 214
Debenhams Co., 46
Decorative Furnishing, 78
Decorator, The, 61
Delano Hotel (Miami), 291
DeMille, Cecil B., 71
Democracity (New York World's Fair, *1939*), 120, 122, 123, **124**, 181
Department of Commerce, 9
Department of Public Works, 181
Des Moines (Iowa), 221
Design This Day, 277
Designing for People, 277
Dessau, Germany, 14
Detroit (Michigan), 19, 25, 84, 95, 156, 279
Deutsches Theater (Berlin), 25
Dewey, John, 201
Dickson, Dorothy, 46, 47
Disney, Walt, 148, 149, 150, 152
Disney World (Florida), 7, 149
Disneyland (California), 149, 150, **153**
Display World, 261
Divine Comedy, 25–27, **26, 27, 28**, 30, 106, 158
Divine Comedy Theater, 27, 30, 107, 108
Dodge and Castle Co., 41
Dodge & Dodge Durango. *See* Chrysler
"Dream of Fair Women, A" (*Follies*), 47
Dreamland (Coney Island), 104
Dreyfuss, Henry, 6, 7, 13, 50, 85, 257, 274, 279; Democracity / "City of Tomorrow," 120, 122, 123, **124**, 181; Influence of Bel Geddes, 31–33, 277, 291; Train design, **34**, 114, 116, 282
Du Pont Chemicals, 238
Duff Gordon, Lady Lucy, 33, 43, 44, 48, 50
Duncan, Isadora, 27
Dvořák, Anton, 103
Dymaxion Dwelling Machine, 111

Earl, Harley, 157
East Lynne, 72
East River Ferry Terminal, New York, 180
Eastman Kodak Co., 32
Eden Roc Hotel (Miami), 291
Edison, Thomas, 103
Egyptian Theatre (Los Angeles), 75
Eiffel, Gustave, 103
Eiffel Tower, Paris, 103, 181
Einstein Chair (Robert Wilson), 293
Electricity Hall (Columbian Exposition), 103
Electrified Farm (New York World's Fair *1939*), 122
Electrolux Group, 251, **254, 256**, 257
Elyria Chronicle-Telegram (Ohio), 178
Empire State Building (New York), 65, 180, 192, 197
Enchantment, 74
Enemies of Women, 76

Engineering News, 95
EPCOT Center (Experimental Prototype Community of Tomorrow, Florida), 149, 152
Eternal Road, The, 66, 125–126, 159
Evans, Maurice, 166
Evening Graphic, 91
Evening Post, 92, 197
Evening Transcript, 39
Exposition Internationale des Arts Decoratifs et Industriels Modernes, Paris, 4, 9, 10, 280

Fairbanks, Douglas, 30
Fairyland (Oakland, California), 149
Fallingwater (Pennsylvania), 195
Fantasyland (California), 149
Federal Emergency Administration of Public Works, 128
Federal Housing Agency, 227
Federal Telephone and Radio, 283
Federal Theater Project, 30
Federation Hall (New York), 120
Feet of Clay, 71, 74, **76**
Ferris, George, 103
Ferris wheel, 103
Field and Stream, 255
Fifth Avenue Gallery (Joseph Urban, New York), 6, 31, 216, 279
Firestone Inc., 128, 270
Fishel Co., 50
Fitzgerald, F. Scott, 77
Five O'Clock Girl, 85, 193
"Flash Gordon" (Alex Raymond, King Features), 111, 112
Flushing Meadow, New York, 120, 179
Folies Bergère, 42
Fontainebleau Hotel (Miami), 291
Foote-MacDougal Restaurant Corp., 68
Ford, Henry, 156, 279
Ford Building (New York World's Fair *1939*), 120
Ford Laboratory (Dearborn, Michigan), 214
Ford Motor Co., 156, 157; Model A, 156; Model T, 156, 157
Fortune, 32, 252, 255, 277
Foster, Norman, 195, 203
Fountain of Light (Chicago World's Fair), 108
Four Hour Lunch Club (Joseph Urban, New York), 23, 194
4D Zoomobile (Fuller), 111
Fox Film Corp., 72, 235
Franco Prints, 49, 237, 273
Frank Silk Mills (New Jersey), 49, 237
Frankel, Evan, 60
Frankel, Paul, 4
Franklin, Benjamin, 103
Franklin Simon store (New York), 8, 260, 261, **262**
Frazer-Nash Research Ltd., 6, 128, 163, 165
Freud, Sigmund, 18
Frigidaire Corp., 251, 257; Frigidaire Exhibit (New York World's Fair), 139, **137, 138**, 249, 252, **255**
Fuerst, Rene, 107
Fuller, Buckminster, 111, 172
Fulton Theatre (New York), 75
Futurama (New York World's Fair *1939*), 116–117,

120–143, **134, 135, 136, 140,** 156, 257, 286; Afterlife, 33, 146–149, 152–153, 162–165, 168–169; Building, 130, 293; Connection to Shell Oil, 173, 175, 177; Frigidaire Exhibit, **138,** 249, 252, **255;** Futurama cars, **129,** 130, 168, 283; "Highways and Horizons" exhibit, **132;** Reviews, 139, 141; And Robert Moses, 181–185
Future City (Conklin & Rossant), 172

Gallup, George, 121
Gallup polls, 121, 123
Garden of Paradise, The, 42, 76, 235
Gardner, Isabella Stewart, 42
Gaumont-British/Gainsborough, 47
Gehry, Frank, 203, 293
General Electric Co., 32, 123, 152, 249, 250, 252, 290; GE refrigerators, 8
General Electric Building (New York World's Fair *1939*), **121,** 123, **131,** 149, 152, 181, **255**
General Motors Corp., 139, 141, 156, 157, 159, 163, 165, 168, 216; Buick, 6, 128; Buick Series 40, 163; Buick Y-Job, 157; Firebird III, 166; And Futurama, 120, 128, 130, 146, 173; Motorama, 165, **165,** 166, **167,** 168; Oldsmobile, 165, **165,** 168
General Motors Pavilion (New York World's Fair *1964*), 148
German Luftwaffe, 113
Gershwin, George, 85
Gershwin, Ira, 85
Gest, Morris, 68
Gibson Girl, The, 44
Gielgud, John, 224
Gingerbread Castle (Hamburg, New Jersey), 150, **151**
Glaser, Milton, 293
Glen Eden Wool Carpets, 293
Golden Gate Bridge, San Francisco, 192
Goodyear Tires, 8, 128
Gorelik, Mordecai, 277
Graham-Paige Co., 128, 158
Grand Palace (Cairo), 279
Grand Union supermarkets, 293
Grauman, Sid, 75
Graves, Michael, 293
Gray, Terence, 107
Great Depression, The, 2, 85, 94, 111, 198, 199, 204; Effects on Urban and Bel Geddes, 30, 75, 105, 180, 219, 215
Great Hall, the (Chicago World's Fair), 105
Greater New York Federation of Churches, 128
Greenwich Village Follies, 44
Griffith, D. W., 25, 71
Gropius, Walter, 14
Guggenheim, Solomon, 216
Guggenheim Museum (Bilbao), 203
Guggenheim Museum (New York), 216
Gypsy Ball (New York), 50, 51

H. C. Price Co., 199
H. J. Heinz Co., 273
Hagenbund exhibition hall (Vienna), 20, 235
Hall of Science (Chicago World's Fair), 105
Hall of the Soviets (Moscow), **205**

Hamburg (New Jersey), 150
Hamlet, 112, 123, 158, 246
Hammerstein, Oscar, 60
Hansel and Gretel, 39, **149,** 150
Harlem, 181
Harper's Bazaar, 32, 44
Harrison, Wallace, 203, 227
Harrods Ltd., 46
Hart, Moss, 2
Hartman Trunks, 247
Harvard Traffic Research Group, 175, 177
Harvard University, 69, 283
Harvard University Stadium, 28
Haussmann, Baron Georges Eugene, 181
He and She, 237
Hearst, Mrs. William Randolph, 50–52, 56
Hearst, William Randolph, 23, 53, 76, 240, 290; And Urban's architectural designs, 195, 237, 240; And Urban's movies, 72–74, 235
Heatter, Gabriel, 95
Helen of Troy, 24, 71–72
Henry Hudson Bridge, New York, 180
Herald Tribune, 240
Hire's Root Beer, 270
Hitler, Adolf, xii, 14, 126, 146
Hocus Pocus, 71
Hollywood Bowl (Los Angeles), 30
Hood, Raymond, 23, 69, 105, 279; Association with Urban, 194, 224, 227, 246, 279; Influenced by Urban, 197, 203
Hoover, Herbert, 9, 104, 156, 257
Hoover vacuum cleaner, 32
Horizons, 30, 159, 214, 215, 221, 249, 252; Aerial Restaurant, 209; Airplane, 112–113, **113,** 161; Cars, 130, **160,** 161, 168, 283; House, **220,** 221; Influence, 32, 102, 111, 112, 147, 152, 277, 279; Ship, 274, **275;** Train, **114**
Hotel Gibson (Cincinnati), **62,** 63, 86
Hotel Manhattan (New York), 85
Hotel Pennsylvania (New York), 85
Hotel Review, 47
Hotel Sherman (Chicago), 84
House and Garden, 240, 244, 255
House of Tomorrow, **218,** 221, 247, 252
Houseman, John, 72
Housing Corporation of America, 221, 230
Howland, A. E., 181
Hudson cars, 157
Hughes, Howard, 113, 225
Humperdinck, Engelbert, 150
Hutton, Edward F., 44, 51

IBM Corp., 6, 271, 283
I'll Tell the World, 122
Imperial Academy (Vienna), 19
Imperial Jubilee (Austria), 18, 23; Pageant, 22
Industrial Design, 250, 277
Ingraham Alarm Clock, 257
Intercontinental Air Liner, 113, **113, 160**
International Film Studios (Cosmopolitan), 72
International News Service, 72
International Style (Architecture), 201, 204, 274

LNWHICH, 25, 107
Iron Men, 72, 193, **194**
Italian National Exposition (Milan), 279

J. Walter Thompson Advertising Co., 181, 221, 226, 269
Janice Meredith, 74, 77
Japanese Ball (New York), 51, **51**
Jeanne d'Arc, 157, **158**
Jefferson, Thomas, 103
John Deere tractors, 32
Johnny Spielt Aus, 43
Johnson, Philip, 201, 282, 293
Jones, Robert Edmond, 4, 27, 41, 246
Joseph, Emperor Franz (Austria), 21
Journal of Commerce and Commercial, 178
"Joy of Life, The" (Ziegfeld Theatre), 60
Jugendstil, 20, 235
Julius Caesar, 30
Just Imagine, 172

Kafka Chair (Robert Wilson), 293
Kahler, Wood, 46
Kahn, Albert, 214
Kahn, Ely, 61, 194, 279
Kahn, Otto, 197
Kaufman, George S., 2
Kaufmann, Edgar, 195
Kaufmann Department Store (Pittsburgh), 262
Kay Jewelers, 265
Kern, Jerome, 46, 60
Kharkov, Ukraine, 204
Kinetoscope Parlor (New York), 103
King's Views of New York, 192
Kingsley, Sidney, 125
Kitty Hawk, North Carolina, 123
Klaw & Erlanger Productions, 47, 234
Klein, Calvin, 8
Klimt, Gustav, 260
Koller, Dr. Otto, 113
Korda, Alexander, 112, 160
Kraetsch, George, 221
Kristallnacht ("Night of Broken Glass," *1938*), 126
Krutch, Joseph Wood, 122

La Boheme, 42
La Mancha, Spain, 54
La Rue Restaurant (New York), 85
Ladies' Home Journal, 221, 247, 249
Ladies Refreshment Salon (Central Park, New York), 88
Lady Be Good, 85
LaGuardia, Mayor Fiorello, 97, 180, 181
Lake Worth, Florida, 56
Lapidus, Morris, 33, 265, 291
Lazarus Laughed, 246
Le Corbusier (Charles Edouard Jeanneret), 192
Le Gallienne, Eva, 157
Lee Lash Studios, 41
Lempicka, Tamara de, 10
Lever House (New York), 199
Levittown (Pennsylvania), 217, 227
Lewisohn Stadium (New York), 27, **29**

Libby-Owens-Ford Glass Co., 186
Libeskind, Daniel, 203
Life, 33, 71, 147, 178, 186, 187, 230, 244
Light, The, 108, 109
Lincoln Center, 180, 203, 209
Lindbergh, Charles, 30, 261
"Little Mermaid, The" (Anderson), 42
Little Old New York, 76
Loewy, Raymond, 31–34, 44, 112, 123, 251, 273, **276**, 277, 291; Bel Geddes' influence on, 14, 116, 168, 250, 257, 274, 278–79; Competition with Bel Geddes, 7–8, 270–271; And Studebaker Avanti, 166
Lohengrin, 38
London (UK), 13, 14, 43, 46, 47, 88, 98, 112
Long Island (New York), 65, 91, 94
Long Island State Park Commission, 179, 181
Long Island University, 189
Lord and Taylor (New York), 261
Los Angeles (California), 11, 74, 75, 78, 227, 228
Louisiana Chronicle, 178
Louisiana Purchase, 20, 106
Louisiana State Capitol, 197
Love Letter, The, 84
Loy, Myrna, 143
Lucas, George, 111
Luce, Henry, 2
Lucille's of Hanover Square (London), 43
Lucky Strike cigarettes, 270
Luna Park (Coney Island), 51
Lutyens, Sir Edwin, 22
Lyon and Healey (Chicago), 260, 262
Lysistrata, 123, 246, **247**

Machine Art Exhibition, 281, 282
MacKaye, Percy, 28, 106, 107
MacKaye, Steele, 106, 107
Mackintosh, Charles Rennie, 31
Macmillan, Prime Minister Harold, xii
Macy's Home Store (New York), 98
Madigan, M. J., 181
Madison Square Boys Club (New York), 127
Madison Square Garden (New York), 51
Madrid, Spain, 291
Maeterlinck, Maurice, 38
Magazine of Light, 246
Magic Chef stove, 249, **250**
Magic Kingdom (California), 150
Magic Motorways, 30, 147, 178, 277
Magic Skyride (New York World's Fair *1964*), 148, 149, 152
Majestic Radio, 283
Malaga, Spain, 85
Mallin Furniture Co., 8, **43**, 235, **236**, 238, **238**, 240, **278**
Man Who Came Back, The, 72
Man Who Married a Dumb Wife, The, 41
Manhattan (New York), 84, 172, 187, 267, 286; Skyscrapers, 65, 72, 180, 192–193; Model of, 148
Manhattan Crystal Palace Exhibition (New York), 110
Manhattan Room (Hotel Pennsylvania, New York), 85
Manhattan Tray and cocktail shaker, 10, **11**, 248, 282
Mann, Thomas, 204

Manship, Paul, 260
Mantle, Burns, 123
Mar-a-Lago (Palm Beach), **52**, 52–54, 290
Marble House, The (Newport, Rhode Island), 53
Marceau, Marcel, xi
Marshall Plan, 152
Massey, Raymond, 112
Master School of United Artists (New York), 73, 277
Maumee River (Ohio), 182, 189
Mayflower Hotel, 84
McClintock, Dr. Miller, 175, 177, 178, 182
McCreary store (New York), 261
McGovern Construction Co., 225
Melba, Nellie, 38
Mercury, 116
Metal Arts, 246
Metropolitan Museum of Art, 6, 193; Architect and the Industrial Arts Exhibition, 193, 237, 244, 279–282
Metropolitan Opera House/Met, The, **3**, 42, **149**, 156, 203, 290; Urban plans for, 39, **40**, 65, 195, 197, **198**, 246
Mexico Goes to Market, 71
Meyer & Holler, 75
Miami, FL, 85, 95, 291
Mickey Mouse, 150
Midnight Frolic, 46, 47, **48**, 50
Milan, Italy, 279
Milford, Connecticut, 225
Millennium Dome, London, 98
Miller, Arthur, 14
Mills Industries, **272**
Minneapolis Journal, 49
Miracle, The, 4, 25, 30, 107, 126, 128, 175, 246, 259; Film, 75; Production, 65–69, **66**, **67**, 125
Miracle in the Evening, 123, 277
Miracles Ahead!, 114, 147
Modernism, 199, 203, 231, 273, 291, 293; American Modernism, 9, 10, 14, 32, 96, 108; Architecture, 203, 274; Bel Geddes, 25, 201, 221, 230, 237, 238, 283; Urban, 42, 75, 238, 244, 263
Monna Vanna, 42
Morgan, J. P., 197
Morgan Library (New York), 197
Mori's Restaurant (New York), 23
Morris, Benjamin, 195, 197
Morris, William, 20, 31
Moscow (USSR), 204
Moses, Robert, 173, 178–182, 187, 189, 209, 290; And World's Fairs, 180
Mount Fuji, Japan, 51
Mount Kisco (New York), 221
Murchison, Kenneth, 197
Muschenheim, William, 203
Museum of Modern Art/MoMA, 6, 18, 279, 281–282, 283, 293
Museum of the City of New York, 148–149
Music Box Revues, 44
Musical America, 197
MV Kalakala, 274

Nabisco (Kraft Foods Ltd.), 271, 273
Nash cars, **5**, 128, 164, **164**, 165, 168

Nash-Kelvinator, 252
Nation, 122
National Aeronautics & Space Administration (NASA), 35
National Beauty Pageant, 98
National Broadcasting Company (NBC), 284, 286, 290
National Cyclopedia of American Biography, The, 106
National Planning Conference (*1937*), 175, 181
Natural History Museum (Toledo), 185
Nature Fellowship (Hagenbund), 20
Neo-Gothic style, 203
Neutra, Richard, 173
New Amsterdam Theatre (New York), 42, 47, **48**
New Deal, The (Roosevelt), 111, 180
New Jersey Highway Commission, 181
New Orleans (Louisiana), 78
New School for Social Research, 7, 8, 96, 102, 274, 287, 290; And Bel Geddes, 219, 270; Urban's design, 199–204, **200**, **202**, 206, 217
"New World Symphony, The," 103
New York American, 56
New York Central Railway, 34, 116
New York Evening Post, 54
New York Herald Tribune, 56, 146
New York Journal and American, 99, 141
New York Morning Telegraph, 234
New York Planning Commission, 181, 187
New York Police Department, 127
New York Post, 139, 143, 197
New York School of Fine and Applied Art, 250
New York Society of Engineers, 146
New York State Pavilion, The, 193
New York Story, 71, 72
New York Sun, 50, **131**, 178, 181
New York Times, 19, 120, 163, 192, 248; Reports on Urban, 65, 88; Reviews of Bel Geddes, 125, 175, 225, 270
New York Times Book Review, 278
New York Times Magazine, 209
New York World's Fair (*1939–1940*), 31, 95, 116, 156, 177, 179, 248; And Democracity (Dreyfuss), 32, 123, **124**; And Frigidaire exhibit, 252, **255**; And Futurama, 120–123, 128, 149–150, 152, 173, 293; And influence, 149, 152, 168, 181, 286–287; And political context, 146; And Rocketport (Loewy), 112, 123
New York World's Fair (*1964*), 148, 149, 152
New York World-Telegram, 187
New Yorker, 4, 31, 195, 197, 246
News, The, 182
Nixon, Richard, 53
No Foolin', 84
Nobel Prize, 204
Notre Dame Cathedral (model of), **136**, 175

Oakland (California), 149
Oasis Club (Palm Beach), 54, 56
O'Brien-Fortin, 225
Odets, Clifford, 111
Offenbach, Jacques, 112
Official Guide Book to the Fair, 121
Olds, Ransom E., 123
On The Twentieth Century, 34

O'Neill, Eugene, 14, 69
O'Shea, William, 89, 91
Otis, William, 110
Outline of History, 120
Owens-Corning Fiberglass Co., 186

Packard cars, 147, **160**
Pageant of St. Louis, The, 28
Palace of the Soviets (Moscow), 204, 208
Palais Royale Dance Hall (New York), 85, 87
Palm Beach (Florida), 4, 23, 75, 84, 88, 280, 286;
    As scenery, 51; Urban's architecture, 53–57, **55**, 91,
    228, 267
Palm Beach Bath and Tennis Club, **53**, 54, 56, 91, 228
Pantages Theatre (Hollywood), 11
"Parade of Progress (Futurama)," 147
Paradise Ball (New York), 51
Paramount Movie Theater (Palm Beach), 71, 75, 267
Paris Exhibition (*1925*), 4, 9, 10
Paris Exposition (*1889*), 103
Paris World's Fair (*1900*), 20
Park Avenue Restaurant (New York), 8, 91, **92**, 96, 97,
    244
Park Lane Hotel (now the Hemsley, New York), 71
Park Theatre (New York), 76, 77–78
Parker, Conway, 46
Parliament of Religions (Columbian Exposition), 106
Passing Show, The, 44
Pathe Film News, 182
Patriot, The, 222, **223**, 224
Pearl Harbor, 283
Pelléas and Mélisande, 38
Peninsular Engraving Co., 19
Penn Central Station (New York), 116
Pennsylvania Railroad, 34, 116
Pennsylvania Turnpike, 146
Pentagon, The (Washington), 147
People's Theater, WPA, 121
Pepsodent toothpaste, 273
Perisphere, The (New York World's Fair, *1939*), 120,
    121, 122, 123, 181. *See also* Democracity
Persian Ball (Palm Beach), 56
Peter Pan, xi
Philadelphia (Pennsylvania), 187, 221
Philadelphia Public Ledger, 209
Philco Company, 249, 279, 283, **285**, 291
Photo Journal, 241
Pickford, Mary, 74
Piscator, Erwin, 204
Pittsburgh (Pennsylvania), 18, 81, 84, 86, 195, 262
Pittsburgh Plate Glass, 95
Place de la Concorde, Paris, 181
Plainfield Courier-News (New Jersey), 178
Playbill Restaurant (Hotel Manhattan, New York), 85
Plaza Hotel (New York), 8, 85
"Pore Judd Is Dead" (*Oklahoma*), 32
Post, Marjorie Merriweather (Mrs. E. F. Hutton), 23,
    52, 54, **55**, 56
Postman's retail chain, 265
Power, Tyrone, 30
Princess Anne, 274, 276
Prospect Park (Brooklyn, New York), 179

Racine (Wisconsin), 216
Radio City Music Hall (New York), 69, 95, 203
Radio Corporation of America (RCA), 257, 283, 284,
    284
Radio Corporation of America Building (Rockefeller
    Center, New York), 11
"Railroads on Parade" (New York World's Fair *1939*),
    123
Rainbow Girl, The, 234
Rand, Sally, 110, 122
Rathauskeller (City Hall Restaurant, Vienna), **21**, 22
Ray, Man, 11
Reader's Digest, 221, 247
Reagan, Ronald, 35
Red Dress, The, 237
Reinhardt, Max, 4, 25, 30, 63, 65, 68
Reinhardt Theatre, **64**, 65, 107, 195, 203, 263
Rembrandt, Van Rijn, 125
Reptilia, 71
Republican Party, 179
Research Laboratories Exhibit (New York World's Fair,
    1939), 152; And Display, 123
Restless Sex, The, 72, 73, 75
Revere Co., 225, 226
Rialto Theatre (New York), 75
Richard Mansell House (Mount Kisco, New York), 221
Ringling Brothers Barnum and Bailey Circus, 7, 98, 99
Ritz-Carlton Hotel (New York), 50, 51, 56
Rivoli Theatre (New York), 75
Road Builder's News, 146
Roadtown (Chambless), 172, 173
Roberts, Mary, **242**
Rochester (New York), 182
Rochester Democrat and Chronicle, The, 187
Rock-a-Bye Baby, 46
Rockefeller, John D., 209
Rockefeller Center (New York), 11, 197
Rockefeller Institute (New York), 227
Rockefeller Plaza (New York), 277
Rocketport Exhibit (New York World's Fair *1939*), 112,
    123
Rodgers, Richard, 32
Rohe, Mies van der, 65
Rome Bed Co., **239**, 240
Roosevelt, Eleanor, 128, 187
Roosevelt, Franklin, 111, 116, 180
Rose, Billy, 122
Rose Room (London), 44
Rowe Manufacturing Corp., 271
Roxy Movie Theatre (New York), 75
Rugged Individualist, The, 237
Rush City Reformed (Neutra), 173
Russell, Henry, 38

Saks Fifth Avenue (New York), 261
Sales Service News Letter, 146
San Francisco (California), 92, 187, 279
San Francisco Bulletin, 74
San Simeon (La Cuesta Entcantada) (California), 53
Sandow, Eugene, 107
Sans Souci Hotel (Miami), 291
Saturday Evening Post (Detroit), 178

Savoy-Plaza Hotel (New York), 71, 85
SC Johnson (Johnson's Wax), 216
Scandals, 44
Scenitorium (Columbian Exposition), 107
Schine, J. Myer, 227
Schine Theatrical Enterprises, 227, 228
Schlemmer, Oscar, 14
Schlesinger and Mayer store (Carson Pirie Scott, Chicago), 9
Schneider, Helen Belle, 25
School of Design (Bel Geddes, New York), 277
Scientific American, 68, **223**, 224
Sea Lion Amusement Park (Coney Island), 104
Sears Coldspot refrigerator, 250
Sears Roebuck & Co. Catalogue, 19, 250, 268
Seattle (Washington), 274
Seattle World's Fair, 209
Secessionist School of Artists (Austria), 20, 173
Servel Electronics, **255**
Service Air Station, 183
Seurat, Georges, 39
Seven Lively Arts, 193
Shakespeare, William, 27, 28, 30, 166
Shell Oil, 32, 123, **124**, 128, **136**, 173, 185, 261; "City of the Future"/ "City of Tomorrow," **135, 140,** 174–178, 261; And Robert Moses, 178–182
Show Boat, 60, 84
Shubert production, 44, 237
Silver Ball (New York), 51
Simmons Bedding Co., **239,** 240, 247, 273, **280**
Simon, George, 260
Simonson, Lee, 4, 41, 246
Singer Sewing Machine Company, 32
Sistine Chapel (Vatican), 60
Sixth Avenue New York studio (ABC), 284
Sky Ride (Chicago World's Fair), 104
Skylab (NASA), 7
Skyscraper cocktail shaker, **11**
Sleeping Beauty's Castle (California), 7, 149, 150, **153**
Smart Setback, 46
Smith, Governor Al, 179
Soda King siphon, **248**
Sorrows of Satan, The, 71
Space Needle (Seattle), 209, 211, 214
Spectatorium (MacKaye), 106
Spirit of St. Louis, The, 30
Spruce Goose airplane, 113
Sputnik satellite, 166
St. Louis (Missouri), 20
St. Louis Art Museum, 146
St. Louis World's Fair (*1904*), **20,** 20–21, 28, 106
St. Regis Hotel (New York), **12,** 13, 88, 98
Stalin, Joseph, 111
Standard Gas Equipment Co. (SGE)—and stoves, 8, 249, **252,** 253, 255, **255,** 273, 290
Standard Oil, 32
Star Trek, 35
State Power Authority (New York), 179
Statue of Liberty, The, 43, 103, 192
Steichen, Edward, 11
Steinway Pianos, 32
Stern, Isaac, 14

Stone, Edward Durrell, 221
Strand Palace Hotel (London), 13
Strand Theatre (New York), 75, 85
Strauss, Richard, 18
Strong, Josiah, 172
Studebaker Avanti (Loewy), 7, 166, 168
Studio, 23
Stylist, 255
Sullivan, Ed, 91
Sullivan, Louis, 199
Sunday Journal, 235
Sunday News, 139
Sunday World, 50
Sunoco Inc., 128
Sunrise Building and Mall (Palm Beach), 75, 228, 267, 268, **268**
Sunshine Biscuits, 271
Swampscott (Massachusetts), 39, 41, 84, 277

Tammany Hall, 97
Teague, Walter Dorwin, 31, 32, 33, 279, 291
Technicolor, 75, 146
Technirama Theaters, 75
Tempest, The, 28
Temple of Music (Chicago World's Fair), 107, **108, 109**
Tennessee Valley Authority, The, 180
Tetrahedronal City (Fuller), 172
Texaco Skychief Gasoline, 32, 183, 290
Theatre Arts Monthly, 68, 107, 269
Theatre Guild, 69
Theatre Magazine, 237
Theatres, 41, 60, 81, 267
Things to Come, 112, **113,** 114, 115, 116, **160,** 277
Think, 269
Thompson, Walter, 32
Thunderbird, 19
Tiffany, Louis Comfort, 8
Tiffany & Co., 9
Tiger Room (Hotel Sherman, Chicago), 84, **86–87**
Time, 2, 293
To New Horizons, 146
Toledo (Ohio), 182, 185, 187, 279
Toledo Blade, 182, 186
Toledo Chamber of Commerce, 187
Toledo City Plan, 182
Toledo Counter Scale, 214–215, **215**
Toledo Plan, 184, 187
Toledo Scale Company, 182, 214–216, 217
Toledo Scale Factory, 214–215, **216,** 217, 219
"Toledo Tomorrow," 182–189, **184, 186, 188,**
Toledo's Natural History Museum, **188**
Too Much Is Never Enough, 291
Toronto, Ontario, 148
"Traffic of the Future" (Shell Oil Advertising), 173
Traffic Research Bureau (Harvard University), 181
Transportation Zone (New York World's Fair *1939*), 123
Travel and Transportation Building (Chicago World's Fair), 104
Triadic Ballet, 14
Triborough Bridge, New York, 179, 180
Trifari & Krussman, 50

Trip to the Moon, A, 112
Trump, Donald, 53
Trump Tower (New York), 268
Trylon, The (New York World's Fair *1939*), 120, 123, **138**
Tsar Paul I, 222
Tupperware, 238
Twentieth Century, 32, **34, 114**
Twentieth Century City, The, 172
Twentieth Century Limited, 116, 282
Tyler, George, 42

Ukrainian State Theatre (Kharkov), 204, 206, **206, 207,** 208
Under the Red Robe, 72
U-Need-A Pack Co., 271
Union Pacific Railroad Co., **114,** 115, 116
United Nations–buildings (New York), 189, 203, 209, 218
Universal Studios (Hollywood), 71
Upholsterer and Interior Decorator, 244
Uptown Chamber of Commerce (New York), 181
Urban, Gretl, 60, 74
Urban, Mary, **24**
U.S. Army, 114, 147
U.S. Army Corps of Engineers, 147
U.S. Information Agency, 14

Valley Upholstery Ltd., 247
Van der Rohe, Mies, 14
Vanderbilt, William K., 53
Vanities, 44
Vanity Fair, 44, 46, 54, 68
Variety, 95
Vaux, Calvert, 88
Veblen, Thorstein, 201
Verdi, Giuseppe, 38
Verne, Jules, 112
Vidor, King Wallis, 72
Vienna, Austria, 13, 18, 20–22, 38, 235, 240
Vienna Polytechnic (Austria), 19
Vietnam War, 294
Vieux Carre (New Orleans), 78
Virgil (Publius Marcus Vergilius Maro), 26, **28**
Virginia Ferry Co., 274
Vogue, 32, 44, 49, 54, 240
Volkswagen cars, 168
Vollmoeller, Karl, 65

Wagner, Richard, 38
Waite, Colonel Henry, 183
Waiting for Lefty, 111
Waldorf-Astoria Hotel (New York), 71, 156, 166
Walker, Jimmy, 88–89
Walker, Ralph, 194
Walkman radio, 2, 284
Wall Street, New York, 110, 192, 195, 180
Walter Thompson Agency, 32
Wanamaker store (New York), 261
War of the Worlds, The, 112, 111–112
Ward, Montgomery, 268
Washington, D.C., 7, 146, 153, 187, 192, 225
Washington, George, 120

Washington Post, 293
Washington Square Players, 39, 41
Water Theatre (Chicago World's Fair), 108
Weaver, Pat, 286
Webber, Andrew Lloyd, 125
Welles, Orson, 111, 112
Wells, H. G., 112, 120–121, 128, 248
Westchester Cinema (New York), 80, **80**
Whalen, Grover, 182
Wheatsworth Biscuits, 150, **151**
When Knighthood Was in Flower, 74, 76
Where, 166
White, Clarence, 260
White, George, 44
White City (Columbian Exposition), 8, 102, 104, 106, 172
White House, The (Washington, D.C.), 128, 173; Winter White House, 53
Whitney Museum of American Art (New York), 282
Wiener, Baron von, 23
William Penn Hotel (Pittsburgh), 86
Williams, Tennessee, 204
Wilson, Edmund, 201
Wilson, Robert, 293
Wilson, Woodrow, 192
Wiltern Theatre (Los Angeles), 11
Winston, Norman, 225
Wizard of Oz, The, 104
Woman's Journal, 281
Women's Home Companion, 269
Women's Wear Daily, 261
Woolworth Building (New York), 175, 192, 193
Works Progress Administration (WPA), 30
"World Finder, The" (MacKaye), 106, 107
World Trade Center (New York), 192, 294
World War I, 39, 19, 71, 282; Effects, 9–10, 38
World War II, 14, 32, 38, 182, 204, 217, 226; And Bel Geddes, 71, 120, 147; And Dreyfuss, 7; Effects, xii, 153, 187
World's Fair. *See* Chicago (*1933*), New York (*1939* and *1964*), Seattle (*1962*), St. Louis (*1904*)
Wright, Frank Lloyd, 33, 110, 172, 227, 290; And Bel Geddes, 215–216; Relation to Urban, 23, 194–195, 198, 199
Wright Brothers, 123
Wyler, William, 128

Yardley Co. (UK), 50
Yonkers (New York), **24,** 240; And Urban's house, 253
Yonkers Studio (Joseph Urban), 84, **86**
Young Diana, The, 74, 235, **236**

Zander the Great, 74, 75
Zephyr train, **114,** 115
Ziegfeld Follies, 42, 47–53, 75–76, 88, 107, 241, 290; And Marion Davies, 72, 75–76; And Urban, 42, 43, 44, 54, 234, 260; Imitations of, 44; Urban's productions, **3,** 44, 47–49, **49,** 50, 75–76, 157, 237
Ziegfeld Theatre (New York), 8, **61, 62,** 69, 98, 195; Reviews of, 60, 61, 77; Urban's variations on, 63, 65, 84
Ziegfeld, Florenz, 42–50, **48,** 60, 63, 88, 107